A GREAT FACE FOR RADIO

THE ADVENTURES OF A GLOBAL
SPORTS COMMENTATOR

JOHN ANDERSON

A GREAT FACE FOR RADIO

THE ADVENTURES OF A GLOBAL
SPORTS COMMENTATOR

FOREWORD BY
TERRY BUTCHER

First published by Pitch Publishing 2013
Originally published by Know the Score Books 2009

Pitch Publishing
A2 Yeoman Gate
Yeoman Way
Durrington
BN13 3QZ
www.pitchpublishing.co.uk

A CIP catalogue record is available for this book from the British Library

ISBN: 978-1-909178-88-5

Jacket Design by Simon Williams at feastcreative.com

Typesetting and origination by Pitch Publishing

Printed and bound by CPI Group (UK) Ltd, Croydon, CR0 4YY

CONTENTS

To Carolyn, Becky and Katie

Curing the pain of separation
with the joy of return

And in memory of my favourite
grumpy northener David Oates,
for whom a two word epitaph
says it all: Top Bloke

ACKNOWLEDGEMENTS

I would like to say a big thanks to the following people who, by virtue of their help, guidance, friendship and stubborn refusal to leave the hotel bar, ensured that there was never a dull moment on the many trips we have shared together:

Nigel Adderley, Matthew Allen, Jeremy Armstrong, Marc Aspland, Stuart Barnes, Rob Beasley, Adrian Bevington, David Bond, Stephen Booth, Steve Bower, Mark Bradley, Eric Brown, Joanne Budd, Mike Burgess, Terry Butcher, Bob Cass, Ian Chadband, Andrew Cheal, Dave Clark, Mike Collett, Nick Collins, Elliot Cook, Martin Cooke, John Cross, John Curtis, Shaun Custis, Ian Dennis, Rob Draper, Jon Driscoll, Andy Edwards, Phil Edwards, Scott Field, Andy Fraser, Olly Foster, Tony Gale, Andrew Gidley, Doug Gillon, Tim Glover, Ian Gordon, David Harrison, Steven Howard, Stuart Hutchison, Mike Ingham, Tom Knight, Tony Lawrence, James Lawton, Bill Leslie, Richard Lewis, Martin Lipton, Tony Lockwood, Mick Lowes, Tony Mabert, George Matheson, Kevin McCarra, Dom McGuinness, Duncan McKay, Phil McNulty, John Mehaffey, Glenn Moore, Tim Morgan, Kaz Mochlinski, Tim Moynihan, Charlotte Nicol, David Oates, Michael O'Neill, Vikki Orvice, David O'Sullivan, Andrew Parkinson, Jayne Pearce, Jonathan Pearce, David Pearson, Dickie Pelham, Mark Pougatch, David Powell, Jim Proudfoot, John Richardson, Stuart Robinson, Mike Rowbottom, Brian Scott, Steve Scott, Caroline Searle, Pete Simmons, Chris Skudder, Owen Slot, Caj Sohal, Guy Swindells, Graham Taylor, Andrew Titheridge, Simon Turnbull, John & Keith Warren, Julian Waters, Neil Webb, Peter Wenmann, Nigel Whitefield, Mark Whittle, Richard Williams, Steve Wilson, Henry Winter, Dave Woods, Rob Wotton and Alastair Yeomans.

In Memoriam: Danny Fullbrook.

I would like to thank all my friends at talkSPORT for affording me the privilege of working with them at World Cup 2010 and Euro 2012, especially Moz

Dee, Matt Smith, Steve Morgan, Mike Bovill, Liam Fisher, Dennie Morris, Mark Saggers, Adrian Durham, Ian Danter, Jonathan Norman and Giles Carruthers.

Hats off to Henry Winter for adding his endorsement to the book and Terry Butcher for his wonderful foreword.

Finally, my most sincere thanks go to Paul and Jane Camillin at Pitch Publishing for rescuing the project, keeping the faith with it and allowing me to waffle on through six more chapters.

You can follow John Anderson on Twitter @GreatFaceRadio.

John Anderson
October 2012

FOREWORD

by Terry Butcher

When John Anderson asked me to do a foreword I replied:

"I was never a foreword, I was a defender."

But nevertheless I very am happy to be writing these words, as this book had given me a lot of laughs and brought back some very good memories of my days on the road with the England media pack.

As any former pro will tell you, nothing can ever replace the thrill of playing football for a living, especially when it's at the highest level. But when the ankles, knees and, in my case, gashed forehead could no longer take any more punishment, at least I had the trusty jawbone to fall back on. I could still talk a good game and so I did the next best thing to actually playing and spent ten years following the England team as a summariser on *BBC Radio 5Live*. It was great to be able to travel the world freed from the inconveniences of discipline, training, curfews and drinking bans.

During that time I met many other like-minded souls who specialised in talking about football by day and slurring drunkenly about it, and everything else, by night.

I don't know exactly when I first ran into John Anderson; it was probably in some dimly lit bar in Eastern Europe that we'd both been attracted to by the prospect of cheap beer and loud music. He's a fan of punk and new wave and I'm firmly in the heavy metal camp, but there were a few mutual points in between that we agreed on. Theoretically we were rivals in broadcasting terms too, with me representing the BBC and John working for Independent Radio News (IRN), but we hit it off straightaway and those few beers, wherever it was, were the first of many. In the years that followed we got sloshed in Sofia, tanked in Tirana, hammered in Helsinki and blotto in Baku.

We often used to sit in a little radio enclave on the plane and trade insults en route to our latest assignment. I remember we were once waiting for take-off to somewhere or other and discussing a Sky TV programme called *The Match* in which Graham Taylor managed a group of celebrity players in a game against a team of former professionals. One of the celebs was Olympic gold medal winning sprinter Darren Campbell.

"He's not a bad player is he, Butch?" John ventured.

Quickly and without thinking I replied "yeah, he's quick."

Within seconds of my realising how absurd this stark statement of the bleeding obvious must have sounded, John had broadcast it down the entire corridor of the plane and I spent the rest of the flight being mercilessly slaughtered by him and everyone else on board.

I proceeded to try and counter the humiliation by chanting "no surrender to the IRN" very loudly, only to be threatened with expulsion from the plane by an irate steward who feared that a drunken England hooligan had somehow sneaked onto the media charter flight.

Happily I later got my revenge as I blasted him off air and almost off his feet by standing in front of his satellite transmission dish in Macedonia which is one of the many tales he has chosen to share with the publication of this memoir.

John Anderson does like the odd beverage or two from time to time, as previously stated, but he is one of the hardest workers I have ever seen and who only raised a glass when all his tasks and requests had been completed. I have been very lucky to share his company and consider John to be one of my closest pals in football and the media, though he really does have one of the best faces for radio!

I hope you'll enjoy his stories as much as I have.

Terry Butcher

INTRODUCTION

"Can I carry your bags?"

I always try and avoid dinner parties.

I don't have anything against the actual concept; I'm sure many people can derive huge enjoyment from them and all the very best if you are one of them. It's just that, despite having carved out a reasonable career as a professional broadcaster, I am hopelessly disinclined towards the concept of small talk, take little interest in the everyday lives of people who I have barely met and struggle to deal with the petit bourgeois etiquette of such gatherings.

I will happily pile into summer barbecues and winter piss-ups in which tried, tested and carbon dated mates gather for a night of food, friendship and Fuller's London Pride. However, as soon as someone utters the dreaded but inevitable phrase "mmm, something smells good" or starts talking about cars, careers or curtains, I take on the persona of a doomed hedgehog, trapped in startled horror by the intense sodium glare of social, culinary and parental one-upmanship.

I'm talking about the sort of event beloved of NCT mothers and IT fathers who wander around in sandals crapping on about timeshares, organic rhubarb (most likely grown in their allotment) and Nigella bloody Lawson. Despite your best efforts to camouflage yourself by leaning up against something roughly the same colour as your shirt and not moving an inch, eventually someone will bound up enthusiastically and start asking vacuous questions about your life. This, of course, is a wholly transparent ploy designed at manoeuvring the conversation around so that they might be able to offer you supposedly fascinating insights into their own.

The manifestation of this is a series of seemingly polite inquiries which, though harmless to many people I'm sure, have the effect of sending me into paroxysms of mental anguish as I try and suppress the urge to give a brutally dismissive response instead of the glib but socially acceptable ones which are *de rigueur* in such situations.

I shall illustrate what I mean by following each question posed in this typical conversation with the actual answer I give and then, in italics, the thought which I was valiantly bottling up inside.

"So what sort of car do you drive at the moment?"

"A Renault Scenic."

A blue one. Cars are functional items, no more worthy of discussion than combination boilers or pressure cookers.

"I love this track, isn't Annie Lennox amazing?"

"It's not really my cup of tea if I'm honest."

Frankly I'd rather listen to the sound of my own teeth being spat into a steel bucket.

"We're considering a loft conversion."

"Oh, that's a good idea. More space and all that."

That's funny because we're thinking of having ours converted back into a loft.

"What are your children interested in?"

"Painting, music and reading."

Watching telly, eating sweets, kicking the shit out of each other and refusing to go to bed.

"Tarquin's starting tap-dancing classes in August."

"Is he really? Good for him."

Poor little sod.

"We've joined the local Roman Catholic church, so Lucinda can get in at St Ignatius."

"It's so hard finding the right school, isn't it?"

In which case my dearest wish is that it is sold off and converted into a multi-storey car park the day before she's due to start.

But there is one polite enquiry which trumps all others for invoking a peculiar combination of resignation and sheer terror. The one which, you just know, is going to hopelessly derail his feeble attempts to start banging on about his annual bonus, business trips to Dortmund and company Lexus.

"So what do you do for a living?"

Now, don't get me wrong, I am proud of what I do and enjoy doing it immensely. I know plenty of people within the industry with whom I can chat endlessly about the joys, wonders and pitfalls of international sports journalism and share fabulous memories of our days on the road. I also have a strong group of lifelong friends who don't really give a shit about any of it, never have and, hopefully, never will. People with whom you can discuss the truly important topics such as the Hubble space telescope, seven-inch singles, the 1970 Brazil World Cup team or who is the most attractive ex-member of the *Neighbours* cast.

But I always feel uncomfortable discussing work with people I hardly know. It's difficult not to sound big-headed when you describe what you do because it is often perceived as impossibly glamorous and exciting. I was in a pub once with a mate talking about football and I mentioned something that some England player had said to me during an interview. Suddenly, out of the blue, someone on a nearby table shouted: "bloody name dropper".

So, forgive me if my attitude seems unnecessarily harsh, but I really do struggle to cope when confronted with the giddy excitement of a 43-year-old high-flying advertising exec who's "more of a rugger man really" but nonetheless insists on grilling you over a bottle of ghastly continental lager in the mid-August drizzle of an Islington patio.

The subsequent discourse is always the same and I've seriously considered handing out a printed sheet with the following exchange reproduced on it to save time. Dull Man can simply read the sheet and go back to discussing tap-dancing and Catholic schools while I can continue to annoy my wife by skulking around on the margins looking generally uncomfortable and out of place.

"I'm a sports journalist."

"So which paper do you work for?"

"I don't, I work in radio."

"Who for?"

"IRN."

"The IRA?" (laughs hysterically while spraying me with his last mouthful of Nastro Azzurro).

"No, Independent Radio News."

"Never heard of it."

"It's an agency service that provides all the independent radio stations in the UK and some abroad with their national and international news and sport."

"Producer are you?"

"No, reporter."

"So do you actually go on the radio?"

"Yes."

"What sort of things do you cover?"

"Olympics, World Cups, England games home and away, world title fights, Wimbledon – that sort of thing."

"Blimey. Can I carry your bags?"

CHAPTER ONE

"So how did you get into that then?"

Once we've got through the items on the printed sheet, this is always the next question.

I'd love to be able to tell you that I'd spent my entire formative years as a radio obsessive, whiling the days happily away listening intently to *Radio Four* while my evenings would be taken up with following the football on *Radio Two* and attempting to replicate the measured tones of Peter Jones and Bryon Butler in readiness for the day when I would take my place among the pantheon of broadcasting greats. Alas it would be a complete lie. If I'm honest, I've still never listened to *Radio Four* in my life and assiduously avoided football coverage on the radio so that I wouldn't know the scores when I watched the television highlights.

In fact virtually the only radio I was really exposed to in my formative years was music programmes like Nicky Horne's *Your Mother Wouldn't Like It* on *Capital* and, of course, John Peel's wonderful show on *Radio One*. As my hair and my flares grew ever longer and wider I harboured dreams of a career in rock'n'roll. But, having failed to get beyond *Three Blind Mice* on the recorder at primary school, my total lack of musical ability was finally confirmed to me when I was given a small drum kit as a birthday present as a teenager and couldn't even master that. I did briefly appear in a secondary school band called 'Benedict Ferret and the Farting Pixies', but John Bonham I was not.

After several more thwarted attempts at rock stardom (be eternally grateful that you have never heard of 'Technicolour Yawn', 'The Epic Flares' or 'The Opal Fruits'), I decided that a career in rock journalism would be the next best alternative. I always enjoyed creative writing at school and, as an avid reader of the weekly music papers, the idea of reporting from gigs, reviewing albums and interviewing rock stars seemed irresistible.

Oblivious to the fact that this sort of job went to ultra-trendy people with their fingers on the very pulsebeat of popular culture, I would fire off missives to *Sounds*, *New Musical Express* and *Melody Maker* in the hope of attracting their attention:

> Dear Editor
> I like music and would be great on your paper. I'm generally able to catch up with the latest musical fads and trends within no more than six months of them becoming fashionable; in fact I had all of the first four Sex Pistols singles well before the end of 1978.
>
> I got grade A at English O level and would be willing to cut my hair and wear straight trousers if the job so demands. I like new wave bands like the Stranglers (Doors-esque don't you think?) but am still into Floyd, Zeppelin, Genesis etc. I feel I would be a hard working and punctual member of your team.
> Yours in rock,
> John M Anderson

Needless to say, Julie Burchill, Tony Parsons and Charles Shaar Murray were spared the ignominy of seeing their picture bylines being blown off the features pages by a 17-year-old Guildford Grammar School boy with a copy of the *NME Encyclopaedia of Rock* under one arm and *Dark Side Of The Moon* under the other.

I ended up leaving school with hopeless A level results, a complete lack of interest in further education and a fast track to mediocrity. Regrettably though, beer doesn't pay for itself and so after several months on the dole I had to swallow my pride, buy a hideous blue suit and step out into what irritatingly smug people still refer to as 'the real world'.

The reality for me was Crown Life Insurance, which was located in the unimaginatively-titled Crown House, a seven-storey, square edifice which looked like a giant Oxo cube afloat in the ghastly stew that is Woking town centre. I started on £2,250 per annum and spent three and a half years there as a Pensions Administration clerk. But all the time I harboured vague dreams of an exotic life somewhere beyond Guaranteed Accumulation Pension Funds and Contracted-Out National Insurance Contributions.

The chance to realise those dreams came when one of my insurance colleagues Steve Newson (still a friend to this day) came running into the office waving a newspaper cutting from the pages of that esteemed organ of local reportage, the *Surrey Advertiser*. In between the weekly digest of reportage from a none too demanding news patch ('Mysterious Re-Appearance of Park Bench', 'Badger Numbers Down in Peasmarsh', 'Man Had Cannabis in Secret Pocket') he had spotted a student recruitment ad posted by Highbury College of Technology in Portsmouth. They had recently launched a post graduate diploma course in radio journalism and he reckoned I should give it a go.

Despite singularly falling short on the post graduate stipulation, I eagerly replied. Two weeks later I received a pack containing an application form and some radio scripts along with instructions to send a demo cassette to the college. I borrowed a microphone off a friend who was in a band, plugged it into the amplifier on my stereo and, with a release of the pause button on my cassette deck, so began my five-year journey from the 4th floor of Crown House to a commentary position at the Olympic Stadium in Seoul.

The main objective of the demo was to assess the candidates' vocal qualities, but the scripts were deliberately designed to contain awkward names and pronunciations to separate the Trevor McDonalds from the Aimi McDonalds (squeaky-voiced Scottish actress in case any reader aged under 40 is confused).

One was a story about a house fire involving a woman called Elsie Yeo which I correctly read as Yo rather than Yee-O. I'd remembered a Gillingham striker called Brian Yeo, who'd played against my team Watford during our 1970 FA Cup run (we won 2-1) and 'Yo' is how Frank Bough had pronounced it on *Grandstand*. Nice one Frank; I still reckon that's what got me in, since everyone else assumed it rhymed with Leo. That and the fact that, vocally, I was marginally closer to Trevor than Aimi.

Highbury College was about as unlovely a seat of learning as you could possibly imagine. This was not a place for dreaming spires or inspiring dreams. Nestled uncomfortably alongside a stretch of dual carriageway where the A27 meets the M27, it was dominated by one of those ominous-looking tower blocks you normally only see in documentaries about Cold War Poland. The whole place looked as if it had been designed by a group of remedial class toddlers armed only with a pile of cornflake packets and a tube of Pritt Stick. The star turn in the canteen were cheese and potato pies, made out of the bits of cornflake packet the kids had left over, filled with pus.

The course itself was run by a ceaselessly cheerful and hugely amiable but utterly clueless former local newspaper reporter who'd never worked in radio in his life. He was 'assisted' by an ex-BBC local radio man who, I firmly believe, had been frozen cryogenically in the days when broadcasters wore dicky bows to announce the BBC Light programme and was then lovingly defrosted every Tuesday to take our practical radio sessions.

Much of these sessions consisted of sifting through great wads of Yellow Pages-sized local council minutes and then attempting to transform these environmental health, planning and sanitation policy documents into snappy voice reports (known as voicers). We called them 'dog-shit stories' and, however well written, they would have bored even the most annoyingly upbeat of listeners into a coma midway through the first sentence of the intro.

Every weekend we were set a practical task as a kind of homework. I once went with a load of mates and a tape recorder to the Bristol Beer Festival to do a vox-pop with the clientele. More astute readers will have already spotted the inherent flaw in this otherwise brilliantly mapped out exercise. Naturally the results weren't exactly Sony Award-winning material: "get it doon yer fuckin' neck . . . down in one, down in one, down in one . . . tits out for the lads . . . and (to the tune of *Guantanamera*) puke in a minute, he's gonna puke in a minute," etc.

Mind you it was much better than the efforts of two of my Kate Adie aspirant classmates who decided to ambush punters in a Colchester shopping centre and canvass their thoughts on the recent American invasion of Grenada. Quite apart from the fact that the opinions of old ladies with baskets full of Mr Kipling Almond Slices carry little relevance in the gung ho world of American imperialism, our pair of intrepid newshoundettes had made one basic but devastating error. They tried to be clever by releasing the pause button on the tape machine to activate the recording immediately after they'd asked the question. This was a wholly understandable ploy given that it would ensure that only the answers were recorded and thus the whole piece would be much easier and quicker to edit later on.

Unfortunately they got it the wrong way round on the first attempt and so, instead of a fascinating discourse on Reagan-era foreign policy, the resultant recording went like this:

"What do you think of the American invasion of Grenada?"

"What do you think of the American invasion of Grenada?"

"What do you think of the American invasion of Grenada?"

"What do you think of the American invasion of Grenada?"

"What do you think of the American invasion of Grenada?"

It made my collection of drunken football chants sound like a BAFTA award-winning *South Bank Show Special*.

However, despite managing to avoid the wooden spoon on that particular exercise it was becoming increasingly and quite understandably obvious that, in the eyes of the course tutors, I was not destined for great things.

The saving grace was that I was the only one in the group of 15 who showed any real interest in sport and so I developed my own niche writing and presenting all of the sports bulletins on the campus radio station *Highbury FM*. We would showcase our work by broadcasting it across the college in a bid to entertain and inform the assembled rabble of goths, geeks, waifs and wasters that made up the population of this hotbed of academia. To use an astronomical comparison: if you imagine the sun as the worst radio station you've ever heard in your life, we were at the far edge of an as yet undiscovered galaxy the light from which will eventually reach the earth in 23.5 trillion years' time.

The real bonus of the Highbury course was that we were sent on attachment to a couple of real radio stations for work experience, one BBC and one independent. As I was totally skint I applied for *County Sound* in my home town of Guildford as the ILR station so that I could stay rent free at my Mum's. It was an inspired choice. At the time this was a brand new station with state of the art facilities, a brilliant town centre location and a young and enthusiastic team of reporters led by news editor Malcolm Deacon with Nick Collins, who's now *Sky Sports'* Chief Football Correspondent, in charge of the sports desk.

Although the studio complex was brand spanking new by mid-Eighties' standards, the subsequent advances in broadcast technology are such that it would resemble the set of *Jurassic Park* today. Everything nowadays is digitally recorded, digitally mixed, digitally edited and digitally put to air. Apparently they're currently working on a programme which allows journalists to digitally have a piss without leaving their desks.

Back then reporters went out on stories with giant Uher reel-to-reel tape recorders which were the size of a family pack of Ariel washing powder and the weight of three copies of the *Sunday Times Illustrated Atlas of the World*. You had to inject a Balco laboratory full of steroids just to lift one. They were notoriously temperamental too, and at times for no good reason they would throw a hissy fit and flatly refuse to record anything at all. You'd be grilling your subject in a fair-minded but no-nonsense manner when you'd glance down to see the level meters dancing a merry jig while the reels had ground to a halt. Or, alternatively, the reels would be whirling around in blissful orbit with the meters lying flatter than a Dutchman's allotment.

Even if you were lucky and your interview actually found its way onto the delicately spooled reels of quarter inch tape, you were then faced with the complicated, and sometimes hazardous process of editing the interview. In order to do this you needed a mass of bits and pieces that would flummox even the most resourceful of *Blue Peter* presenters. Red leader tape, yellow leader tape, green leader tape, editing block, razor blades, chinagraph pencil, splicing tape, notepad, pen and adhesive labels. Newsroom stationery cupboards resembled a small branch of Robert Dyas.

Once you'd transferred the tape onto a larger machine and plugged in the headphones you were ready to go. You could find the point at which you wanted to edit the tape by manually pushing the tape reels backwards and forwards in a similar way in which club DJs do with vinyl records (we were hip-hop pioneers in many ways). The next step was to mark the spot with the chinagraph pencil and this was where the trouble started.

Now you may remember that Douglas Adams in *The Hitchhiker's Guide to the Galaxy* wrote of a planet inhabited by all the lost biros which had unaccountably disappeared from homes and offices. What he failed to point out was that this planet was orbited by a small moon made entirely out of the chinagraph pencils which had vanished from radio newsrooms. There was simply never one around when you needed it. Even if you'd lovingly placed one on top of the editing block it would have gone next time you looked down. Grown men (myself included) would run around in circles, their faces gnarled with anger and frustration, apoplectically screaming: "WHERE THE FUCK ARE ALL THE CHINAGRAPHS?" I swear if Lord Lucan had just given an exclusive interview about how he'd kidnapped and eaten Shergar, it would have missed the next news bulletin while the reporter spent half an hour searching in vain for a chinagraph pencil with which to edit the clip. The simplest thing was to abandon the search and use a biro.

The next step was physically to cut the tape at the desired points at either end of the edit with a razor blade, discard the bit in between, and then join the tape together with the splicing tape so that the cough or swear word or libellous outburst was removed.

I can illustrate this with the use of the slash key as the razor blade. Take this example:

Your quote is: That John Anderson is an absolute arsehole for God's sake.

You edit thus: That John Anderson is an absolute // arsehole for // God's sake.

Then thus: That John Anderson is an absolute God // 's sake //.

And hey presto: That John Anderson is an absolute God.

The dangerous bit was trying to cut the tape cleanly without severing your finger in the process. Many of the editing blocks had been lying around for years and the specially-designed grooves where you made the incision had often become full of dust, grit and bits of severed finger. So sometimes the blade would hit a divot, forcing your hand to jerk upwards causing you to slice through one of the fingers on the other hand which was holding the editing block. Newsrooms would resemble military field hospitals.

"Have you got that piece ready for the lunchtime programme?"

"Yes, I'm just mopping up the blood now."

Shorter clips were transferred onto cartridge tapes or 'carts' as they were known. If you're old enough you may remember those eight-track tapes featuring *Neil Diamond's Greatest Hits* or *The Best of Kenny Rogers,* which were sold at petrol stations in the 1970s so that truck drivers from Kettering could imagine they were driving a Winnebago through the Blue Ridge Mountains, stopping off only to pick up a hitchhiking Dolly Parton. These were similar, but often didn't 'fire' or would grind to a sudden stop halfway through the piece of audio. "That's one small step for man, one giant…" "I have in my hand a piece…" "Baggio steps up and…" That sort of thing.

The other problem with carts was that you couldn't simply record a new track over the existing one.

The tape inside had to be wiped clean first. This involved pushing them backwards and forwards inside a strange magnetic device for several minutes in order to erase the previous recording. Very often the job didn't get done properly, so bits of sound that hadn't been completely erased would create strange burping sounds underneath the new piece of audio.

Where there is discord may we burp harmony. Where there is error may we belch truth.

However all of this seemed like the ultimate in cutting edge technology as I prepared for my first ever crack at a proper shift at a real radio station. The night before I started my first day at *County Sound* I was cleaning my teeth with all the vigour of a young man who is out to impress, when a particularly brusque bout of head shaking caused my glasses to fly off into the air and land in the wash basin with a terrifying crash followed by an even more horrifying tinkle (I realise that may come across as an oxymoron since seldom has a tinkle been described as horrifying, but the sound of it still gives me nightmares). Since suffering from an astigmatism as a child I've always had very poor eyesight and have worn glasses since I was about five years old, so this was not the most promising of scenarios. When I looked down through the blur of my partial vision I saw the crystalline remains of my only pair of prescription lenses twinkling up at me in a million pieces. I felt as if my career was, almost literally, disappearing down the plug-hole before it had even started.

Luckily my Mum lent me her reading glasses, which improved matters slightly. So, leaving her to squint through her *Daily Mail*, I reported for duty on my first ever newsroom shift looking like a cross between John Lennon and Mrs Merton. Throw in the hawk-eyed 20/20 vision of Blind Pew and I was a real contender.

I explained the situation to Malcolm, who luckily saw the funny side. Thankfully my temporary blindness hadn't affected the key skill needed by any first-time newsroom dogsbody; I was still able to produce a reasonable cup of tea whenever required. It transpired that Malcolm had worked at the same BBC station as my cryogenic college lecturer and asked me what I thought of him. Suddenly I'm back at the dinner party. Do I give Mr Frosty a right coating or try and be polite? For all I know he could be Malcolm's father-in-law.

So I valiantly went for the non-committal, straight down the middle approach:

"Er well, we didn't really see eye to eye."

To my joy and relief came the reply:

"Not surprised, stupid old tosser. I couldn't stand him."

Those two weeks in the new studios atop the Friary Shopping Centre in Guildford and, more importantly, directly above the Blackfriars pub, taught me more about being a radio journalist than 17 consecutive years at Stalag Highbury could ever have done. Nick Collins, in particular, took me under his wing and gave me loads of brilliant advice about the sports side of things which stood me in good stead for years to come.

During my two weeks at *County Sound* there was a bank robbery at the local Tesco which was right next door to our studio. With all the senior staff out on other stories, another trainee was sent to get some reaction and returned half an hour later proudly describing the great interviews she'd got from shop staff and eyewitnesses. She went off into an editing booth to prepare the material for broadcast but a minute later there was an anguished and ear piercing shriek. We rushed in to see what the matter was and she tearfully pointed down towards her tape machine. In her hurry to get across to the story she had mistakenly laced up the machine with a spool of blank red leader tape, which was edited onto the end of interviews to bring them to a halt, instead of proper magnetic tape which carried the actual sound. I was then rushed out of the building in her place and got the actual material which went to air. Among the other big jobs I undertook for *County Sound* were interviewing a tearful bride-to-be whose wedding dress had been incinerated in a dry cleaning accident at Sketchleys, and talking to two

Farnborough boys who'd rescued a pensioner's dog which had become stranded on a frozen lake.

My BBC attachment was at *Radio Bristol* which was older, shabbier and less relaxed than *County Sound* but much more speech orientated and so offered me the chance to do programme features as well as straight news. I was sent on a number of interesting and diverse stories to show what I could do. One involved covering a photographic exhibition which is tough going on radio, but the highlight was a trip on the Orient Express. Okay, it was only between Bath and Bristol, but it was a great pleasure and privilege to get a free ride. I interviewed the oldest and most experienced guard on the train who gave me a guided tour of the carriages and referred to me throughout as 'sir' which was a nice touch. I also followed Princess Anne around Weston-super-Mare (not as a stalker I hasten to add). She was on an official visit of some sort and I had to describe the action . . . (effects lickspittle Nicholas Witchell whisper): "Her Royal Highness resplendent in a summery orange two piece, topped by a tangerine hat with matching tassels."

The chance to do sport couldn't come quickly enough.

The *Radio Bristol* newsroom wasn't the most cheerful and dynamic place in the world. At times it resembled a mausoleum, but I seemed to do pretty well there. The lugubrious news editor described me as "one of our better students" which, coming from him, was high praise indeed. Unfortunately I blotted my copy book when, on the last day of my scheduled stint, he called me over to his office: "I'm delighted to announce that we'd like to extend your stay by a couple of days so that you can work as a runner on the weekend breakfast programme. I'm afraid there's no money in it, but it'll be a great experience and you can help out with the sport if you like."

On any other day I would have bitten his arm off and thanked him profusely for his generous offer. But this was Friday 18 May 1984.

"Sorry I can't, I just can't."

He looked up, no doubt expecting me to announce sombrely that a dearly loved, aged relative had passed away and that I had to be back for the funeral.

"It's the FA Cup final tomorrow, my team Watford are playing Everton. I've waited all my life for this and my Dad's got a couple of tickets. I have to be at Wembley to cheer the golden boys on as it's probably the only time they'll ever get there. Sorry."

Even though Watford lost 2-0 I don't regret that decision. When the team came across to applaud us at the end clutching their losers' medals, a chorus of *We'll Support You Evermore* broke out. I just welled up, tears streaming down my face; it was the last time I cried in public.

When I got back to college I was hauled into the tutor's office.

"What's this about you snubbing a generous offer from *Radio Bristol* in order to attend a soccer match?"

I was past caring by then, I'd had a taste of what it's like to work as a proper broadcast journalist, where it really mattered, and I knew I could do it.

It's very probable that, in the 25-year history of Highbury College's Post Graduate Diploma Course in Radio Journalism, I'm the only person ever to have failed the course. I was certainly the first. In the years that followed they used to hold up some of my work as shining examples of how not to do it. Everyone else in my year passed with flying colours, but hardly any of them ended up in broadcasting.

The college wanted me to re-submit parts of the coursework so that their 100 per cent batting average of course passes would be maintained but I couldn't be arsed and just wanted to prove them wrong. At the same time I was very fearful that my failure would come back to haunt me and that I'd blown it once and for all. The end of my course coincided with the release of the first Smiths album and heaven knows I was miserable at times, but nothing changes as fast as your luck and eventually the phone rang.

CHAPTER TWO

"Stan Laurel on a bad day."

The call was from *County Sound* who wanted me to help out on their breakfast show from Monday to Friday. It meant ridiculously early starts and all they could pay me was £8 per week in expenses, but it was a foot in the door and I was thrilled to accept. My advice to budding broadcasters even now is take anything that's offered however low-paid, menial or unsociable because if you're any good it's bound to open a few more doors.

The fact that I was paid only expenses meant I also qualified for the dole although, eventually, my old Crown Life mates organised some temping work for me which kept me afloat. It was a hectic schedule though: up at 5am for a 5.45 start at the radio station. Work there until 9am and then go for a driving lesson before arriving in Woking at midday for an insurance shift until 5.30pm.

I had trouble adjusting to the early starts at first, being by nature a lazy git who never gets going until mid-morning. But at least I had this fabulous new invention called (and how quaint it must sound to the iPod generation) a portable stereo, to keep me going. I used to take great pleasure in picking the most inappropriate music for the prevailing conditions. I'd be trudging through an arctic gale in three inches of snow at the crack of dawn listening to *Summer Breeze* by the Isley Brothers, but on warm and sunny July days I'd go for *New Dawn Fades* by Joy Division.

The harsh grind eventually took its toll and on one particular day my timetable went like this:

0500 Rise
0545 Radio shift starts
0900 Radio shift ends
1000 Driving lesson
1200 Insurance work starts
1730 Insurance work ends
1731 Pop into the Red House for one very quick drink before going home
2305 Leave pub
2310 Board train for 8 minute journey to Guildford
0025 Wake up at Portsmouth Harbour
0520 Board train for Guildford
0650 Report for duty an hour late with a monster hangover

This should have been a chastening experience, a cautionary tale that drink and work don't mix and that the responsibilities of your job must always come before any social temptations. Unfortunately, like 99 per cent of journalists, my reaction was: 'Fuck me, I can do this with a hangover. Game on.'

Years later my fellow commentator and long-time travelling companion Jonathan Pearce and I would coin a deliberately ironic and oft-repeated phrase. The most common usage of this would be around 3.30am in a nightclub in somewhere like Izmir or Katowice five hours after we'd vowed to have an early night. One of us would suggest another beer and back would come the reply: "You know me, I never drink the night before a big game."

My most spectacular hangover ever came in Hong Kong on England's Far East tour just before Euro 96. A few of us had enjoyed a stupendous night at a bar called Carnegie's which played amazing music and positively encouraged people to dance on the bar. I was among the last to leave at around 5am. Four hours later I got a call saying Peter Beardsley had announced his international retirement and that the FA were staging a press conference with manager Terry Venables at the hotel as we spoke.

I jumped out of bed, threw on some clothes, grabbed my tape recorder and headed towards the lift. When I got downstairs I saw *Radio Five's* Mike Ingham had already started his interview with Terry and hovered around waiting for my turn.

When Mike had finished Terry glanced up only to be greeted by a figure who looked as if he'd just stumbled in from a downtown soup kitchen after a particularly arduous day of begging; shirt out, hair sticking up all over the place, unshaven and with eyes like the proverbial piss-holes in the snow.

"Hi Terry, can you do a piece for IRN?"

"Bloody hell son, what have you been doing? I'll tell you what, you go and sit over there and have a nice cup of tea, sort yourself out and I'll come back once I've spoken to all the newspaper guys. Dear me, you look like Stan Laurel on a bad day."

Fair play to him, he saw the funny side and did return as promised, so I got my interview. I'm not sure certain subsequent England managers would have been quite as understanding.

This was the same trip in which several of the England players got in real trouble for the infamous dentist's chair episode which involved late night drinking at another of Hong Kong's many watering holes. Some of them then caused damage to the interior of the plane which took them home. I still feel a slight tinge of guilt at the sanctimonious tone of some of my reports in the days that followed, as I berated footballers for bringing shame upon the nation with their drunken antics.

Back in 1984 the thought of crossing the world to cover England games was not so much a pipe dream as the product of a 24 hour LSD binge with Syd Barrett and Timothy Leary. But I was content to plough my way through the possibly unique role of dividing my days between appearing in local news bulletins in the morning and organising the termination of liquidated companies' pension schemes after lunch. I'd spend my Saturdays helping out on the *County Sound* sports show, lifting the national football reports from Independent Radio News, writing scripts and reading out the racing results, which was my first ever taste of live broadcasting. As with many things, the first time was a terrifying, fumbling, nerve-wracking affair, lacking any kind of composure or finesse.

"Haydock 3.15 . . . f-f-first number twelve L-L-L-Lucky Lad . . . t-t-ten to one."

And, to complete the analogy, it was over as soon as it had begun, although I very gradually improved.

Finally, no doubt wearied by my cajoling, badgering and puppy-like enthusiasm over a post-show pint or two, Nick Collins agreed to send me to cover my first ever live football match. It was a real clash of the titans and a local derby to boot; Farnborough Town v Fleet Town in the Surrey Senior Cup at the Theatre of Dreams that is Cherrywood Road. Sadly the press facilities there didn't quite match up to those at the Emirates or Old Trafford. We'd broadcast our reports over the telephone in those days and the nearest one was in a small kitchen in the clubhouse with a tiny window through which you could only see half of the pitch. So I had to sit in a nearby seat making notes and then rush back inside to file whenever the studio rang in or to dial out if there was a goal.

Fleet, who were the minnows in this epic knockout tie, scored after only five minutes, so off I went: "Sensational start at Cherrywood Road ... Fleet have taken a shock lead against mighty Farnborough ... "

When Farnborough equalised 15 minutes later I was halfway through describing that goal when an old boy tapped on the window and shouted: "We've got a penalty!" Sod's law dictated that it was at the end I couldn't see, but I didn't want to lose the moment.

"As I speak, Farnborough have a penalty ... a foul in the box and ... " I realised I had absolutely no idea who was taking the spot-kick and so with one hand over the mouthpiece I quickly hissed: "Who's taking it?" "Smithy" came the reply. Back to the phone: "Smith steps up ... " I could see and hear the fans cheering " ... and scores . . . Farnborough have the lead." For the record they went on to win 5-1 and I'd got through it reasonably well.

In the weeks that followed I visited more of football's cathedrals: places like Sutton United, Leatherhead, Woking, Ash United and Egham Town. It's amazing to think now that a small independent radio station in Surrey would devote so much of its time to covering what, in some cases, was very minor non-league football. It wasn't just us though, all over the country ILR stations were going head to head with their BBC counterparts on Saturday afternoons.

Commentators of the calibre of Clive Tyldesley, Jonathan Pearce, Steve Wilson, Guy Mowbray and Jim Proudfoot were all products of this belief that a local station's purpose was to serve, inform and reflect its local community.

Nowadays you could stick a witless DJ with a mid-Atlantic accent into a small studio on the North Pole, call it WANK FM and simulcast Celine Dion, Snow Patrol and Leona Lewis on constant rotation to every independent station in the United Kingdom and nobody would notice the difference.

"It's just coming up to 5 o'clock, we'll have three seconds of news and then it's back with a classic from Peter Andre."

In fact I think there is, or has been, a station based in Guildford called The Eagle. What the fuck's that all about for Christ's sake? Unless I've missed something, the town isn't renowned for its proliferation of aquiline birds of prey. I can only assume that, given the station's dismal middle of the road music policy, this is some sort of tribute to Don Henley and Glenn Frey. To steal a song title from one of my heroes, Mark E Smith of The Fall, it's the war against intelligence.

Having got the first game under my belt without embarrassment or calamity I felt I was on an upward spiral and it wasn't long before I made my League debut.

County Sound, though based in Surrey, claimed north east Hampshire as part of its catchment area and followed the fortunes of Aldershot, who were in the old Division Four.

The regular Shots man was unavailable one Saturday and so I was sent to Layer Road, Colchester for my first taste of the big time. Aldershot very generously allowed me to travel with the players and staff on the team coach and join them for a light lunch at a hotel en route. The players would sit towards the rear of the coach while the entire press contingent (myself and Martin Creasey from the *Aldershot News*) would occupy two seats at the front.

By my standards this was Hollywood style glamour; mixing with real footballers and getting free scrambled egg on toast. The biggest name in the squad was the veteran defender Ian Gillard, who won three England caps during a long career with QPR in the 1970s. I felt like I was rubbing shoulders with royalty. The captain Ian McDonald nicknamed me Curly because of my supposed resemblance to the *Coronation Street* character. A grossly unfair comparison in my opinion, but at least it wasn't Hilda or Vera.

Anyone who's ever been to Layer Road would concede it isn't the most plush of arenas, indeed Colchester have now relocated to a modern, out of town stadium, but to me it felt like the Nou Camp. I was sat in a proper little press box with exclusive use of a phone, next to the local newspaper guy who actually had his photo on the back of the programme. Aldershot lost 2-0 with Colchester legend Tony Adcock scoring both goals.

The following week I was on hand to witness a seven goal thriller (the old clichés are the best) in the 4-3 home defeat by Darlington. I became a regular covering Aldershot in the weeks that followed but also something of a curse. The Colchester game had been in September 1984 and I subsequently travelled to such footballing hotspots as Newport County, Hereford, Leyton Orient, Swindon and Southend with the club, as well as reporting on many of the home games. But I didn't see them win until New Year's Day away at Torquay.

I'd just failed my driving test for the first, but not last, time and there were no trains that day, so midfielder Paul Shrubb, who lived close to me in Guildford, kindly agreed to pick me up and take me to Aldershot to get the team bus. It was a ridiculously early start, so I had to leave my mates in the pub on New Year's Eve at 10.30 and was in bed by 11 o'clock. It remains the only time I've not seen the New Year in properly.

I waited at the end of my road looking out for a smart footballer's car, a Merc maybe or a BMW. After a while a battered, white painter and decorator's van pulled up alongside me and Shrubby poked his head through the window. These were very different times; nowadays a decent League Two player might be on about £150,000 a year, which is more than most people earn and certainly enough to afford a pretty nifty set of wheels. Shrubby's football salary alone wasn't sufficient to bring up a young family and he needed a second trade. When he wasn't winning balls he was skimming walls.

He was only a little fellow, but ended up in goal that day after regular number one David Coles got injured (no such thing as sub keepers back then). He played a blinder as Aldershot won 3-1 and after the match the club chairman treated all of us to a slap up meal at a local restaurant. It was a brilliant way to start the year in which I'd take my next big step career wise.

I loved every minute of my time at *County Sound* and will be eternally in the debt of Malcolm, Nick, Hugh Kirby, Guy Phillips, Kerry Swain and all the others who gave me such a brilliant start in broadcasting. But I was still on £8 per week expenses plus the Crown Life money and needed to get a full-time job.

I would apply for every ad that came up for news or sports reporters in the pages of the *Media Guardian* and *UK Press Gazette* as well as sending out my CV on spec. One of the lessons I quickly learnt, and still abide by as a freelance today, is never to take rejection personally. In no time at all I had amassed a large wad of letters informing me that my services were not required. The BBC, being the BBC, had a standard format with which to rebuff any unwanted advances. The parts in brackets are mine, I should add.

Dear (insert name of over optimistic no-hoper)

We have now considered all the applications received for the post of reporter at (insert name of station followed by bureaucratic reference number).

As a result I am sorry (relieved) to tell you that we are not placing your name on the shortlist of candidates to be invited for interview (we've known all along who's getting the job and were merely fulfilling our legal obligation in advertising the post in the first place).

I hope you will not have been too disappointed (we're certainly not) and I should like to thank you for the interest you have shown (now go away).

Yours sincerely.

V. Bland, News Editor

(until a job in national radio comes up)

At least the rejection letters from ILR stations, though just as dispiriting, had a more personal touch. So well done to the likes of *Devonair*, *Severn Sound*, *Hereward*, *Broadland*, and *Mercury*. Although they're doubtless now better known as BASH FM, CRASH FM, WALLOP FM, WHIZZ FM and DULL FM.

The same phrases kept cropping up in these letters: 'We have no vacancies at present' (we can't even afford new chingraph pencils). 'We'll keep your letter on file' (in the same place as we file the crisp packets, half-eaten sandwiches and pencil shavings). 'We wish you every success in the future' (whoever you are). 'It is not our policy to have trainees on the news staff' (unfortunately slave labour's been abolished).

In fact I sent off so many letters that I lost track of what I'd applied for, to whom and where. There's a good chance my postman still gets back spasms from the sheer weight of correspondence he was forced to shuttle back and forth at that time.

In the end my perseverance paid off and I received two positive responses in a matter of days. *Chiltern Radio* wanted to interview me for a news reporter job at their station in Dunstable and *Signal Radio* in Stoke-on-Trent had a vacancy for a sports editor.

I've always adopted a wildly enthusiastic approach to interviews. I don't see them as nerve wracking stuffy affairs and have always believed that if you can get a laugh out of the people across the table you're in with a great shout. It obviously worked in this case because I was offered both jobs. *Chiltern* carried the tantalising prospect of having Watford FC on their patch but, whereas their job entailed mainly news with a bit of sport thrown in, *Signal* had grander plans. They wanted me to reshape their entire sports output which included presenting their programmes on Fridays and Saturdays, as well as running the desk and covering games.

I'd never been to the Potteries before and plenty of my fellow southerners had been quick to slag the place off and tell me what a dump it was. I decided to travel up to Stoke the day before the interview at *Signal*, so that I could get an impression of the place and thus, hopefully, impress the interview panel with my knowledge of the area. A few minutes after I'd settled into my seat on the train an outlandishly dressed middle-aged lady sat opposite me. As I glanced up from my paper I realised that it was none other than the husky voiced star of *Carry On Screaming*, Fenella Fielding. I spent the remainder of the journey struggling against the urge to adopt an over the top Kenneth Williams nasal tone and shriek 'frying tonight' loudly down the carriage.

Once I arrived at the station I followed road signs for Stoke, assuming this would be the city centre, and quickly found Stoke City's then home the Victoria

Ground, but there seemed to be little else of any note there. The sprinkling of little shops had begun to close for the evening and there were hardly any pubs or restaurants, bar a couple of fish and chip shops and some dreary back street locals. I was beginning to fear that my friends were right and I'd stumbled into the arse-end of the world. Of course, assumption is the mother of all fuck-ups, and I should have checked before jumping to the conclusion that Stoke was the cultural heartbeat of the city.

I got the job and was soon to discover that the commercial centre of Stoke-on-Trent is in Hanley, where you can eat, drink and be merry to your heart's content. So, happily, the kind of regional one-upmanship adopted by my southern mates proved to be utter nonsense and something I always consciously avoid regardless of where I am in the world. Unfortunately you also get that attitude shown towards London by some northerners and it's born out of total ignorance and ludicrous stereotyping. Okay, Stoke-on-Trent is never going to rival Rio, Cape Town or Sydney in any beauty contest, but, as far as I was concerned it was the promised land.

CHAPTER THREE

"I'm glad we've spoiled your night."

"I hope it's not too much for you."

Those were the ringing words of endorsement I received from *County Sound's* Programme Controller as I left the station for the last time bound for the Midlands.

I wasn't too bothered. He was typical of the witless, patronising wallies who were in charge of the musical output of ILR stations in the mid-1980s. They can best be summed up in a hastily adapted version of the old joke:

Why did the Programme Controller cross the road?

To get to the middle.

Their safe as houses, stick to what you know attitude paved the way for the carnival of blandness that is the majority of local radio today. They were almost always 'Smashy & Nicey' types with rubbish haircuts and a pathological aversion to anything original, challenging or even mildly controversial. They would employ idiot savant disc jockeys (or presenters as they laughably insisted on being called) whose job it was to spout inane drivel in impossibly contrived accents in between spinning records by Hall & Oates, Sade and A-ha. They were in the thrall of record company reps who would ply them with free gifts in return for championing the latest no-hope pop acts. Worse still, they would parade around in cap sleeved T-shirts or ghastly satin tour jackets bearing the names of bands they'd never even heard of.

"I didn't know you were into The Fields of the Nephilim."

"Freebie, innit?"

Can you imagine an Arsenal fan happily wearing a Spurs shirt because it didn't cost them anything?

The *County Sound* PC's valedictory statement served as an inspiration; there's nothing better than proving your detractors wrong.

Mercifully though, the *Signal Radio* newsroom was staffed by people who did want to take risks, provide alternatives and challenge convention. And that was a fairly radical stance media-wise in that part of the world at the time.

Stoke-on-Trent is a funny old place. Virtually every single toilet you've ever pissed into was fashioned there, in keeping with the area's rich tradition of ceramic production pioneered by Josiah Wedgwood and Royal Doulton. The once thriving mining industry was in its death throes when I arrived; bitter clashes between police and picket lines had broken out at local collieries during the miners' strike the year before.

Early in my career at *Signal* we were invited to visit a local pit and actually descend into the coal face itself. Imagine if they'd left the London Underground as it was when the tunnels had first been dug in the Victorian age and you might get an idea of what it was like. Even with 20th century technology it was a stifling experience as we choked our way through the dust, grit and darkness into tiny access routes where thousands of men had spent their entire working lives chiselling in cramped conditions to help the rest of us enjoy the benefits of consumerism. A friend of mine told me his grandfather's palms were still black from the soot more than twenty years after hanging up his Davy Lamp and that no amount of washing could remove the stains.

That day down the mine often returns to me whenever I hear broadcasters in exotic locations moaning about meaningless friendlies or old fashioned commentary positions or the fact that they can't see one of the corner flags. Listen mate, you're doing something most people would give their right arm to have a crack at, so if you don't like it, fuck off and let someone else have a go.

So, given that a vast majority of the population of Stoke-on-Trent owed their living to pot banks and coal pits this was, unsurprisingly, a fiercely working-class, hard knocks, down to earth environment, very far removed from my home town of Guildford, where the number of shoe shops in the High Street alone would have left Imelda Marcos on a life support machine.

It was said at the time that Stoke-on-Trent had the greatest proportion of people who were born and also died there than any other city in the UK and it certainly has a shed load of indigenous eccentricities. Its conglomeration of six separate communities (Stoke, Hanley, Burslem, Fenton, Longton and Tunstall) is collectively known as the Five Towns and the main road in and out of the city, the A500, was known as the D road because of its shape, even though it actually looks like an inverted C.

The people were great, though, once you'd managed to pick your way through the local accent, which seemed to be an unholy alliance of Scouse, Manc and Brummie. There were endless linguistic quirks. The word 'to' was seldom used as a preposition while the definite and indefinite articles were often scorned too, hence: "I'm going shop", while 'to' was often substituted by 'for', as in: "I'm going shop for get sweets". 'Don't' for some reason came out as 'donna'.

I once told a newsroom secretary not to talk so loudly on the phone:

"Donna fockin' tell me what not do," came the reply.

I used to amuse myself by constructing improbable sentences in Stokie-speak. My favourite was:

"Donna forget go donner kebab shop for get donner kebab."

'Lend' and 'borrow' were inexplicably juxtaposed e.g. "can I lend a fiver off you?" to which the answer is: "I'd love to help you out but the constraints of the English language render such a transaction impossible." Words like 'cook' and 'book' were pronounced as if they had seventeen o's in the middle, all women over 40 called you 'duck' and all blokes under 30 called you 'youth'. I truly hope this is still the case.

Signal had been launched in 1983 as a rival to the well established *BBC Radio Stoke*; a station so set in its ways you imagined the music was still played from wax cylinders on a Regal Zonophone. Their presenters made those satin-jacketed ILR buffoons look like John Peel. One of their star turns was a bloke with an organ (don't titter) who would set up at a local Darby and Joan club or Women's Institute meeting and play requests for the old folks. Now, this would have been a wholly admirable enterprise had it merely been in private for charitable purposes but, inexplicably, the results were broadcast at peak times on the station:

"A very good afternoon, we're live at Wolstanton Miners Welfare, where the local Women's Guild are taking a break from their bring and buy sale to enjoy some jolly tunes. Mavis from the oatcake shop says she'd like to hear *Tip-toe Through The Tulips*, so this one's for you."

I always wanted to sneak in at the back and shout: "Can you play *How Does It Feel To Be The Mother Of A Thousand Dead?* by Crass or, failing that, anything by the Dead Kennedys?"

Faced with their first ever competition for listeners, *Radio Stoke* put up a large advertisement at the side of the road close to the *Signal* studios. The slogan read (I kid you not) '*BBC Radio Stoke, we're up Hanley, duck*'

The local paper, the *Evening Sentinel* (or Evening Senile as we called it) was even less progressive if that were possible. Rumour has it that the first edition was discovered on an archaeological dig in the late 1800s and had been typeset by John Caxton himself. In any event it took an immediate and irrational hatred of anything to do with *Signal Radio*.

So, in the autumn of 1983, Stoke-on-Trent's genteel, laissez-faire broadcasting and journalistic landscape was shattered as *Signal Radio* gatecrashed the scene like one of those Facebook 'trash a mansion' parties so beloved of precocious teenagers with too much money and inadequate parental supervision.

The station's HQ was a converted building not far from the railway station. It had been lovingly designed by a panel of experts to include two big on air studios, a production suite, offices for executives, an open plan area for programming staff, an engineering department and a garage for the OB vehicles. Unfortunately, no-one had made any provision for a newsroom and the whole site was duly constructed without one. With a six- strong news staff to accommodate, a hasty reappraisal of the space available had to be made. And so it was that *Signal Radio* announced, with great pride, the opening of its brand new, up to date, state of the art news . . . corridor.

This narrow channel which ran along the length of one side of the building was at its narrowest point about six feet wide and at its widest about nine. Anyone reversing their chair without due care and attention was in danger of inadvertently kneecapping a cherished colleague. Occasionally someone would be stupid enough to try and use the newsroom as an actual corridor. They'd stride in wearing a look of smug arrogance only to hobble out at the other end bruised and battered; the very same face now transformed into an ugly, contorted mix of agony and rage. It was a bit like a spindly-legged winger trying to dribble his way through a back four comprising Chopper Harris, Tommy Smith, Neil Ruddock, and Julian Dicks (with Vinnie Jones as the holding midfielder). Seasoned potholers would have thought twice before attempting to squeeze through its confines and if you tried to design a prison along the same lines, you'd have had hardened lifers up on the roof hurling slates quicker than you could say "spatially challenged".

As for the fixtures and fittings, one long workbench ran along the left hand side, atop which sat five clunky old typewriters just about visible amid a mountain of waste paper. The editor's desk jutted out at right angles following the contours of the wall at the end. Think of a poorly designed and desperately ill equipped B&Q galley kitchen, only with tape recorders instead of white-tops.

I first stepped into this architectural monstrosity in mid-April 1985 at the age of 24 and enjoyed a halcyon two and a half year spell there. In those days of incremental pay structures I was a Journalist Local Radio Grade One (JLRI), commanding a head-spinning salary of £9,665 per annum. The first thing I did was get highlights put in my hair, buy a black leather motorbike jacket and virtually empty the Lotus Records alternative rock section.

My cohorts were news editor Chris Moore, reporters Rob Beasley (now one of the country's leading football writers), Sue Bookbinder (formerly of *BBC Radio Five Live*), Paul Sheldon (who spent an amazing 25 years in the news corridor before finally winning parole) and Jackie Wheatcroft (whose teenage son, I believe, is now a professional footballer who was once on Stoke City's books). Or as they were more commonly known, in the finest British tradition of imaginative nick-names: Mooro, Robbo, Booko, Shello and Wheato.

I also had a sporting partner in crime in the diminutive, rotund shape of garishly-coutured workaholic George Andrews, a legendary Midlands soccer and speedway man who, in the 1960s and 70s, had been billed rather incongruously as 'top local DJ Andy Best, spinning all your northern soul favourites'. He still did the odd gig and I once went to watch him compere a show by soul legend Edwin Starr at a small club in the city. I'm sure the late, great Edwin took to the stage with many an MC's resounding build up ringing in his ears. But I doubt any of them ever topped George who, with his gift for finding the wrong words at the right time yelled:

"Ladies and gentleman get off your feet and on your seats for Mr Edwin Starr."

He (George, not Edwin) was known as the Hofmeister Bear, in homage to the ursine, pork pie-hatted 1980s beer commercial character to whom he bore an uncanny resemblance, even down to the exaggerated gait. Even now people come up to me and say:

"Have you seen The Bear lately?"

Small details such as George's age, home address, marital status and offspring would forever remain a tantalising mystery.

"Come on George, tell us, are you married?"

"Not so's you'd notice."

"Any kids?"

"Fucking hell, Wolves have signed Steve Bull from West Brom, what a waste of money."

He was an absolute diamond. If Port Vale were away at Torquay on a wind-swept Tuesday night in mid December he wouldn't need to be asked twice. "Steady ride," he'd shout as he left the building, only to return 15 minutes later after realising he'd forgotten his tape recorder.

One time he went to do some interviews at Crewe Alexandra, another of the local clubs, and sensibly decided to check the recording had worked before returning to base. He put the Uher machine on to the roof of his sponsored car (a tasteful metallic blue Renault with 'Ando 257 Sport' emblazoned down each side), clicked the play button and all was well. After a quick thank you and goodbye to Ros, the ever friendly and helpful Gresty Road secretary, he drove off.

As you've probably guessed, George had left the ground with the machine still on top of his car and somehow managed to get about two and a half miles before it finally slipped off and crashed into the road. Twenty minutes later we got a call from a lady in a phone box near a roundabout on the A500 who had had to swerve to avoid this airborne recording device but, bless her, was more worried about getting it back to us.

She kindly offered to take it into the local police station so that we could retrieve it.

George duly returned to the newsroom.

"Forgotten anything George?"

"Don't think so, why?"

"Tape recorder?"

"Oh fuck, aye. Must have left it at the ground."

"No, you've left it in a tangled mass of metal, plastic and magnetic tape on a grass verge near Barthomley, but it's now in the safe hands of the Cheshire Constabulary."

He went back to collect it, the station engineers somehow managed to put it back together and the tape recording survived. Later that day when we were compiling the evening news programme someone asked George if the interview was finally ready for broadcast. The response summed up his whole attitude to life in general:

"Oh aye, no problem."

As well as Crewe and Port Vale (who were both Fourth Division at the time) we covered the big local team, Stoke City, who were then in the First Division, although not for long. The 1984/85 season saw the club win only three matches, totalling a meagre 17 points to set a new record for the least successful season in the history of English top flight professional football. They scored just 24 goals all season and relegation had been well and truly clinched by the time I arrived towards the end of the campaign.

On my first day at the station I was quite nervous and hoping for a nice quiet shift learning the ropes, trying to be polite and getting to know my new colleagues and surroundings. Unfortunately within about an hour of my arse hitting the seat the sports desk phone rang. It was Stoke City informing me that the manager Bill Asprey had been sacked. Suddenly my nerves turned to terror. I'd only arrived in the area the night before, I knew no-one at the club and no-one knew me. Fortunately Rob Beasley, primarily a news reporter but who covered many of Stoke's matches, went off to do the live outside broadcast from the ground while I wrote the obits and began the speculation.

It wasn't my biggest ever baptism of fire (more of that later) but I felt a little embarrassed by my rather hesitant reaction to a big, breaking story. I'm sure there were a few at the station who felt Chris Moore's faith in appointing an inexperienced outsider was beginning to look like a massive gamble that wasn't going to pay off.

Funnily enough, my predecessor as sports editor had had to cover the departure of the previous boss Richie Barker the season before. They crossed to him for a live update from outside the ground and he was obviously very nervous about the whole thing. His opening line passed into *Signal Radio* legend:

"I can confirm this morning's rumours are true. Stoke City manager Richie Barker has been shot . . . er . . . er . . . er . . . sacked."

The first few days were pretty hard going. I was confident in some ways but not especially outgoing; hopeless at starting up conversations and a little nervous when thrown into new situations. I was subjected to a series of practical jokes at the hands of Messrs Beasley and Sheldon which amused them more than it did me, but this was par for the course.

At the end of the first week I was invited to a party thrown by the station in honour of the station's record librarian, who was leaving. I remember a ring of people dancing to some record or other and, every now and then, someone would be chosen to go into the middle and strut his or her stuff while the others cheered them on. Most were brilliant and utterly uninhibited, throwing shapes learnt through a lifetime on the dance floors of Northern Soul clubs.

As a teenager I'd been used to Guildford house parties where most of us would spend the whole night in the kitchen in our cheese cloth shirts drinking cans of Party Seven and discussing the latest punk releases, while the dopeheads sat crossed legged on the floor of the adjoining breakfast room skinning up and listening to Steve Hillage or Planet Gong. So Gene Kelly I was not, but reluctantly I took my turn in the centre of the circle and spent a hugely embarrassing ten seconds shuffling around uncomfortably to *You Spin Me Round* by Dead or Alive. It was a bit like one of those old fashioned film scenes where a khaki clad white hunter in a pith helmet stumbles upon a long lost tribe of colourfully painted African headmen wielding their spears, and politely enquires if anyone knows where you can get a nice cup of tea.

Mercifully this party long pre-dated the advent of camera phones and camcorders so there is no documented evidence of my first and last attempt to emulate Pete Burns. But it was a very enjoyable occasion and I slowly began to become a part of the *Signal Radio* fraternity although, on this showing, their acceptance of me was inspired by pity rather than admiration.

Incidentally, the girl in whose honour the party was held was called Anthea Turner. I wonder what happened to her?

I wasn't due to start presenting the sports show until the start of the new football season, so I had the summer in which to bed in. For a short spell I lived in a rented room in a house owned by a trendy woman with lots of equally trendy friends who would come round and talk about art installations, jazz clubs and macrobiotic diets while I was trying to watch the football.

I tried to be patient, civil and understanding, but finally snapped during the legendary World Snooker Championship final between Dennis Taylor and Steve Davis. A nation was glued to what was developing into one of the greatest contests ever televised in this or any other sport, but unfortunately the unbearable tension and drama was lost on a group of her friends who plonked themselves down on the sofa. They began to complain about how boring it was, how the players looked stupid in their bow ties and why couldn't they turn over and watch something else. There was one guy in particular who went on and on and on about it until finally I could take no more. Of course as a paying guest in someone else's house one should always respect the rights of people to express their views while accepting that not everyone has the same tastes and that their opinions were just as valid as mine. Well bollocks to that. I rose from my chair, turned round and shouted words to this effect:

"Listen mate, if you don't shut the fuck up I'm going to get a snooker cue and shove it so far down your throat that you'll be shitting 147 breaks for the rest of your life."

It did shut the lentil eating, tea-cosy hatted, satchel carrying wanker up, but, suffice to say, I was swiftly struck off the yoga and mime workshop invitation lists and soon seeking new accommodation.

During that summer I met a young *Signal Radio* trainee presenter called George Vjestica or 'VJ the DJ' as he was known, who shared my taste in indie music and was well connected with the local rock inner circle (such as it was in Stoke at the time). One of the perks of working at *Signal* was that we could fill our boots from the vast array of records in the station library's 'chuck out bin'. These were the records sent into the station by record companies which were deemed by the satin jacket brigade as being not quite bland or middle of the road enough for general airplay. Such subversive and controversial acts included REM, The Cure and Echo and the Bunnymen. I occasionally flick back though my vinyl collection, many of the LPs bearing a *Signal Radio* sticker and the legend 'Promotional Copy Not For Resale' and wonder whatever became of The Mighty Lemon Drops, Balaam And The Angel, Flesh For Lulu, The Leather Nun, Strawberry Switchblade and the Close Lobsters. They're probably all accountants now. George, incidentally, became a session guitarist of some repute and has worked with KT Tunstall, Nick Cave and Bernard Butler as well as touring with Groove Armada and getting engaged to a 23-year-old model. Bastard.

I went down from Stoke to London for the Live Aid concert with George. It always makes me laugh when they dredge up all these Z list celebrities with their memories of the event on those nostalgia programmes as they drone on and on about Queen and Princess Diana and Bob Geldof. My most vivid memory of the world's biggest rock show was being part of a large section of the crowd playing 500-a-side volleyball with a teddy bear while Paul McCartney plunked his way through an instrumental version of *Let It Be* after his microphone cut out.

We were also often given tickets for shows at the Hanley Victoria Hall and other, smaller music venues in the area. I saw some great gigs during my time at *Signal* like The Smiths, The Fall, OMD, Big Audio Dynamite, The Stranglers and Prefab Sprout as well as some not so great ones such as Doctor and the Medics, the Armoury Show, and, inexplicably and to my eternal shame, David Cassidy. "Come on, it'll be a laugh," someone said. It wasn't.

The most memorable was Sigue Sigue Sputnik at a small club George used to DJ at called Shelley's in Longton in 1986. The London-based band were briefly the *enfants terrible* of rock with their pink hair, gyrating female backing vocalists and the singer's fishnet facemasks. Looking back it was sheer panto, but after reports of riots breaking out at their shows, the tabloid dailies were positively incandescent with righteous indignation as evidenced by their 'The Sick Group Perverting Our Pop Kids' style headlines. The Shelley's gig was only the fourth they'd ever done and I went along with a tape recorder not to capture their 'unique live sound', but in case I needed to interview outraged punters after another night of sexual abandonment and violent disorder. I needn't have bothered; the only thing the audience were outraged about was the band's lame theatrics and third rate cyberpunk. They were booed off stage after only four songs and didn't return.

I picked up the *Sun* the next day, only to read about how the gig had degenerated into a sordid sex show with drugged up fans jumping onto the stage in scenes of near copulation with members of the group in full view of shocked and disgusted teenagers. Total bollocks of course, but as they say, never let the facts get in the way of a good story.

The following year I did get my chance to report on a full scale rock riot. That year's perverters of pop kids were New York rappers the Beastie Boys. They'd caused a storm by allegedly poking fun at some disabled children at an airport and had a stage act which involved topless, caged go-go dancers and a giant inflatable penis. Needless to say the red tops were having a field day. I loved the single *Fight For Your Right To Party* and had fished their excellent debut album 'Licenced To Ill' out of the *Signal* chuck out bin.

My girlfriend, now wife, was living in Liverpool at the time and got tickets, so I went up to the city's Royal Court theatre to see what all the fuss was about. It was one of those nights where you could smell the danger; I'd later experience the same feeling many times when travelling the world with some of the hideous scum that follow the England football team. You just know it's going to kick off. It was soon pretty clear that many of the people in the crowd were scallies who'd gone along simply to show these brash Yank rappers a thing or two. After about three or four songs, beer cans, lighters, coins and other stuff was being thrown at the stage. We were in the stalls and more items were raining down from the balcony including several seats. One of the Beastie Boys unwisely reacted to this by hurling a beer can back into the crowd, hitting a young girl in the face. Cue pandemonium. What had been a light drizzle of bottles and cans suddenly became a torrential downpour, people were piling towards the exits in terror as the promoter pulled the plug on the gig.

I got hit on the back by a beer bottle as I fled out of the venue and ran straight across to the nearby studios of *Radio City* (where my erstwhile *Signal Radio* colleague Sue Bookbinder was on the late shift). I filed some eyewitness reports for them and for IRN which ended up as a lead story on the national news. I had always dreamed of being a rock critic, but both concerts I'd covered as a reporter had ended prematurely with only about eight songs between them. Maybe I was better off in sport.

* * * * *

My new sports show began in autumn 1985 and coincided with the arrival of former England captain Mick Mills as Stoke City's new manager. He was incredibly helpful to me (as were John Rudge at Port Vale and Dario Gradi at Crewe) as

I stumbled my way through the early weeks of the news season, presenting a one hour preview show on Friday evenings and the four hour programme between 2pm and 6pm every Saturday alongside one of the DJs who did the music while I concentrated on the sport. We didn't have any commentary rights, so the four hours were a mixture of music and updates from 'around the grounds' both nationally via IRN and with our own team of reporters (Rob Beasley at Stoke, George Andrews with Vale, the late Mike Calvert following Crewe and Chris Godwin covering non-Leaguers Stafford Rangers). We had landlines at the local grounds which meant we could broadcast from there in studio quality, but away games were almost always done on the phone. This led to occasional disconnection and crossed lines, such as when I was covering a midweek Crewe game at Burnley and one of the reports featured a row between a bloke and his irate girlfriend going on in the background.

"Nil nil at Turf Moor . . . *you've been seeing that slag haven't you?* . . . Gary Blissett had a chance in the 14th minute . . . *but I still love you, Donna* . . . Pemberton was booked for dissent . . . *how can I ever trust you again?* . . . it's been a disappointing game so far. Burnley nil Crewe Alexandra nil . . . *Donna, please, she means nothing to me.*"

Sometimes we would rely on the services of local agency reporters to cover the away games for us if they were too far flung even for George Andrews. Many of these were old dyed in the wool newspaper men who sounded (and doubtless looked) like Arthur Mullard or Les Dawson. And they often had no idea of what was acceptable in a radio broadcast. I remember one guy repeatedly referring to "the two coloured lads on the bench", while another summed up a particularly dreadful goalless draw with the words: "This was the sort of game that makes you want to go home and batter the wife." One even came out with "Port Vale one up thanks to Phil Sproson, that's Sproson spelt capital S . . . P . . . R . . . O . . . S . . . O . . . N", thinking he was filing copy back to a copytaker in a newspaper office somewhere.

We had this gimmick, which we'd unashamedly nicked off *Piccadilly Radio* in Manchester, whereby if there was a goal at one of our featured games, we'd play a jingle in the middle of the record before cutting away to the ground for an update. There was: "It's a gooooaaallll" for good news and "Ohhhhh nooooo" for bad. Sometimes it would go slightly awry.

"We're going to interrupt David Platt's new single there because Kylie Minogue has just scored at Boothferry Park."

The national material was supplied by IRN who were very much allied to the London station LBC and we had to lift reports directly from the output of their Saturday afternoon programme *Sportswatch* which was piped in to all the independent stations. The problem was that they only covered matches involving London clubs so there would be some rather strange and enforced editorial decisions:

"Ian Rush has just put Liverpool two goals up at Old Trafford, but let's go back to The Den and find out how Millwall are getting on against Charlton."

As well as being the sports editor I was also expected to fill in on news at *Signal* when it was quiet on our desk. This was a far stronger and grittier news patch than Surrey and north east Hampshire and I got the opportunity to cover much bigger stories than I had been used to at *County Sound*. One example was the brutal murder of a prostitute in one of the city's red light areas. Rob Beasley and I decided to go out there the following evening to see if there were any girls brave or desperate enough to be back out on the streets so soon after the tragedy. Depressingly there still were, but we got some really emotive interview material which made national news headlines.

I also turned political correspondent for a week. Newcastle-under-Lyme, a town separate from Stoke-on-Trent but bordering so close as to be almost part of it, had a by-election while I was there which was great fun to be involved in. I interviewed former Prime Minister Edward Heath and Labour front bencher Roy Hattersley who was a really nice bloke. After he'd done his bit on tape we sat for half an hour discussing Sheffield Wednesday and curry houses which, frankly, was far more interesting than the political stuff.

On the night of the election itself I was in the Town Hall working as a roving reporter looking out for key figures to interview as part of a special programme which was going out live throughout the evening. I remember waiting to talk to somebody or other when I was barged in the back by a fat bloke with a camera crew in tow.

"Vincent Hanna BBC, Vincent Hanna BBC, let me through," he kept shouting.

I later learnt he was the doyen of television by-election coverage and had apparently been present at every count since Pitt the Elder first came to power. At the time though, I didn't have a clue who he was, other than seeming to me a rude, fat bastard who was trying to push in. So I decided it was a bye-bye election as far as he was concerned and told him I wasn't moving for anyone and he could wait his bloody turn. As Oscar Wilde once noted: 'The antiquity of an abuse is no justification for its continuance.'

As a result I had to do the whole interview with this enraged, sweaty mass leaning against my back pushing, shoving and muttering furiously under his breath. It's a stand that I have always taken; don't let anyone, however important they think they are, try and muscle in on your interview.

Generally though, unlike Mr Hanna, I wasn't a heavyweight news journalist and most enjoyed doing the quirky off-beat 'and finally' stories which often provide a smile at the end of a bulletin.

Rob Beasley, Paul Sheldon, Sue Bookbinder and I were forever looking at absurd ways of making these light-hearted pieces more amusing. We once did a story about a particularly dim-witted burglar who would take his dog out with him on jobs and eventually got caught after leaving the animal outside a house as he fled after being disturbed. The police found his name, address and telephone number on the dog's collar and duly collared the felon.

We decided, given the ridiculous nature of the story, that it would be more fun to immortalise this in verse rather than provide a normal voice piece. And so the report went something like this:

There was a young burglar called Bob,
Who took his dog out on a job.
He broke into a house
As quiet as a mouse
And found lots of stuff he could rob.

His plan was going all right,
As he rummaged around in the night,
But he turned round and fled
In terror and dread
When somebody turned on the light.

And as he ran off in a state,
The coppers arrived just too late,
But they soon had their man
And he was thrown in the can
'Cos he'd left the dog tied to the gate.

Another one we had fun with was the case of a group of Cheshire naturists who'd been told they could no longer use a particular piece of ground for their sports activities after local residents complained to the council that unsightly patches of flabby and wrinkled flesh were sometimes visible from a busy nearby road.

The group's crestfallen president called the newsroom to ask if we could publicise their search for a replacement venue in which they could enjoy an innocent game of badminton or volleyball *au naturel*. This was, he insisted, a serious matter and not the sort of thing to be sniggered at or used as an excuse for any cheap smut or innuendo. We assured him that, as responsible journalists, the last thing we would ever want to do is humiliate, belittle or offend, and that we would treat the story with the respect and subtlety it deserved.

So Rob Beasley and I got our heads together and came up with the following opening line:

"And finally . . . nudists in Crewe are looking for a new place to hang out."

To be fair we did stop short of our original intention of describing the president as "the naturist group's big nob" but, inevitably, the phone rang within seconds. "You haven't heard the last of this", "I'll be on to the management", "never been so insulted", blah blah blah. I think at one point Rob said, "keep your shirt on mate . . . oh no you can't can you?" which hardly helped matters. Of course we never heard any more about it and my dearest wish is that the Crewe nudies are happily ping-ponging away in some idyllic glade as we speak.

We also ran the story of an extremely attractive local woman who was claiming unfair dismissal after being sacked as a tour guide for a coach company when they discovered that she had a second career as a glamour model and had appeared naked on the pages of a top-shelf men's magazine. The boss of the firm in question came in for an interview clutching a copy of the offending publication. Seething with righteous indignation, he walked up with a face like thunder, opened the mag out at the centre spread and slapped it down on the desk in front of us.

"Do you think this sort of thing is acceptable?"

"She looks more than acceptable to me mate," I replied.

We finally did get a warning from the Programme Controller though when I voiced a feature about the success of bodice ripping romantic novels complete with Sue Bookbinder faking an orgasm in the background. Mind you, the same bloke once told a presenter to remove the audio of Neil Armstrong's "one small step" speech from a promo on the grounds that "the sound quality's very poor".

But this was as nothing compared to the furore we caused at one of the station's Christmas parties. We had become such a close knit group by then that we decided to liven up the event by forming a band. Rob was a very competent singer and guitarist and I, fancying myself as the Keith Moon of north Staffordshire, took the drum stool. Simon, one of the engineers, played bass, with Booko and Shello on backing vocals, augmented by presenter Chris Lowe and a cracking lad who worked in admin called Neil Thompson. As a mark of disrespect to the incumbent leader of the 'free world' we were called President Reagan's Aids (note spelling).

Our set featured a handful of easy to play cover versions (Dr Feelgood's *Milk and Alcohol* was definitely one) and the climax of the show was a punk version of *White Christmas* (nicked off a Stiff Little Fingers B-side) which went down a storm, and a revamped adaptation of *No One Is Innocent* by the Sex Pistols which did not.

Neil, Rob and I had sat in the bar of our home from home, the Roebuck pub, and come up with a new set of lyrics for the song which poked fun at certain members of the station's presentation and management staff. The chorus of the song set out our stall:

> God bless President Reagan's Aids,
> What a load of shite,
> But if you haven't got a sense of humour,
> We're glad we've spoilt your night.

All was going well, with the victims enjoying the good natured piss-taking until the last two verses (and I've altered the names to avoid them any further embarrassment).

The first concerned a DJ who had recently been banned from driving for being over the limit, a story which had made the front page of the *Evening Sentinel,* who always enjoyed rubbing our noses in it:

> God bless Tommy Tyler,
> Drink driving's what he likes,
> So it's bye-bye to your sponsored car,
> And on your fucking bike.

The second lampooned a member of senior management, about whose appearance there had often been rumours:

> God bless Gerald Watson,
> He thinks he's Mr Big,
> But we know his little secret,
> He wears a fucking wig.

Almost as soon as Rob had said "thank you very much, goodnight" we saw poor 'Gerald' leading his sobbing wife out of the room, his face red with rage, while 'Tommy' the banned DJ was equally incandescent.

Unbeknown to us, the management had invited a large group of board members, sponsors, advertisers and other local worthies to the party and were less than pleased to see their own staff ritually humiliated by a bunch of musically challenged journalists in black leather jackets. Apparently they were considering disciplinary action against us at one stage, but the thought of the fun the local rag would have with that story probably put them off.

I'd been at the station for two years by that stage and had had an absolutely brilliant time. I did my first ever football commentary at the Victoria Ground when Stoke City reached the fifth round of the FA Cup and lost to eventual winners Coventry City. The Stoke side that day featured Lee Dixon, who would go on to play for Arsenal and England before becoming a first-class television pundit. The city was great, the people were fantastic, the programme was a success and I'd met my wife Carolyn thanks to one of the guys who helped out on my sports show, who casually told me:

"I went to college with a really nice girl who supports Watford, she's coming down this weekend."

His loss was my lifelong gain. The first thing I ever said to Carolyn when she arrived in the studio at the end of a programme was:

"If you're not doing anything else can you go and get the chips love."

Inexplicably this was the start of a beautiful relationship.

You can look at local radio two ways. Either you lay down roots, bed in, enjoy the quality of life and stay put, or you use it as a platform to venture on into the wider world, cover bigger stories and go to bigger events. I was of the latter persuasion and an intriguing newspaper advertisement had caught my eye, this time in the *Media Guardian*:

'Independent Radio News are seeking an enthusiastic and knowledgeable sports reporter to join its London based team. Must be prepared to travel abroad as part of the job.'

CHAPTER FOUR

"Rimpick Star–Yon."

So it was that in October 1987 after another hyperbolic and high octane interview I was hired in a dual role working for both IRN in its capacity as the provider of national and international sports coverage and LBC as the speech station for London.

This plunged me right into the heart of Fleet Street, which was just beginning to head towards the end of its journalistic heyday, although had not yet imploded into the inglorious strip of insurance companies and cappuccino bars it is today. The LBC/IRN HQ was in Gough Square, opposite the house where the 18th century essayist and lexicographer Samuel Johnson had lived and within convenient staggering distance of his favourite pub the Olde Cheshire Cheese. This fine hostelry was located on a site where pints had been pulled since 1538 and not even The Great Fire of London or the drunken antics of an endless stream of pissed up hacks had threatened its position as a cornerstone of life in the so-called street of shame.

The legendary basement (some would say bunker) at Gough Square housed the journalistic nerve centre of both operations. IRN provided news bulletins on the hour, every hour, which most independent stations took in those days and its proud motto was 'never wrong for long', meaning that if you made an almighty fuck up you could at least put it right within the next 59 minutes. I'm told certain other organisations have adopted this as their motto, but we definitely thought of it first and anyone leaving IRN was presented with a T-shirt bearing the slogan.

Whereas *Signal's* newsroom had been narrow and congested, this one was large, open-plan and computerised. The staff were a generally well educated and liberal bunch who, nonetheless, displayed a near Neanderthal approach to post-shift refuelling. This was before the days of all day pub opening hours, but you could still drink round the clock if you knew the locale well enough. The boozers in nearby Smithfield market kept unusual hours to cater for the changing shifts of its meat workers and, for a small fee, you could join 'The Workers', a little club just behind Gough Square, which by virtue of its private status was not subject to the licensing laws. It's rumoured that several members of staff discovered the secret of perpetual motion by rotating endlessly between newsroom and pub.

There was a heady mix of editors, producers, presenters, reporters and researchers at Gough Square, all vying for space and status within this windowless world and they generated feverish levels of noise and activity. Shouting, swearing, fighting, random acts of violence, destruction of equipment, tantrums and other extremes of ergonomic behaviour weren't so much frowned upon as actively encouraged. Cartridge tapes, notepads and other items of office stationery seemed to be perpetually flying through the air; thrown, like the thunderbolts of Thor, by irate staff, while great cardboard boxes of discarded copy paper would be booted skywards Jonny Wilkinson style, showering everyone in yesterday's news. Many of the workforce conversed in a unique language comprising only personal pronouns, expletives and the very occasional verb, e.g.: "You fucking arsehole, you wanker, I'll fucking twat you, you tosser." Sometimes even the pronouns and verbs were considered surplus to requirement: "Fuck, shit, bollocks, fuck, fuck, shit, wank."

It was not unusual to walk down the stairs into the newsroom and find a full scale game of cricket being played out between two rows of desks with a litter bin at each end for the stumps. The batsman would wield one of those large cardboard tubes that normally houses a rolled up poster while the bowler would begin his run up in a nearby corridor and burst through the door like Freddie Flintoff wielding a ball fashioned out of lovingly entwined rubber bands.

As you edged gingerly towards your seat you'd either be poleaxed by a beautifully middled cover drive or greeted with a banshee-like cry of: "Get out of the fucking way, I can't see the mid-wicket boundary."

If such a scene were to be re-enacted today, some Human Resources knobhead would contact the Health and Safety Executive who would doubtless close down the entire operation within seconds and send us all on an anger management course where we'd be invited to confront our 'aggression issues' using only the medium of mime. Back then, a passing management figure would merely have chuckled and shouted: "Fine shot McGarry."

Actually I didn't pluck that name out of the ether; it's a respectful nod to the legendary news editor Vince McGarry whose propensity for swearing would make even the most foul-mouthed of troopers run blubbing to his Mum and who, along with his partner in crime Steve Gardiner, was the driving force behind the regular basement Test matches and most of the mayhem which exploded around Gough Square. Give them a breaking story, though, and they were the best in the business.

Other luminaries included the inspired Aussie Rob Sims, the sagely John Sutton, the generally sanguine but occasionally explosive Rick Thomas, the oasis of calm amid the storm that was Gary Donovan (coincidentally now a near neighbour of mine) and the totally bald, but totally inspired Tony Cook who suffered from alopecia but positively encouraged jokes about his lack of hair.

One time a colleague of Tony's spotted a familiar-looking bald dome in front of him as he descended the stairs towards the Gough Square basement. Without hesitation he jumped down a couple of steps, leapt on to his victim's shoulders and began slapping the shining pate just like Benny Hill used to do with that little old guy during the final credits of his show, when he was taking a breather from chasing scantily clad models through a London Park.

"Hey Cookie, you bald twat, how's it going?"

A sense of horror then engulfed the cheerful slapper as he looked up and was confronted not by workmate Tony Cook but former Olympic gold medal winning swimmer Duncan Goodhew, who'd come in for an interview. Profuse apologies followed and Duncan, to his eternal credit, saw the funny side. Good job it wasn't Yul Brynner.

I was just short of 27 when I arrived at IRN, which made me by several years the youngest of a sports team which was led by the hugely likeable and laconic editor Mike Porter. He'd lived a very varied life and was great value in the pub after work, but if you wanted to know anything about football you had to ask someone else as he had little interest in anything other than rugby and boxing.

In addition to the normal desk and presentation duties each reporter had a specialist sport which was their passport to the big events at home and abroad. Steve Tongue was number one in football, aided by Andrew Gidley who also covered tennis, Nick Peters did golf, Colin Turner racing and Dominic Allan, who sadly died in 2007, followed cricket. Dominic's brief meant that he hardly ever spent any time in the office as he'd cover the home series in the summer and head off to Australia, the West Indies, Pakistan or wherever in the winter.

In fact I had begun to wonder whether he actually existed since it was nearly six months after I'd joined that we finally got to meet. Dominic was an extraordinary figure whose capacity for drink was as legendary as his wit, which was so dry that he could drain a swimming pool with two carefully chosen words. A huge, lavishly-bearded Scot with a military background who'd boxed for his regiment, he drifted into broadcasting in his forties after a career as an actor in the early days of television. More often that not Dominic had found himself cast as a fog-shrouded policeman holding a flashlight in the opening scene of 1960s episodes of *Doctor Who*. As he prowled around an alleyway, he'd suddenly turn around at the sound of a dustbin being overturned.

"Is somebody there? . . . Aaaaaaarrrrrrrrggggggghhhhh!!!!!!!!!!!"

Within seconds he'd been vaporised by an irate cyberman (is there any other type?) and all that would be left of him was a smoking patch of neutralised sou'wester. I think he also fell victim to an alien avenger in the rubbish 1970s children's sci-fi series *The Tomorrow People* which starred the drummer out of Flintlock, the world's most unlamented pop group.

Dominic enjoyed an even shorter role in *The Railway Children* in which he played one of the policemen that took the family's Dad away in the opening sequence. Sadly, his only speaking line was cut from the subsequent video and television versions of the film and so his 15 seconds of fame were lost forever. It was also rumoured that he got on the shortlist of auditions for the part of nautical fish fingers guru Captain Birdseye, although given his stern exterior and refusal to suffer fools gladly, it's hardly surprising that the role went elsewhere. You can imagine the audition:

"Aye, aye Capt'n Birdseye, how about serving us up some tasty treats?"

"Sorry young man, I'm rather busy at the moment having a drink with an old friend, so would you kindly bugger off?"

The small screen's loss was radio's gain though. Dominic, though Scottish and fiercely proud of it, had a southern English accent and what a wonderful, rich, authoritative voice it was. Imagine, if you will, Luciano Pavarotti reporting from Lord's rather than singing at La Scala.

However, the faultless professional tones which graced the airwaves would often descend into a series of unintelligible mumbles, groans and grunts after a few pints of bitter (always in a jar with a handle) in the Cheshire Cheese as he'd go into one of his amusing, but long-winded anecdotes about life on tour. I think of him whenever I see the *Fast Show* character Rowley Birkin QC and wonder whether, somewhere at the back of the saloon bar, Paul Whitehouse was lurking with a notepad.

"Hhhmbbphhrrr...Second Test at Port of Spain...hhhhmmmphrrrrgggghhpphh . . . 173 for 2 . . . ffppphhhhlllppggghhrrr . . . rain stopped play . . . rrhhhhmmm

. . . went to the bar . . . phlllllppppprrrr . . . ended up in a skip . . . mmmhhhp-prrrrrggghhmmpph."

Dominic was off in some faraway land, doubtless with a huge hangover, on the first day I arrived at IRN. I remember Mike Porter was flicking through the diary and noticed that the name Colin Jackson had been scribbled down as being a guest for an interview that afternoon.

"Who the hell's Colin Jackson?" he asked.

"He's a Welsh 110 metre hurdler, won a bronze medal at the World Championships in Rome this summer," I replied, eager to look alert and knowledgeable.

"Right, well you can interview him then."

And so it was that after this rigorous selection and vetting process I became, by default, IRN's athletics correspondent, a job which would take me to five Olympic Games in the next 17 years.

I was born in an Olympic year, 1960, and have always been fascinated by the event. Tommie Smith's black power salute, Bob Beamon's jaw dropping long jump and David Hemery's hurdles gold medal in Mexico in 1968 are among my earliest sporting memories. As a seven-year-old I followed the action via the fuzzy black and white pictures and phone quality commentaries that crackled into our living room at odd times of the day. I even kept a scrapbook on those Games as a primary school project, cutting out grainy newspaper pictures of boxer Chris Finnegan and sailor Rodney Pattisson which were crudely glued down and bestowed with horribly misspelt captions.

Being the child of an English father and a French mother, the highlight of the games saw the family gathered round our small TV set to watch the women's 400 metres final, a showdown between Britain's teenage golden girl Lilian Board and her French rival Colette Besson. It was a fantastic race which was won, to my Mum's delight and Dad's consternation, by the underdog Besson amid a cacophony of screaming and shouting which may have prompted some of our neighbours in Northcote Crescent, West Horsley, to fear that the Sealed Knot Society were re-enacting the Napoleonic Wars in the lounge of number 83.

Every subsequent Olympics conjures up a moment in time for me. Four years after Mexico I was on holiday in Brittany when news of Valery Borzov's sprint double, Mark Spitz's domination in the pool and the horrors of the Olympic Village massacre filtered through from Munich via tiny TV screens in local bars and three-day-old copies of the *Daily Mail*.

By Montreal in 1976 I had just completed my fourth year at grammar school and was on a scout camp in Devon. Apart from taking up smoking and drinking on a full time basis and literally bumping into Eric Clapton on the dodgems in

Plymouth, the trip was memorable for the radio commentary of Trinidadian Hasely Crawford's surprise win in the 100 metres. Years later I went to Trinidad for one of my best friends' weddings and absolutely everything there had been named after the man who was the first competitor from the island ever to win a gold medal. We flew to Tobago on an aeroplane called the Hasely Crawford and the main Stadium in Port of Spain also carries his name. I'm sure if you look hard enough you'll find the 'Hasely Crawford Sauna and Massage Parlour' or the 'Hasely Crawford Drug Dependency Drop-In Centre'.

By 1980, a year out of school, I was an aimless low level insurance orderly, rushing home to watch Allan Wells, Seb Coe, Steve Ovett and Daley Thompson triumph in Moscow. The 1984 Los Angeles Games coincided with my summer of breakfast shifts as a trainee at *County Sound*.

Because of the time difference between LA and London, much of the action from the Games took place in the small hours of the morning which was a godsend for radio as listeners would wake up to all the Olympic news, hours before the TV highlights and a day ahead of the newspapers. One of my jobs was to take in the reports being fed from IRN and prepare them for the news and sports bulletins. My knowledge of the Games meant I was able to make sound decisions on the editorial strength of stories, audio selection and running orders on behalf of presenters who weren't necessarily sports experts, earning valuable Brownie points.

I wasn't in the newsroom when Mary Decker and Zola Budd famously tangled in the 3,000 metres final in Los Angeles. Instead I followed the action, beer can in hand, from a pavement outside a Camden TV shop in the midst of a drunken sprawl around north London. If anyone had suggested at that moment that I'd actually be at the next Olympics in Seoul as a commentator and reporter I'd have drugs tested them for LSD, magic mushrooms and methylated spirits. But, just four years later and on the grounds that I had heard of Colin Jackson, I was asked to cover the world's biggest sporting event in an exotic, far flung location on what was to be my first ever foreign assignment. Up to that point, a four-day trip with *Signal Radio* to the Isle of Man on a pre-season tour with Stoke City represented my most glamorous 'send'.

Whereas the BBC routinely staffs the Olympic Games with more people than there are in the entire Great Britain team, Independent Radio News dispatched two of us to the Far East. I had to fulfil the roles of commentator, reporter, producer and engineer. NBC probably sent three people along to sharpen the pencils.

To adapt an old joke:

How many IRN reporters does it take to change a light bulb?

None. I'm too fucking busy doing everything else.

My travelling companion was Michael O'Neill, a news reporter who'd joined the company on the same day as me, but who I didn't really know from Adam. I knew even less about South Korea. My only impressions of the country came from watching episodes of M*A*S*H and, given that the series had been filmed in the wooded hills just north of Hollywood, I might as well have been going to Mars.

Before the trip I had to have various inoculations and vaccinations, including a particularly nasty one for cholera. This consisted of a nurse producing a hypodermic needle the length of a javelin and jabbing it into my backside with the kind of force that Tessa Sanderson would employ in a warm-up throw. Almost immediately my buttocks became two separate entities. One of them remained the normal, slightly rounded, pliant mass of tissue we've come to know and love, while the other stiffened up instantly becoming as hard as teak and throbbing with a pain which felt like the Drummers of Burundi had been using it during a particularly aggressive workout at the WOMAD Festival.

The agony didn't end there. I remember going home, cooking some dinner and settling down in front of the TV as comfortably as I could with only one arse cheek in service. Tilting slightly to the left, I was just about to swallow my first mouthful of food, when my appetite completely vanished, I started to shake and sweat and my temperature went from normal to Chernobyl in about three seconds as a tiny dose of the disease worked its way around my bloodstream.

We travelled to Seoul in economy class via Tokyo and by the time we got to Kimpo airport, Michael and I were getting on famously. The first thing that struck us on arrival was the feeling that the whole city had been liveried for the Olympics. You couldn't walk three paces without seeing the five rings, the Seoul logo, the Games' cartoon tiger mascot or gigantic posters of the star performers. Everything looked pristine and new and the venues stood proud like the gleaming, architectural splendours of some hyper-advanced alien planet. You half expected Captain Kirk, Spock, Bones and Scotty to beam up on the forecourt of the Wendy's burger bar registering plenty of human activity on their tricorders. Gresty Road and Vale Park seemed light years away.

We were billeted at the Press Village, a collection of high rise housing blocks which had been specially built for the event and, once the Games were over, would provide cheap homes for Korean families. There were three of us in one apartment; myself, Michael and a very helpful freelance reporter called Andy Edwards who was working for Capital Gold and whose vast knowledge of athletics I regularly tapped into. One of the rooms was bigger than the others and had a larger bed so I invoked the ancient and unwritten law and claimed it on the grounds that 'I sat on it first'. A short distance away was the Athletes' Village which housed the competitors and was separated from us by an enormous mesh fence topped with barbed wire and policed by gun-toting security guards stationed in wooden turrets. It was like a cross between *Brookside* and *Colditz*.

As far as was possible, each of the nations were housed along with their compatriots but everyone mingled at the various restaurants, shops and bars. We established base camp at the Bier Stube which was the compound's very own authentic German bar, the sheer absurdity of which was a constant source of wonder. It was a half timber, half canvas construction, its walls bedecked with enormous steins, cuckoo clocks and pictures of the Matterhorn (yes I know it's not in Germany, but they obviously didn't). There was one long bar at the end and rows and rows of wooden benches to which pimply Korean YTS trainees in lederhosen would bring plastic glasses of frothy lager and plonk them in front of bemused hacks from Ecuador, Senegal and Papua New Guinea. It was obviously better than the bar in the Athletes' Village and became particularly popular with competitors who had been knocked out in the first round on the opening day of their events and were, as tradition dictates, spending the rest of the Olympics on the piss.

The breakfast hall was great too. It's rare in life that you have the privilege of witnessing a true microcosm of the people of planet Earth in all their complex and disparate cultural guises. Here, under one roof, you had representatives from almost every nation in the world, clutching plastic trays and queuing together at one gigantic global buffet.

I've never been a great one for breakfast; most of my mornings had begun with a cup of tea and a Marlboro Light until I had the good sense to cut out the fags a few years before. However when you're covering such a massive event it's advisable to eat as much as you possibly can first thing, as it could be your last proper meal until midnight. So I'd force down cereal, toast and fruit while observing the rituals around me in awe and wonder.

It struck me as incredible how a group of creatures from the same species, with roughly the same metabolisms and biological structure can vary so greatly in their eating habits. It was 8am and you'd see people grazing from great bowls piled with red cabbage or tipping yogurt made from yak's milk onto a heap of what looked like sawdust. Others would be stuffing down chicken livers with small cubes of dried vegetables resembling dishwasher tablets or dipping cream doughnuts into mugs of steaming Bovril-like liquid. It was mesmerising. I mean, I've got three cats who all eat the same homogenised gloop from the same packet. You don't get the tabby one saying: "Well, actually I prefer tomatoes."

Anyone who's ever covered an Olympics will tell you that transport is the key issue. The host city will increase in population by as much as ten per cent with the influx of competitors, media and fans and if you can ferry them around quickly and efficiently you've won half the battle. Once you start delivering pissed off journalists to the wrong venue at the wrong time you'll be guaranteed bad press for the duration (Atlanta, Georgia this means you and more of that anon).

Seoul did a pretty good job. Everyone bearing the laminated accreditation pass went free on the public transport system which was clean, slick and efficient, but of course the language and different alphabet still made things tricky. To the Western eye the place names were all in hieroglyphics and by the time you'd satisfied yourself that the station sign corresponded to the squiggle on the map in your media guide the train was halfway to the next destination. Mind you a similar thing happens in Germany where words are constructed like Lego and you simply don't have time to read the place names. The German word for a tram stop is actually longer than the platform itself (*strassenbahnhaltestelle* in case you're wondering).

However after spending the first couple of days stumbling around blindly you soon get the hang of it and after a couple of weeks you become so familiar with the surroundings that locals would come up and ask *you* for directions:

"First National Bank of Korea? No problem love. Take the next left, over the bridge by the massage parlour, go past the John Bull English pub and it's on the right, opposite the 60 foot poster of Florence Griffith-Joyner. You can't miss it."

With the Press Village being on the outskirts of the city though, it was often easier to get to and from the venues in a cab which were plentiful and cheap although not without their own pitfalls. You'd hail a taxi and say "Press Village, please" only to be greeted with a quizzical look as the drivers repeated the phrase over and over again, shrugging their shoulders and wearing a furrowed brow. Eventually we worked out that that you had to state your desired destination in Korean cabbie-speak. For example, Press Village became "Press Willie-Gee" and Olympic Stadium was pronounced "Rimpick Star-Yon".

Cabbies are the same the world over. Having established that you wanted to go to the Rimpick Swimpool he'd take you via the most convoluted route, all the time nattering away, oblivious to the fact that you had absolutely no idea what he was talking about:

"D'you know what, I had that Juan Antonio Samaranch in my cab last week… bleedin' foreigners coming over here running our Olympics."

I once nearly caused an accident by interrupting one of them on the way home from a drunken night out and shouting "Kim Young-Nam", the name of a Korean wrestler who'd thrilled the nation by winning their first gold medal of the Games the night before. The driver got so excited at the very mention of the name of his new hero, that he instantly started shouting the name back while clapping and tooting his horn so enthusiastically that he only narrowly avoided an oncoming bus. Putting your life in the hands of foreign taxi drivers is an occupational hazard, but, I'm happy to say, my fears that I would end my days being scraped off the central reservation of a motorway in Bratislava have, thus far, remained unfounded.

Everyone in South Korea, incidentally, was called either Kim, Young, Lee or Park which was quite confusing. If you had to find someone called Mr Lee it would only narrow it down to around ten million people. It was easier to adapt their full names into an English approximation so that you'd remember who was who. I remember we met two girls called Kim Un-Yon and Kim Ji-Nih who were thereafter referred to as Kim Onion and Jean Genie.

A few years later we came up with similarly themed joke:

"I hear Manchester United have signed a Korean winger."

"Really, who?"

"Young Lee Sharpe."

In a bid to help confused visitors, hundreds of young Korean volunteers were recruited to help with translations. They wore little badges which said 'I Speak English' or 'Ich Spreche Deutsch'. Unfortunately even the simplest question in that particular language, for example, "where's the nearest toilet?" would be returned with a look of utter confusion. With my French background I even approached a girl whose badge boasted 'Je Parle Francais' only to discover that, compared to her, I was Michel Platini. Frankly she'd have been better off with a badge which said 'Je ne comprends rien'.

The real problems came when dealing with important matters like commentary positions and phone lines which had been pre-booked for us through the European Broadcasting Union. This was a Swiss-based company which acted on behalf of the continent's major TV and radio companies and brokered the transmission rights issues to major events. Our membership of the EBU entitled us to 'rights holder' status which granted unlimited access to any venue and the right to broadcast from it. 'Non rights holder' status basically meant you had to cover the Games from the nearest car park. In the years that followed I would come to rely heavily on the expert advice of EBU officers Arlette Dumont, Giles Kennedy and Javier Tola. Their almost saintly patience at my endless stupid requests and general lack of personal organisation eventually led me to forgive the company for inflicting the *Eurovision Song Contest* upon the continent.

If only they'd been the people running the main Olympic Stadium in Seoul.

We got there the day before the opening ceremony to find our reporting position completely empty; no monitor, no telephone, just the desk itself. We embarked on a seemingly endless trawl through the bowels of the Olympic Stadium which recalled the scene in one of my favourite films, *This Is Spinal Tap*, where the spoof rock band get lost in a labyrinth of passageways in some American sports arena and can't find their way to the stage. This, incidentally, was to become one of the recurring themes of my travels with IRN. Eventually we located the people in charge of the press positions and they produced a large plan of where each broadcaster was located within the stadium and pointed to the spot where we'd just been:

"Ah, yes, IRN, EBU position 32. Everything good."

"No, everything not good. No line, no telephone, no monitor."

"Yes, says here. Monitor, phone very good."

"But there isn't actually a phone there."

"Yes, yes phone here, look on paper."

By now my mood had gone up a gear from cheerful to no-nonsense.

"No, no, it's on the paper but it doesn't exist in reality."

"Yes is there. Look, look."

By now I'd gone from no-nonsense to ballistic.

"Look dickhead, I know it's on your fucking map, but it's not actually there is it? Are you telling me that I'll have to broadcast to the British Isles using a fucking piece of paper?"

At this point he got extremely agitated and upset.

"You use curse words, you use curse words . . . is very bad."

"I'll do more than use fucking curse words if I don't get my fucking phone you fucking tosspot."

Eventually the phone appeared of course but this was a depressingly familiar routine which has been played out all over the world and I apologise if I come across as a bad-tempered, arrogant, foul-mouthed despot. It's just really difficult when you're tired, jet-lagged and under pressure, to keep a lid on your temper when you're prevented from doing your job just because a load of poorly organised bureaucrats can't do theirs. It's a bit like Basil Fawlty trying to get through to Manuel.

"Please try to understand before one of us dies."

A well-travelled ITN cameraman had a wonderful phrase when confronted with communication problems in foreign countries:

"Do you speak English or am I going to have to shout?"

At least we didn't have to bribe them to get ourselves set up which is what used to happen in certain countries prior to the break-up of Eastern Europe. There'd be some giant Polish Telecom worker holding a bare wire in his hands with a look of pure menace and you'd have to negotiate a price before he'd connect you to the outside world. I never used to venture into the old Eastern bloc without a fistful of dollars, a couple of cartons of Marlboro Lights, dozens of packets of chewing gum, sweets and chocolate and a job lot of England badges and pennants.

Nowadays almost everyone in radio uses ISDN lines to broadcast from live events or satellite phones for on-the-spot reporting. I won't try to explain how it works as it's far too boring (if you really want to know type 'Integrated Services Digital Network' into Google or Wikipedia, but don't expect to ever find a girl-friend). Basically it works on the same principle as a phone except in studio quality on a digital line via a decoder and portable mixer. The problem with telephones is that the microphones in the handset are very cheap and nasty and give poor quality sound. It's fine for ordering a pizza but not so great on live broadcasts.

Before ISDN came along there was a gizmo called a Comrex, through which you could bypass the crap mic in the phone thus improving the sound quality. You had to be able to unscrew the handset on an old fashioned phone or get into the point on the wall and fix crocodile clips to the connections from which wires would lead into the Comrex box. This was about the size of a weighty hardback novel (*Harry Potter and the Deathly Hallows* for want of a better example) and incorporated a mixer into which you could plug a decent quality microphone and headset. This was easier said than done, though, especially if you're like me and can't even change a fuse without setting fire to the house. I would keep a set of screwdrivers in my bag in order to make the task easier, but even then it was often a real struggle. If you could take the phone handset apart it was relatively simple, but increasingly phones were being manufactured in moulded plastic and there was no way to dismantle them, so you had to get inside the telephone socket in the wall to set up the Comrex.

Unfortunately hotels are generally designed for the business traveller rather than the intrepid radio reporter and so the phone points were often hidden behind cupboards, wardrobes or built-in units. Many is the time I've had to dis-mantle an entire item of furniture in order to access the point. The result was that various bits of wood, metal, screws, nuts and bolts would be strewn across the floor while the dismantled telephone junction box was dangling out of a square hole in the wall via a couple of wires and attached Heath Robinson style to a strange Harry Potter-shaped box. I can imagine the chambermaid walking in the next morning and thinking: 'Fuck me, I thought Keith Moon had died.'

The other thing about Comrex is that it converted your voice or the audio being fed through it into a strange Dalek-like electronic sound which was then decoded back to normal at the other end.

I used to annoy the sound engineers by introducing the voicer I was about to record in a normal way by saying something like "OK this piece is called Olympics/Anderson. It's 25 seconds long with a standard outcue (i.e. name and location) and it comes in three – two – one . . ." But instead of delivering the report I'd scream:

"You are an enemy of the Daaaaaa-leks . . . you will be ex-term-i-nated."

Childish I admit, but I defy anyone not to do that when speaking into a Dalek voice converter. Try putting on a fez and not doing a Tommy Cooper impression or picking up a feather duster without saying "how tickled I am".

After the initial and inevitable technical hiccups the Olympics began well with Adrian Moorhouse winning the 100 metres breaststroke gold for Britain and I did a reasonable job of what was my first ever swimming commentary. It's a nightmare sport to call accurately, especially in a close finish as they all touch together amid a spray of water and the competitors are barely recognisable under their caps and goggles. Fortunately in the state of the art Seoul Aquatic Centre, which was shaped like a giant armadillo, the touch pads at the end of each lane triggered the giant screen in sequence and I looked up to see the winning time flash up next to Moorhouse's name and was able to deliver the kind of over the top eulogy which was detested by purists and commentating anoraks, but sounded good in news bulletins and upbeat sports programmes.

I make no excuses for putting all the emphasis on the emotion, atmosphere and colour of the occasion, rather than concentrating on the technical aspects of the event. In the heat of the moment I don't think anyone really gave a shit whether there was a slightly lacklustre third turn or a loss of stroke pattern between 75 and 100 metres, but they sure as hell cared that Britain had won its first gold medal of the Games.

The swimmers have always been a really excellent group mediawise and we got some great interviews and reaction pieces. Moorhouse, Nick Gillingham, who got a silver in the 200 metres breaststroke, and butterfly bronze medallist Andy Jameson were really fantastic blokes and made covering their events really easy and enjoyable for us all.

Two years later another swimmer, James Parrack, came out with one of the best reactions I've ever received to a glib interview question. He'd just finished second in a final at the 1990 Commonwealth Games in Auckland and I said to him:

"Well James, you've come away from the Commonwealth Games with a silver medal, where does it go from here?"

"It goes back in its box, into my bag, off on the plane and eventually onto my mother's mantelpiece."

We celebrated Moorhouse's victory long and hard in the German bar, trading insults with the Aussies who always regard the swimming as a private battle between themselves and the Americans and hated seeing the Poms grab a slice of the action. The whole experience had given me huge belief that I could cut it as a commentator as well as reporter and I was really looking forward to the athletics which traditionally follows the swimming programme as the main attraction. In particular I couldn't wait to have my first crack at a 100 metres commentary.

Quite an interesting race as it turned out.

CHAPTER FIVE

"Johnson's flying."

Commentating on a 100 metres sprint is a strange, complicated and extremely nerve-wracking experience. There is absolutely no equivalent to it in any other sport. A football match lasts 90 minutes, a Test match five days and even the shortest of boxing contests will offer a minute or so in which to gather your thoughts and choose your words carefully. If you get a goalscorer wrong in a football commentary (especially on radio) you can quickly recover. How many times have you heard phrases like "in fact it was Scholes who got the final touch" or "it might have gone in off the defender"?

In the 100 metres you have less than ten seconds from start to finish. That's it. There's no hiding place, no second chance. In less time than it takes to recite the alphabet you have to follow and describe the positions of the eight runners in the field and correctly identify at least the first three across the line while checking the clock for the winning time to see if it's a record of some kind. You must also consider other noteworthy information such as where the British runners finished and react to unexpected incidents such as someone falling over or pulling up injured.

Most human beings generally speak at a rate of about three words per second; so by the time you've said "and they're away" you've already used up 10 per cent of your allocation. Add "Bolt's got off to a great start but Powell's also going well in lane three" and you're well over halfway through. That leaves about three seconds to untangle a hurtling blur of velocity at the finish line. More often than not there's only a couple of hundredths of a second separating the leading competitors, so you're making judgement calls based on less than the thickness of a vest with the naked eye. There's a worrying amount of stuff that can go wrong.

It seems incredible, nay impossible, now that any commentator with no previous experience would be thrown blindly into the midst of the biggest single event of the biggest sporting show on earth. But that's the unique position I found myself in on 24 September 1988 at 1.30pm local time. I thought about all the times I'd sat watching the Olympic 100 metres in the past, never imagining that one day I'd be a tiny part of it.

Even before the final you sensed that something extraordinary was about to happen, with Canadian world champion Ben Johnson and American reigning Olympic champion Carl Lewis going head to head for the right to be crowned as the fastest man on earth. Johnson had beaten Lewis to the world title in Rome the year before, smashing the world record in a sensational time of 9.83 seconds. But his run up to Seoul had been hampered by injuries while Lewis was in the form of his life and had won the meeting between the two in Zurich the previous month. For added spice, Britain's Linford Christie was hoping for a medal but would have to hold off Lewis's fellow Americans Calvin Smith and Dennis Mitchell.

There's something magical about the stillness and near silence which envelops a stadium of 80,000 people in the seconds leading up to the start of a 100 metres final. It's as if the whole world has gone into slow motion, stopped what it's doing and settled down for a ten second adrenalin rush; the sporting equivalent of a shot of espresso on a sleepy morning. At the end of the day it's only eight blokes trying to see who can get from A to B the quickest, but in order to define the global impact of that moment I've often stolen a TS Eliot phrase. For the next ten seconds the Olympic Stadium in Seoul, South Korea, was 'the still point of the turning world'.

I was glancing down the track at the eight men lining up and desperately trying to remember who was in which lane. I kept whispering the same mantra: "Da Silva one, Stewart two, Lewis three, Christie four, Smith five, Johnson six, Williams seven, Mitchell eight." It's only just struck me now that, apart from da Silva, you couldn't pick a less exotic list of surnames. It sounds more like the roll-call at a Surrey primary school than a gathering of the greatest sprinters on earth.

"Take your marks" – the tannoy boomed out. I'm sure I was more nervous than the competitors as they crouched in their blocks as my grip on the microphone tightened.

"Set" – heart pounding, I waited for the gun and finally, after what seemed like a breathless eternity, off it went. I can remember my words even now:

"They're away in the final . . . Linford Christie got off to a slow start but Johnson's flying . . ."

This, of course, was bollocks. Johnson had indeed produced one of the greatest starts of all time but to suggest Christie's had been sluggish was ridiculous in hindsight, but at that moment, compared to Johnson, he resembled an old age pensioner struggling out of a bath chair.

"It's Johnson . . . Lewis coming up behind . . ."

Many felt that Lewis, traditionally the strongest finisher, might rein Johnson in over the final 50 metres, but the Canadian's start had been so good that there was simply too much ground for him to make up.

"Burp."

At this point the Comrex signal dropped out meaning that there was a split second of dalek interference, but happily the forces for good ensured that their intervention was short-lived.

"But it's Johnson . . . and Johnson wins . . . he's upset the form book. Lewis second and Linford Christie's got a bronze, he'll be delighted with that."

I was very fortunate that the first two places had been about as easy to call as is possible, but equally very pleased to have spotted Christie grabbing third just ahead of Smith to claim a medal for Britain.

"The time . . . nine point seven nine."

I should have gone into raptures about the world record having been smashed in the first sub 9.8 second run of all time. But I didn't. Although I'd got the correct words out, I'm sure I was so incredulous that, in my mind, the clock read 9.97 seconds, which would have been relatively modest. It could have been worse though.

"The time . . . nine point seven nine . . . nothing to write home about."

As first attempts go it wasn't bad at all and I slumped back in my seat relieved, elated and exhausted. I felt like Johnson did as he took his lap of honour and looked up to see O'Neill's beaming face:

"That was fucking great . . . well done mate."

However, I didn't have much time for resting on my laurels. Three days later we got the news that Johnson had failed a drugs test and all hell broke loose. We received a call from London to say the story had been broken by the French news agency AFP, so I quickly bashed out a holding voicer full of ifs and buts and maybes to cover our arses in case this was some kind of gigantic hoax.

Michael, Andy and I then went our separate ways to see what we could find out. I headed for the Canadian block in the Press Willie-Gee (as everyone now called it) expecting them to be able to shed some more light on the story. In the lift I bumped into *Daily Mail* reporter John Burton who told me that the news, though not yet official, had been given credence by a senior figure within the International Olympic Committee's medical commission.

It was the middle of the night in Seoul and most people were asleep, but as I walked across the main square of the Village you could see lights popping on in windows one by one as arguably the biggest sports story of all time began to dawn on a pack of bleary-eyed journalists. The Canadian house was strangely dark but I picked an apartment at random and knocked. A bloke in a dressing gown answered the door.

"Hi my name's John Anderson. I'm from Independent Radio News in London, I'm just wondering if you have any more info on the Ben Johnson story?"

"What Johnson story?"

"He's failed a drugs test."

"WHAAAAAAAAAAAAAATTTT!!!!!!!!!!???"

He shouted to his mate, who shouted to his mate and so on and within minutes it was as if the Oxford Street Christmas lights had been turned on by some Z-list soap opera celebrity.

'Well they're no bloody use,' I thought, and set off in the opposite direction.

My next port of call was the entrance to the Athletes' Village. This resembled Checkpoint Charlie and only those with Athlete or Official accreditation were allowed through the gates. Reporters had to hang around and hope someone interesting would turn up. Given the time of day there weren't many competitors still up and almost everyone was fast asleep in their beds dreaming either of gold medals or the Brazilian synchronised swimming team and blissfully unaware of the drama that was gradually unfolding.

Eventually I sidled up to a tall, lean guy in a USA tracksuit and his jaw dropped as I told him the news. As luck would have it, he turned out to be a member of the American 4 x 100 metres relay team called Emmit King, who'd raced against Johnson many times and gave me one of the earliest athlete reaction interviews.

Back at the Canadian block by now they were all up and dressed and in a frenzy of activity. I interviewed one of their track and field experts to get a perspective from his nation's point of view. At one point he shook his head and memorably said: "Ben Johnson – hero to zero in nine point seven nine seconds." Another Canadian joked that the headlines back home which 72 hours earlier had screamed: 'Canadian Sprints To Golden Glory' would now be changed to: 'Jamaican Sent Home In Disgrace'.

The next day the IOC called a press conference at the Shilla Hotel to confirm the positive test and Johnson's disqualification from the Games. A French press spokesperson called Michele Verdier read from a prepared statement:

'The urine sample of Ben Johnson collected on Saturday 24th September 1988 was found to contain the metabolites of a banned substance, namely stanozolol, an anabolic steroid. The IOC Medical Commission recommends the following sanction: disqualification of this competitor from the Games of the 24th Olympiad in Seoul. Of course, the gold medal has been withdrawn by the IOC."

And that was it, no real details, no elaboration, no follow up questions permitted. As Ms Verdier rose to leave I was among a crowd of reporters (mostly British I hasten to add; if there was a gold medal for being awkward fuckers we'd be home and hosed) who surrounded the poor woman haranguing her for the lack of information and demanding to be told more. When she explained that they had nothing further to say, I shouted aggressively: "Oh come on, you've got to give us more than that."

All of which had been filmed by an ITN camera crew and appeared on *News at Ten* that night. My sister was in the kitchen when her husband suddenly called out: "Get in here quick, your brother's harassing some poor woman in a blazer on the telly."

One of the most enjoyable jobs in Seoul involved doing what we call 'two-ways' in which you are interviewed by a presenter in order to explain a story more fully. I had been appearing frequently on LBC's breakfast show hosted by the legendary Douglas Cameron and suddenly had to become an expert in dope testing. To be honest, at the time I didn't know stanozolol from Stan Ogden but thanks to the knowledge passed on by Andy Edwards, a decent runner himself, I was able to sound as if I'd spent a lifetime in a laboratory whizzing test tubes full of piss round in a centrifuge.

"Well, of course, Douglas, the thing about steroids is they enable athletes to undergo more punishing training schedules and thus build up unnatural levels of muscle bulk. It's similar to how farmers increase meat production in beef cattle. And increasingly the labs are developing masking agents so the athlete can continue his doping regime right up until the start of a competition without fear of detection even in random tests."

If they introduced a random test for blatant plagiarism I'd have been banned for life.

One other notable result of my stint as the breakfast show's resident expert was the glory and prestige of being quoted in the Colemanballs section of *Private Eye* which showcases the cock-ups made by commentators and reporters with this insightful pronouncement: "The more experienced runners, putting all that training and practice into theory."

By now, of course, the Johnson scandal had completely overshadowed everything in the Games and we devoted 90 per cent of our time to covering it. Because we were spreading ourselves so thin, the actual sporting side of the Olympics was getting brushed aside. On the very same day as the now infamous 100 metres, Great Britain had won a rowing gold medal in the coxless pairs without much of a fanfare from us. Oh well, you can't be in two places at once and anyway what were the chances of two blokes called Andy Holmes or Steve Redgrave ever being heard of again? To add insult to injury, when we did announce their moment of triumph it was spoilt by a newsreader describing them as competing in "the cockless pairs".

Mind you, if you think that was bad, someone commentating on the University boat race once apparently said: "What a wonderful gesture, the Duchess has gone over to kiss the cox of the Oxford crew."

As journalists abandoned sleep to chase the Johnson story across Seoul, the villain of the piece himself had slipped out of the back door, pursued by a baying pack of reporters, and boarded a flight to New York. But we heard that his then business manager Larry Heidebrecht was still in town and we set out to find him. Having established that he was staying at one of the top hotels where many of the big names were staying, I dashed out of the apartment to get a cab. On the way I bumped into Simon Turnbull, a north east based athletics writer, and UPI agency man Mike Collett. Simon had competed at a good standard as a runner and was very perceptive about the sport. He was the first person I ever heard questioning Florence Griffith-Joyner's sensational sprint performances that year. With her garish outfits and colourful fingernails, Flo-Jo was the flamboyant queen of the track to many people but Simon always felt there was more to her than met the eye. I'd become friends with Mike after a few too many late nights at the legendary Stompers Club in Itaewon, the epicentre of the city's nightlife.

The club was situated at the end of a narrow street known colloquially as Hookers Hill, which, as the name suggests, was packed with prostitutes who normally serviced the US military personnel in the city, but were having an absolute field day with the thousands of extra visitors flooding in because of the Olympics.

Before you ask, dear readers, the answer to your next question is no, but there were some who did succumb to the charms of the girls who paraded up and down Itaewon's narrow streets. I heard of one foreign journalist who procured the services of a hooker and took her back to his hotel room. Once the deed was done and he'd paid up, she left and he went to sleep. Upon awaking he noticed that she'd left an ornate pair of earrings on the bedside table. Not one to look a gift horse in the mouth, he took them home and gave them to his wife as a present.

Apparently there were plenty of ways of getting your rocks off in Seoul; for example one of the hairdressing salons had a very interesting take on the phrase 'wash, cut and blow'.

Stompers consisted of little other than a large square dance floor with a small DJ booth, a bar and a particularly rank toilet whose plastic door opened out straight onto the open plan area and didn't have a lock. Every now and then the occupant who'd been hanging onto the handle for dear life would let it slip or have it ripped from his grasp by an impatient queuer and the door would fly open and you'd be amused by the sight of someone desperately trying to protect their modesty. To be honest you wouldn't look at the place twice if it were in London, but for some reason this particular club became a magnet for the British press and I met loads of wonderful and helpful people there and established many long lasting friendships not to mention long lasting hangovers.

Mike, Simon and I decided to share a taxi to the hotel which was about half an hour away from the Willie-Gee. When we got there the guards ushered in the other two but held me back. A heavily armed security man pointed at my chest and shook his head. It was then that I realised I wasn't wearing my accreditation. The accreditation pass is one of those rectangular, laminated plastic things dangling from a lanyard that you'll have seen football back room staff wearing while sitting in the dugout at major tournaments. This is your passport to the Games; it carries your photo, organisation details and accreditation status and you need it to access any Olympic venue, including the main hotels. They took the photo at the airport immediately after we arrived, and unsurprisingly after a long flight with two changes none of us looked our best. As well as being unshaven and bleary eyed after too many beers, I was asked to take my glasses off for some reason so the picture didn't look like me at all.

I fumbled about in my bag to see if I had put it there but it was obvious pretty soon that I had left it in the apartment. For some reason, which even now I don't fully understand, I did have my passport in the bag and in a moment of either sheer inspiration or sheer stupidity I held it up in front of the guard's face, shouted "Her Majesty's Press" and sprinted into the foyer. Once inside I dashed off and hid for a few minutes before emerging sheepishly and darting into the lift. I located Mr Heidebrecht's room and a woman answered the door. She told me he wasn't in but I could hear a man's voice on the phone in the background. I jammed my foot in the door and when he finally came over, I shoved the microphone in his face and started asking questions about the case. All I got was a load of non-committal answers and 'no comments', but it was better than nothing and at least I had something to talk about on the breakfast show next morning.

Four days after the infamous race, Carl Lewis, who'd ended up successfully defending his Olympic 100 metres title, albeit in such extraordinary circumstances, was back on the track in the final of the 200 metres. After every Olympic event, the three medal winners are compelled by the IOC to attend an official press conference just before they go on to the medal ceremony itself. Lewis had not actually spoken publicly on the drugs topic thus far, but as long as he finished in the top three in the 200, which barring disaster he would, we'd finally be able to get his reaction to the events of the past three days.

Normally these conferences are held in a special room in the stadium which holds about 100 journalists. The microphones on the top table are fed through a mixer with a plethora of output sockets which you can plug your tape recorder directly into to get the audio. If it was the 50km walk, for example you could probably conduct the whole process in a broom cupboard, but the world and his wife were geared up for the post 200m conference and it was wisely switched to a larger area outside so that everyone could be accommodated comfortably.

As it turned out, Lewis was beaten into second place by his 21-year-old training partner and protégé Joe DeLoach, but, as silver medallist, he was duly obliged to face the world's press. I must admit I had sympathy for young DeLoach who must have felt like a gatecrasher at his own party. An IOC official stood up and announced that Lewis would be willing to take three questions on the Johnson scandal and then we would move on to the 200 metres.

"So could we have the first question please?"

What followed was either the worst piece of journalistic initiative I have ever had the misfortune to witness or a clumsy attempt by the IOC to try and deflect the questioning by planting someone in the audience. A little Korean fellow stuck up his hand and was given the roving microphone as the world held its breath: "Mister Lewis could you tell us how you are enjoying life here in South Korea?"

Gasps of horror swept the assembled hacks and even Lewis's first reaction was to laugh before telling us how great the place was and how he'd been shopping in Itaewon. Eventually, of course, he was asked the question the whole world wanted the answer to. His response was polite, understated and uncontroversial. There was no condemnation, he said he felt sorry for Johnson and hoped he could get his life back in order.

A couple of years later Lewis would reveal in his autobiography, *Inside Track*, that deep down inside he'd really wanted to tear into Johnson and call him a cheat, but had opted for diplomacy. When he visited London as part of a publicity tour at the time of the book's release he came into LBC and gave me an excellent interview as well as signing a copy of the result sheet from the 100 metres which I'd hung onto as a souvenir. When I met him he was on crutches, recovering from an injury. I made him laugh by shouting "race you down the corridor" and running off at full pelt as he hobbled behind.

Having got Lewis's reaction, in truth I was hoping we could now move on from the story which had dominated the world headlines for what seemed like an eternity and move on to more routine matters as I'd hardly slept since the news had broken. Fat fucking chance. No sooner had the Johnson saga finally started to die down than Linford Christie, now elevated to the silver medal, came under the scrutiny of the drugs testers himself. His sample was found to contain traces of pseudoephedrine which, Andy Edwards informed me, was a lesser prohibited substance, not considered as serious as a steroid. Cannabis compared to heroin if you like. Nevertheless Christie now faced the prospect of disqualification and a three-month ban if found guilty. He protested his innocence vehemently, claiming the substance had entered his system via cups of ginseng tea which he'd been drinking during the Games.

So we traipsed back to the Shilla Hotel (yes I remembered my accreditation this time) where the IOC were deliberating whether to send Christie the way of Johnson or uphold his version of events. I actually dozed off a couple of times in a standing position as we waited in a corridor close to the meeting room as the discussions dragged on and on. We took it in turns to creep up to the door and try to earwig what was going on inside. Finally Andy came rushing back.

"He's been cleared, Linford's been cleared."

In the manner of those old black and white films where trilby-hatted reporters dash for the telephones after the conclusion of a court case, Michael ran off to file a voicer from the lobby and I waited around to get the official British Olympic Association reaction from its marvellous and never adequately replaced press officer Caroline Searle. Christie had been smuggled out of a side entrance but Caroline, patient as ever, gave everyone a fabulous interview.

Back in London, IRN had a reporter outside Christie's family's home. He was given the news via a radio car and was first to the door to break the good news to them. With his tape recorder running, he brilliantly captured their noisy reaction in a memorable piece of audio.

It was a huge relief to me, not necessarily because Christie had been reprieved, but because we finally felt we had put the whole saga to bed. And that's where we headed after three days of virtually non-stop dashing about. Suitably rested, the following night we set out for Itaewon. On the way we got fake Yves St Laurent polo shirts made up bearing the legend 'I Saw The Junkie Run'. I've still got mine.

We started at a place called the Passport Club which was a pseudo-upmarket piano bar on the third storey of a high rise building which had a nightclub of some sort on every level. This enabled you to enjoy a strangely vertical pub crawl although I would warn potential visitors to start at the top first and work down otherwise it's a hell of a lot of stairs to negotiate when you're pissed.

On this particular evening the Passport was hosting a karaoke night. This was before the phenomenon had taken off in the UK and we were amused by the concept. Instead of using a backing track, they had a little band in jackets and bow ties playing tippy-tap drums, tinny organ and pedestrian bass which trundled out the songs while locals and tourists squawked along. Occasionally they'd drag out a proper singer to show how it should be done so you'd have Aretha Franklin one minute and the Wurzels the next. I'm not a natural performer and my singing voice is more suited to Death Metal than lounge cabaret but of course we all had to have a go and I shambled through a lamentable version of *Yesterday* by the Beatles. If Paul McCartney had been there he'd have wished he'd never written it.

The highlight though was another Beatles classic, *Lucy In The Sky With Diamonds*, as performed by the house singer. Vocally it was great but she had real problems coping with the pronunciations. Lucy became Rucy and some of the lines made John Lennon's acid-drenched visions seem relatively pedestrian:

"Picture yourself on a boat on a liver."

"Locking horse people eat marsh marrow pies."

And best of all: "Cerrophane frowers of yerrow and gleen/towelling over your head."

After continuing on to the brash, American influenced King Club and, of course, Stompers, we got to bed at 5am. Compared to the events that had just taken place, the rest of the Olympics was going to be a doddle. Whereas the BBC and the other giant broadcasters have a correspondent for virtually every sport, we had to choose our events carefully. Basically, the Games became like a giant treasure hunt as we went anywhere to cover any sport which offered a whiff of British success.

I spent a hugely enjoyable day at the equestrian arena and was strangely compelled by a sport in which I previously had had no interest at all. Captain Mark Phillips was part of the British team which won the Three Day Event silver and was presented with a medal by his then wife Princess Anne which was an interesting angle while Ian Starke and the delightful Ginny Leng won individual medals. I also saw a couple of the hockey matches (though sadly not the final) and knew goalscoring hero Imran Sherwani from my days at *Signal*. He ran a newsagents in Stoke-on-Trent and had been a guest on my show a couple of times. Like the swimmers, the hockey players were a brilliant bunch, absolutely delighted that their sport was getting some long overdue credit.

My main focus was athletics though and I was on hand to capture the medal triumphs of Colin Jackson, Peter Elliott, Liz McColgan, Fatima Whitbread, Mark Rowland and Yvonne Murray (whose then boyfriend Nigel was a fellow reporter and Itaewon regular).

Daley Thompson just missed out on a medal in the decathlon, but declined to share his thoughts with the British public despite my repeated requests for an interview. I have always found this kind of attitude utterly unacceptable. The competitors are icons to millions and represent their country thanks, in no small part, to donations from the public via the BOA's appeal fund. I firmly believe it is their duty to devote a tiny amount of their precious time to co-operating with the media. Thompson had this ridiculous rule whereby he wouldn't speak to you unless you could list the ten decathlon disciplines in order. Can you imagine Gordon Brown refusing to make any public statement until you'd listed every Prime Minister since 1832? I always loved Steve Ovett's response:

"Nine Mickey Mouse events and the 1,500 metres."

As I walked away from my last failed attempt to get a few words out of this undoubtedly brilliant but infuriatingly arrogant man, a smug faced BBC reporter came up and patronisingly sneered:

"You should know he never does interviews."

"Well at least I fucking tried. You'd have looked a twat if he'd changed his mind."

Happily, deadpan Daley was the exception rather than the rule and generally we got the stuff we wanted. Fatima Whitbread told me that, after she'd finished second in the javelin behind East German Petra Felke, the two of them had sneaked into a toilet and enjoyed a crafty cigarette like two rebellious schoolgirls. This was a nice story to send down, but it had a disastrous effect on me, though.

When the Games ended we were queuing for a bus to the airport when one of the Canadians I'd spoken to on the night the Johnson story broke came over with a group of friends and three huge crates of beer. We polished off the cans in world record time and one of the guys offered me a cigarette. I had given up smoking while at college on New Year's Eve 1983 mainly on the grounds that I was too poor to afford it. But I had just come to the end of an extraordinary and sensational first ever foreign send and was still scarcely able to believe that, just four years after walking into *County Sound's* newsroom for the first time, my life had taken such an extraordinary turn. I felt as if, like Fatima, I deserved a moment of indulgence and lit up. As I inhaled I felt a profound sense of joy, achievement and relief. It's not as if having one cigarette is going to hurt me, I thought, I'll just have this one and then quit again.

Sure enough, 12 years later, I did.

The journey home was a nightmare. Pissed out of my brain and by now chain smoking I was repeatedly sick throughout the journey. To make matters worse we were delayed at Anchorage, Alaska of all places, after the plane developed a fault. I spent most of the time in the airport toilet with a variety of complaints, occasionally joining Michael and some other English journalists at the bar although sticking to coffee and Coke.

Apart from a giant, stuffed polar bear in a glass case and the fact that it was minus 200 degrees on the observation deck, my abiding memory of that stop was the fact that the barmaid had the most improbable name of anyone I've ever met before or since. She was called, God's honest truth, Lolita Baby.

Now, throughout the process of writing this book I have used Google and Wikipedia extensively to establish facts and check that my memory isn't playing tricks on me. I have, however, resisted the temptation to do any research on Ms Baby as I dread to think what an internet search of her name would produce. The same also applies to looking up the Swiss football team Young Boys, rock group Big Black or any pub called the Three Cocks.

Happily we didn't need an overnight stop in Anchorage and eventually arrived in London several hours late. I think it was very early in the morning when we touched down. Michael had bought a fake Rolex watch at a stall in Itaewon on the last day and had been proudly showing it off during the flight. Unfortunately for him it said 11 o'clock at night.

CHAPTER SIX

"I've got all my tattoos down the right-hand side."

It was strange returning to the everyday life at Gough Square after a four-week non-stop adrenalin rush. Having just covered arguably the biggest sports story of all time, it was a little difficult to put your heart and soul into Perry Groves's groin strain or the latest transfer speculation at Crystal Palace.

Everyone was very complimentary about the work we'd done in Seoul, we were wined and dined by the management and would hold court in the pub with tales of Itaewon and the Press Willie-Gee.

Michael O'Neill would boast about his stint of active duty in the South Korean capital as rioting students did battle with armed police during the Games. There had been outbreaks of violence before and during the event as the students protested about taxpayers' money being spent on the Games rather than what they saw as more deserving causes. The television pictures looked pretty dramatic. Molotov Cocktails flew at officers with riot shields as young people were hauled off into police vans, the whole area shrouded in tear gas. Michael filed some good stuff in the midst of battle with sirens blaring and explosions going off in the background.

In reality though the whole thing was more like *It's A Knockout* than Brixton or Toxteth. These showdowns were planned in advance and were thoroughly orchestrated affairs. They would take place at a certain venue at a certain time and no innocent civilians were caught in the crossfire since they'd all been evacuated for the afternoon. I offered to go along and add a commentary:

"Good afternoon, welcome to downtown Seoul where this afternoon it's University v Police in a rescheduled match after Thursday's riot was postponed due to rain. The students will give a debut to new signing Pet-Rol Kan while the coppers' defence is bolstered by the return to fitness of Wil-Kik Shit. So the man in the middle, Fuk-Me Ref, will get us underway. Students on the attack . . . but the first flaming Cola bottle goes wide of the police van. Back come the Fuzz . . . great tackle to floor Young-Thik Twit who'll need treatment on that broken fingernail . . ."

During those early days at Gough Square I used to enjoy presenting the sports bulletins live from the on-air studio not least because you'd often end up sitting right next to whoever was the guest for the forthcoming hour of chat. I remember noting how short *Man About The House* star Paula Wilcox is in real life and marvelling at Queen guitarist Brian May's hair. Best of all though was when I was introduced by the presenter to a painfully thin, ashen faced, sunken cheeked old man wearing a cream suit with a freshly cut orchid in the lapel. He grasped my outstretched hand with both his and shook it firmly; I was struck by the piercing blueness of his steely gaze. In a sombre voice, no more than a whisper, he addressed me with the utmost old fashioned politeness:

"It's an absolute pleasure to meet you dear boy."

I almost shivered in his ghostly presence. Not surprising perhaps given that the man clutching my hand with his bony fingers was legendary Hammer horror star Peter Cushing looking every bit like one of his on-screen characters. I hardly dared look up from my notes as I delivered the sports news lest he suddenly come lurching at me with a crucifix.

Once on a late shift I found myself working on a programme hosted by 'Whispering' Bob Harris, whose *Old Grey Whistle Test* show I had watched avidly in the early 1970s. He cued me in with the words:

"And now with all the day's sports news here's John Anderson. . .(snigger) . . . you're not the one out of Yes are you?"

I was fairly used to this kind of thing, given that I had the same name as the lead singer of the preposterous progressive rock monsters (although he spelt his first name Jon) and so I had a ready made reply: "Afraid not Bob. As you can tell I don't have a high pitched Lancastrian accent and have never written a 20 minute song about Topographic Oceans."

I would occasionally fill in for regular presenter Mike Porter when he was unavailable for the *Sportswatch* programme. I loved doing the show, but didn't get on with the producer who was a tennis fan with little or no knowledge of football and an irritating, patronising manner. He would insist on running long, boring interviews he'd done rather than concentrating on the live action and I always felt the programme could have been so much better than it was. This was soon proved true when Jonathan Pearce launched his new, slick, up-front show on *Capital Gold* which left us trailing in its wake.

I was presenting *Sportswatch* on the day of the 1989 Grand National at Aintree. We had no commentary rights but would try and keep a tally of who was leading, who was in contention and who had fallen. I had a little screen in front of me onto which a programme assistant would type in the latest scores and results. During the race he tapped in a message that one of the big favourites, Little Polveir, had fallen and I announced excitedly that he had crashed out. This was in fact a mistake and, using the 'never wrong for long' motto, I quickly apologised and gave out a correction. The horse then went on to win the race. A week later we got a letter from an angry listener who'd backed Little Polveir and was in his car when he heard the horse had fallen. In frustration he ripped up his betting slip and flung it out of the sun roof like confetti. He said when he'd realised Little Polveir had actually won he'd nearly crashed his car. Our mistake had cost him about £500, but we turned down his request for a refund.

In truth, though, I was much happier covering a game than working in the studio and I shared commentary duties with Andrew Gidley on the 1988 FA Cup final when Wimbledon shocked mighty Liverpool. Andrew got to describe Lawrie Sanchez's winning goal but I got the John Aldridge penalty miss.

"Beasant's saved it . . . unbelieeeeeeeeeevable!!!!!!"

The following year I was at Villa Park for an FA Cup semi-final between Everton and Norwich City which turned out to be probably the most depressing afternoon of my entire career. In those days, before everyone had a laptop with an internet connection, we radio reporters who were listening to studio output through our headphones, would filter the news from other matches through to our press box colleagues. The general hubbub would often be punctuated with a cry of, "United are one up at Leicester" or "Tony Gale's been sent off for West Ham."

The main game that afternoon was Liverpool v Nottingham Forest in the other semi at Hillsborough and very early on it became clear that something had gone terribly, horribly wrong. Andrew Gidley was at that game for IRN and I listened to his reports with increasing disbelief. Now, instead of cheerfully calling out football scores I found myself solemnly updating the report of a rapidly unfolding disaster which got bleaker with every update.

"Something's happened at Hillsborough, the players are leaving the field."

"Apparently some Liverpool fans have been injured in a crush at one end."

"Fans are being stretchered across the field on broken advertising hoardings."

"There are reports that some people have died."

"It's now been confirmed that nine people have been killed . . ."

By now fans in the seats nearby were averting their eyes from the game and craning their necks towards the press box. On the occasions the presenter crossed to me I could only report that our game, though still being played, was now a total irrelevance in the context of the situation in Sheffield and the depressing fact was that many of the Everton supporters inside Villa Park, who might have had family and friends at Hillsborough, were obviously unaware of what was going on as they cheered Pat Nevin's early goal.

The post-match interviews were not with Nevin or any of his team-mates, but with the FA chairman Sir Bert Millichip who was at Villa Park and gave his reaction to the tragic news. As I left the ground I could see little huddles of Evertonians hugging each other, some in tears, as the full scale of the tragedy that had befallen the city of Liverpool just four years after Heysel finally hit home. My wife Carolyn, who was working on Merseyside at the time, tied a Watford scarf to the Shankly Gates at Anfield as football united in grief.

1989 was the year I graduated to the ranks of England reporter, at first helping out with covering games at Wembley as a pitchside interviewer. It was a huge thrill to be standing in the Wembley tunnel as the players came out and watching the game from behind the goal among the photographers, even though the vagaries of the English weather meant we would as often as not get absolutely soaked through.

It was the Bobby Robson era and the under-fire England boss was still recovering from a disastrous European Championships campaign in Germany the previous summer, when his team lost all three games and went home after the group phase. A series of lacklustre subsequent friendlies had prompted the famous 'Go, In The Name Of God, Go' headlines and a dismal draw in Saudi Arabia appeared to spell the end for Robson (although the headlines had now changed to 'Go In The Name Of Allah Go'). I was sent to Heathrow to cover the squad's return from Riyadh which saw Robson escorted through the airport by police, pursued by a gaggle of radio and TV reporters.

The whole scene was captured on the back page of the then pioneering *Today* newspaper which carried a wonderful colour shot of a stone-faced Robson, tight lipped as he tried to weather the storm. Foremost among the group of press men and camera crews was yours truly shoving a microphone at him in a forlorn attempt to elicit some form of reaction to the latest calamity. The headline read 'No Hiding Place' with a side-bar: 'Police Rescue Robson In Stormy Homecoming'.

I also managed to annoy Robson's eventual England successor Graham Taylor while he was manager at Aston Villa during their ill fated title battle with Liverpool in 1990. As a Watford fan, Graham Taylor's a real hero to me and I was lucky enough to get to know him a little when he travelled with the *Radio 5Live* commentary team in later years. He's always charming, intelligent and amusing company and while we were on an England trip in Vienna in 2004, *5Live* chief football correspondent Mike Ingham very kindly invited me to an impromptu dinner in honour of Graham's 60th birthday, which was a wonderful evening during which I reminded him of the time I had really pissed him off.

Villa had played very poorly and suffered a 2-0 defeat at Coventry towards the end of the season which put a huge dent in their title aspirations. Graham was never one to shirk his media responsibilities and came out to give his reaction to the assembled radio reporters outside the Highfield Road press room. As was the protocol, the local radio guys would get the first crack of the whip after which time we could ask a few questions of our own. I was becoming increasingly weary of the sycophantic line of questioning from the Midlands based reporters who seemed to be acting as apologists and so, when I got my chance, I waded in with both barrels.

"Graham, what would you say to people who now believe Villa's title hopes are over?"

His response was swift, concise and emphatic: "Bollocks," he said, before bringing the interview to an abrupt end by storming off.

This got picked up by the Press Association and it wasn't long before all the papers were running stories about Graham's 'eight letter response' and suggestions that the pressure was beginning to get to him.

The following day Graham appeared on a *Granada* football programme hosted by Clive Tyldesley who asked him to explain what had happened. Graham claimed I had shoved a microphone under his nose and said something like: "Well that's it, you've lost the title, what do you think of that?" and his terse reaction had been because of my rude intrusion. I was a little annoyed as this wasn't really a fair representation of what had occurred and I wrote to him to clarify the position. Graham, to his eternal credit, sent me a wonderful letter back insisting he was not having a go at me personally and that he perhaps should handle certain interview situations differently.

His final line was a classic.

'I could have given you a five letter response meaning the same thing, but as usual I tend to go on a bit.'

Another example of Graham's good humour was when I met him at Watford near the end of his second spell as manager when things weren't going too well. During the conversation I mentioned that I felt a bit like an unlucky charm for the club.

"I don't get here that often which is probably just as well because they never win when I come," I told him.

His response came as quick as a flash.

"They never bloody win when I come either."

Despite the poor results, somehow Bobby Robson had managed to cling on to the national team job and in September 1989 I covered my first ever England away game, a World Cup qualifier against Sweden in Stockholm. It was the famous 0-0 draw when England got the point they needed to reach Italia 90 and Terry Butcher's white shirt became stained red with blood in an iconic image. Years later I'd get to know Butch really well on the road with England in his guise as a *Radio 5Live* summariser. You couldn't meet a more down to earth character; a big fan of heavy metal music who would always have a few beers with the supporters and never once bragged about his illustrious career. I asked him about that game once and his response was typical: "It looked worse than it was, like cutting yourself shaving really."

The match itself went off well, the atmosphere was good and we were, at last, able to run some very positive England stories. But as I was preparing to leave the stadium I got a call from the news desk to say that some of the England fans had been involved in ugly hooligan incidents in the city centre and that I needed to stay over in Stockholm to cover that story. English supporters had been involved in a battle with a notorious Swedish gang, causing widespread damage to property and misery to citizens.

Unfortunately all my bags had been packed away onto the media bus and were en route to the airport, while some local Abba or Volvo convention meant there were no hotel rooms left in the city. I had my broadcasting equipment, the clothes I was standing in and, given the price of beer in Sweden, only about 10 krona left in my wallet.

Fortunately I hooked up with the BBC reporter Frank Partridge who did have a room and let me kip on the floor and file from his phone. We spent all night scouring Swedish prisons where the England fans were being held overnight before being sent home and got some excellent audio with local police who, like all Scandinavians, spoke good English.

I remember being accosted by a female beggar in Stockholm, who was waving an empty cup and babbling something or other in Swedish.

"Sorry I can't understand what you're saying," I muttered, keen to hang on to what little money I had.

"I said would you be so kind as to give me some money towards a hot meal?" she replied in perfect English.

Confronted by a dosser who had taken the trouble to learn a foreign language, it would have been churlish not to hand over the cash. It also underlined the saying that someone who can speak many languages is multi-lingual, someone who can speak two languages is bi-lingual and someone who only speaks one language is English. Unfortunately my shame at the alarming ignorance of some of my countrymen was about to be compounded.

We got up early to go to the railway station where much of the previous night's trouble had taken place and where these so called 'supporters' were now being herded – disgraced, dishevelled, but still defiant – onto trains headed for the ferry ports and airport. It was the first time I'd had any first hand experience of some of the scumbags who habitually besmirch England's reputation in foreign countries and they really were a hideous, surly rash on the arsehole of humanity. Most of these people do not conform to the tattooed, Doc Martens wearing, skinhead stereotype. Many have respectable jobs and families and live in harmless satellite towns where they are often supporters of the smaller clubs, although their enthusiasm for football is generally dwarfed by their unswerving devotion to ultra right-wing politics which, in their warped vision, purports to honour Queen and country. They are as likely to be snorting cocaine and dropping caps of speed as quaffing super strength lager and prefer casual fashions to replica football shirts. We interviewed a group of these morons and they proudly told us that it had been a thrill to do battle with their Swedish counterparts, or in their words: "It was a right charge when it all kicked off, a real buzz."

They were all wearing Burberry caps which they'd stolen from a local department store and, at 9am, already well into their stash of Stella. Even now I can't look at anyone wearing Burberry without wanting to machine gun them on the spot.

These yobs don't mind doing radio interviews as they provide them with a degree of anonymity and they will often talk enthusiastically about their exploits, but their reactions change dramatically when they're confronted by television cameras. The brazenness and bravado suddenly evaporates once they realise their Mummies and Daddies might end up seeing them on *News at Ten* and there have been instances where TV crews have been attacked to prevent them filming. I knew a cameraman who said he'd rather cover a war story than a hooligan story because at least in the war zone there was some semblance of order with certain lines of engagement drawn up. In soccer riots the violence is completely haphazard, randomly directed and totally unpredictable, making it far less safe for crews to film.

The disgusting behaviour of some England fans was a very constant and depressing feature of my subsequent travels with the national team. Three years later I was back in Sweden to cover Euro 92 which England had scraped into under new manager Taylor. Their first two matches were in Malmo, a largely unremarkable but very welcoming city just across the water from Copenhagen. The Swedish hosts were early pioneers of fan zones, offering cut priced low strength alcohol and musical entertainment in special areas in each city. In Malmo this was located in a very large cobbled square in the centre of town; the weather was glorious and the gorgeous blonde locals added to the party atmosphere.

For two days I mingled with supporters of all nationalities, including English, without so much as a cross word or a raised voice. It seemed as if the Swedes had miraculously found a way to create a festival of football rather than fisticuffs and I thought it only fair to report back on how wonderful the atmosphere was. I interviewed supporters, locals, police representatives and put together a package highlighting a new mood of celebration. I think one of the phrases I used was: "Treat them like animals and they'll respond accordingly, treat them like human beings and they'll show their true human side."

What I should have said was: 'Trust English soccer fans at your peril'.

On the third day I was in the square with a Scottish reporter called Kevin Kelly who worked for that heavyweight organ of journalistic excellence the *Sunday Sport*. I spotted a guy about my age in a 1970s replica Watford shirt and we chatted amiably about the good old days of Stewart Scullion, Barry Endean and Ken Furphy to the general bemusement of those around us. We were joined by some other fans, one of whom raised his glass and said: "To Her Majesty the Queen." When I replied that I wasn't a great one for the royal family it was like watching Bill Bixby turn into the Incredible Hulk. His face went red and he began spitting and snarling.

"You're a fucking disgrace to your nation, you fucking commie wanker."

Several of his mates joined in as the mood very quickly turned nasty. One of them lifted up his shirt to reveal a St George Cross tattoo on the right-hand side of his chest.

"I've got all my tattoos down the right-hand side 'cos that's what I am, right-wing."

He wasn't talking about which position he played in the local pub team.

As I hinted before, you can smell danger in the air sometimes and this was just such a moment. After two days of peace and tranquillity the hardcore nutters had arrived to ensure any feelings of goodwill would quickly be replaced with hatred and contempt.

I looked up and saw that two drunken English yob ringleaders had somehow climbed onto the roof of one of the beer tents and were taunting the crowd. This, we later discovered, was a call to arms and within seconds the carnival scene had descended into chaos. A large group of fans charged forward hurling chairs, bottles and anything else that came to hand towards a line of Swedish police who had hitherto been keeping a fairly low profile on one side of the square. Immediately a posse of police on horseback charged into the crowd forcing myself, Kevin and everyone else to run for our lives. Terrified members of the public who seconds before had been enjoying an ice cream or a drink on a summer's afternoon, were sent scattering and screaming as the missiles continued to speckle the blue skies and smash down onto the cobbles.

The police charge managed to funnel the yobs away from the main square and into a small side street but in the ensuing rampage they smashed shop windows, overturned motorbikes and damaged cars in a grotesque wave of human sewage. It was like a scene from one of those nature films in which a plague of locusts descends on a fertile plain and strips it bare in seconds.

Back in the safety of the hotel, just 12 hours after eulogising the behaviour of the supporters, I was filing my latest piece describing the chaos and panic I had witnessed first hand at the epicentre of this hideous and premeditated outbreak of violent disorder. I interviewed those people who were willing to talk about the incident but many were understandably reluctant. The fact of merely being English was now a source of embarrassment and shame. I tried to apologise for what had gone on, but what can you say to people who came out to celebrate the joys of a major sporting event and ended up standing knee-deep in the wreckage of their own town?

England fans don't even have to be fighting running battles with police to ruin the lives of ordinary people and I've lost count of the number of times their mere presence has destroyed the ambience of pleasant European towns. Down the years I have almost become a professional apologist for the obscene behaviour of

England's minority of committed soccer thugs. It's a painful feeling which I know is shared by all the broadcasters and reporters who regularly cover the England team. However much you try to persuade people that most English people are sensible and decent, deep inside you know they have a perfect right to hate your country. For many of the younger ones it's their first ever experience of English behaviour, and mud sticks.

During France 98 we stayed near England's HQ in a delightful upmarket seaside resort called La Baule which, by French standards, was a very anglophilic place. It had a restaurant called The Salisbury and a gang of us set up base camp at The Sailor, a wonderfully friendly little bar where, as a French speaker, I was unofficial interpreter and we were treated like locals.

Unfortunately it didn't take long for the entente cordiale to be shattered. Before and during England's first game in Marseille a riot broke out involving English and Tunisian fans at an area that had been thoughtfully set up to allow ticketless supporters to watch the game on a giant screen. The scenes of violence were replayed endlessly on French TV and, although you try to kid yourself, things are never quite the same after an incident like that. You simply know that from there on in, everyone pretty much on the whole planet can't wait for England to be knocked out. To be honest I've even felt that way myself at times.

It is this kind of antisocial activity which has led the French, I'm told, to come up with a new nickname for the English. Given the boorish and aggressive behaviour which our country so depressingly exports to our nearest European neighbour, we are apparently now known as 'les fuckoffs'.

Having said that, it's not just England fans who've disrupted games I've covered. Given that England habitually seem to draw Poland in their qualifying groups, I've got to know Katowice quite well. It's a dour town in the upper Silesian coalfields but the Polish national side like playing there rather than Warsaw or Poznan because of the intimidating and hostile atmosphere at the Slaski Stadium. This giant, open bowl of an arena resembles an enormous, bubbling cauldron when Poland are playing, as it brings together the rival supporters of GKS Katowice and Ruch Chorzow who share all the convivial bonhomie of Celtic and Rangers fans.

The first time I saw England play there, in 1993, we walked into the stadium hours before kick-off and noted the presence of two long lines of Polish army soldiers in the stand behind one of the goals. We were discussing how sensible it was of the authorities to cordon off the England fans when a Polish reporter corrected us.

"No, no that is for the locals, England can stand where they want."

Sure enough midway through the first half the Poles started laying into each other with a ferocity that was only matched by the reaction of the army guys who clearly couldn't wait to get stuck in. Within minutes they were baton charging supporters up and down the terrace as missiles flew everywhere and tear gas virtually shrouded one end of the pitch.

England fans, some of whom had been involved in countless riots in the past, stood stock still, huddled together in one corner and cowering in terror. I remember thinking how pathetic they looked, given their self appointed image as the so-called hard men of Europe.

I also remember a game against Turkey at the Ataturk Stadium in Izmir when we in the press box got caught in the crossfire of a hail of projectiles being hurled across the stands. There we were filing and broadcasting away without incident when suddenly we felt coins, lighters, rocks and pens raining down from above. There didn't seem to be any prelude to this and we weren't in an area populated by the most vociferous fans.

I recall *Sky News* reporter Steve Bottomley getting hit on the arm by a lump of concrete and I had to deliver a live bulletin piece while huddled up for safety under my small wooden work top. I dashed out the report and quickly uttered the outcue, "John Anderson, IRN, Izmir" before sticking my head back up over the parapet only to be struck full in the face by an unpleasantly ripe banana. Still it could have been worse.

It turned out that a section of the Turkish fans were protesting against their Football Association and we were in the firing line between them and the VIP box with a vast majority of the missiles falling short.

Another ugly event took place in Bratislava in Slovakia in 2002. To all intents and purposes it is a lovely town, like a miniature cross between Prague and Vienna, full of pedestrianised squares, interesting buildings and cool bars. We spent the first night of our three-night stay at an excellent pub called Kelt which was right opposite the England team hotel and had a great time mixing with the locals and some very well-behaved England supporters.

On the second night I went for a meal with two of my best mates on these trips, Chris Skudder of *Sky News* and Ian Chadband, then of the *London Evening Standard*, both of whom are great company. We found a terrific little place hidden away in the back streets with a wonderful courtyard and had just ordered our starters when Chris's phone rang. Apparently the Kelt bar where we'd had such a nice time the evening before had been transformed into a war zone with rioting England fans being met with plastic bullet fire from the no-nonsense Slovakian police who were the closest thing I've ever seen to Robocop or Judge Dredd.

Once again, we spent half the night running around covering the story. England coach Sven-Göran Eriksson witnessed some of the trouble from his hotel window and famously described it as being like a scene from the Wild West.

To further dampen the proceedings (literally), it started to rain that night and carried on into the day after. There were fears that the game would be called off because of the weather and the pitch was in a pretty sorry state when we got to the stadium. So were the England fans. As ever, many innocent supporters had to suffer because of the actions of the idiot minority and they were escorted like drowned rats into the ground by the Robocops who, by now, were thoroughly relishing their role as enforcers and woe betide anyone who voiced any discontent.

To compound what was becoming a nightmare trip, the lightning took out the main ISDN terminal in the city half an hour before kick-off and so my broadcasting equipment was rendered useless. It was only thanks to the generosity of the *Mail On Sunday's* legendary correspondent Bob Cass, who lent me his phone, that we got anything out of the stadium at all.

England won the game 2-1, but it is remembered primarily for the disgusting racist abuse meted out to Emile Heskey and Ashley Cole. Strangely, the Robocops did nothing to stop the home fans making revolting monkey noises every time either player touched the ball.

After the game we stood in the pissing rain waiting for the interviews, which were obviously dominated by the appalling treatment Heskey and Cole had received. The Football Association's hugely likeable Head of Communications Adrian Bevington who, along with Media Liaison Officer Joanne Budd, was a constant joy to work and relax with on these trips, finally came out. He gave a very eloquent and reasoned FA reaction to the story which I recorded among a huddle of newspapermen. Unfortunately some of the paper guys took exception to my being there on the grounds that – "Oi, it's Mondays only." – Meaning the quotes they were claiming from 'Bevo' were for the sole use of Monday newspapers.

Now there are certain rules of etiquette in these situations and I'm happy to say that I largely abide by them. If, for example, you see a group of Sunday paper journalists talking to a certain player then that is off limits to the rest of us and fair enough too, as they have to get something for the weekend as the saying goes.

It's also perfectly reasonable for the daily papers, whose coverage of a Saturday match won't appear until the Monday, to try and get something a little different from everyone else to try and avoid the endless repetition of the same quotes. Again, just as I would expect them to stay clear of the radio interviews, I would never encroach on a group of daily reporters who are talking to a player.

But when it comes to riots, hooliganism, racist chanting and so forth, there's simply no way the quotes can be held back. The pictures have already gone out live on TV and obviously the story's taken on headline proportions for both news and sport, so how could I possibly, as a radio reporter, 'sit on' the quotes until Monday?

When I heard that 'Mondays only' phrase I'm afraid I lost it completely. There I was having had hardly any sleep, soaked to the skin, filing on a borrowed telephone, working three times as hard as you'd expect to after a game and being told by a member of my own profession who I hardly knew that I shouldn't be doing my job on a story of national importance.

"Who the fuck are you? What gives you the right to tell me not to record this? Are you the new FA Press Officer or what? Fuck off and let me get on with my job."

It was unnecessarily abusive but in the heat (or in fact wet) of the moment I felt justified.

It is sometimes funny the lengths people will go to try and protect their precious quotes (or 'nannies' as they are known in Cockney rhyming slang) given that most of them are on the dull side of soporific. Once, in the bowels of the Stade de France in Paris, I heard an English reporter trying to explain to a Frenchman that he wasn't supposed to be ear-wigging a post-match interview. The Frenchman shrugged in the customary Gallic fashion and feigned either non-comprehension or disinterest as the Englishman made a last gasp bid to explain. "Journaux de Dimanche. Journaux de Dimanche," he shouted, blissfully unaware of how absurd this sounded, given that most of our continental counterparts seem to have a much more liberal attitude toward sharing quotes.

As a TV commentator myself now, it always makes me laugh when you read the Monday newspaper report of a game and someone has lazily trotted out the same quotes from a *Sky Sports* interview conducted half an hour after the match ended. I'm tempted to phone up the reporter and shout:

"Television en directe. Television en directe."

It would be unfair to end this chapter without paying tribute to the thousands of genuine, law abiding football fans who spend a small fortune following England and with many of whom I've enjoyed hugely enjoyable conversations in bars, trains and airports and who truly represent everything that is good about the British sports fan. They never cease to amaze me with their enthusiasm for and knowledge of the game. Many treat football as their passport to visiting places they'd never dream of going to otherwise, but all too often see their attempts to widen their cultural horizons thwarted by the Burberry scumbags.

I am very happy to say that the recent tournaments in which England have participated have shown a vast improvement in the general behaviour of fans and long may it continue, but am I really alone in feeling that Euro 2008 was all the better for England's non-participation?

I even met two Scottish guys in La Baule who were supporting England after their team went out of France 98.

"We're all from the same country after all," was their perfectly logical explanation.

If only everyone could take the same attitude. For some reason football fans seem to need someone to hate as well as love. I've met Leeds supporters teaching their kids vile Munich air crash songs, middle-aged Chelsea idiots revelling in the 'glory' days of 1970s hooliganism, Spurs fans who won't support Arsenal players on England duty and Millwall supporters reducing train carriages to mute fear simply by their aggressive demeanour.

I'm a Watford fan and proud of it but I would never think less of anyone if they told me they supported Luton Town.

CHAPTER SEVEN

"Schi-laaaaaaaaaaaa-ci!!!"

My first major football tournament was Italia 90 when I was lucky enough to spend the majority of my time following Scotland and the Republic of Ireland whose wonderful fans put England to even greater shame. I was part of a four strong team from Gough Square which also included IRN Football Correspondent Andrew Gidley, LBC's Tony Lockwood (a mate to this day whose legendary sense of humour lit up many a foreign trip) and another great pal, IRN News reporter George Matheson. The other three were based with England in Sardinia, which cynics suggested had been deliberately picked to house our national team because of its island status. The logic seemed to be that at least the fans would be easier to control if they were away from the mainland. I'm sure a Napoleonic-style exile on Elba would have been considered if there had been a football stadium on the island. Indeed George, who was on what's known as 'hoolie watch', was on air more often than the rest of us put together in the opening week as England's supporters did their worst once again.

I started with the Scots who were billeted at a lovely place called Rapallo which is just along the coast from Genoa where their first two matches were played. We stayed at a wonderful upmarket fishing village called Santa Margherita de Ligure. The location has become even more desirable since then and was the venue for the wedding of Wayne Rooney and Coleen McLoughlin. It's a little ironic that the king and queen of the Wag/Chav brigade should tie the knot in such a sophisticated and stylish place. A Working Men's Club in Croxteth would have been a more appropriate venue, but apparently it was double booked.

The hotel I was in was very close to a much larger, posher one which had a lovely outdoor swimming pool, which we would sneak into and use. One of the residents there was the UEFA chairman Lennart Johansson who was in town to support his country Sweden who were in the same group as Scotland along with Costa Rica and Brazil. 'Big Len' as we dubbed him was a huge bear of a man but very approachable. Unlike the detached and aloof mandarins at the Football Association, you could leave a message on Johansson's answerphone at UEFA HQ in Switzerland and he would always call you back personally, however trivial or irritating the inquiry. On this particular excursion he put in plenty of hours on the sundeck between his official engagements and I sidled up to him one day and asked if I could do a general piece talking about the tournament as a whole and he agreed to meet me for breakfast the next morning.

That night we got reports of the first outbreak of widespread disorder among England fans on Sardinia. Some supporters had wrecked a couple of bars on the island and fought battles with local riot police in depressingly familiar scenes which were headline news on Italian TV. When I arrived for my interview with Johansson he looked up from his newspaper, shaking his head in desperation.

"What is wrong with these people?" he said. I told him I only wished I knew.

On the record he spoke at great length and with great regret about the previous night's trouble and suggested at one point that England should be thrown out of the tournament if the violence persisted. Even as he said the words I knew this was the radio equivalent of a money shot and the clip was rapidly turned round and run as a world exclusive as the most powerful man in European football suggested his FIFA counterparts should give England one last chance before booting them out of the World Cup before a ball had been kicked.

He'd have had no such trouble with the Scottish fans who descended upon the area in droves with their kilts, orange wigs and, in some cases, bagpipes. The locals were utterly captivated by these clansmen who treated them to impromptu singalongs and joined in the wild celebrations when Italy won their opening match against Austria. Now, no-one can tell me that the Scots drink less than the average English fan, in fact they probably drink more. And yet their behaviour generated warmth, comradeship and celebration. At one point I spotted the Scottish comedian Stanley Baxter in amongst a group of Tartan Army foot soldiers treating passing motorists to a Highland Fling. In fact the only Scotsman who came close to causing any trouble at all while we were there was Rangers striker Mo Johnston who was accused of singing a sectarian song at a group of supporters from his former club Celtic.

It has to be said, though, that a good portion of the Scottish media party were considerably less friendly than their fans and seemed to resent the infiltration of English interlopers within their ranks. Accordingly a wee clan of us Sassenach reporters quickly teamed up and huddled together on the tiny ferryboat which took us on the short ride across the beautiful sun-drenched little bay in the Ligurian Sea from Santa Margherita to Rapallo for the daily press conferences at the Scotland hotel. As daily commutes go, it certainly beat the 07.52 from Basingstoke to Waterloo hands down.

One of these conferences took the form of an open day where you could mingle with the players and get interviews ahead of the opening game against Costa Rica (surely a banker even given the Scots' woeful World Cup record). When I approached Johnston he gave me the shortest interview I've ever had, although it was my own fault. I rather foolishly decided to wade in with the sectarian allegations instead of softening him up with questions about the game and then dropping it in at the end. I got as far as:

"Mo, there have been a few allega . . . "

But before I could finish the sentence he turned tail and scarpered and I learned a quick lesson in how to approach interview situations. If I'd have saved the most awkward question until last I would at least have had some football stuff in the can. As it was I had nothing.

The match itself entered the great litany of Scotland's depressingly frustrating World Cup under-achievements. It was played at the Luigi Ferraris Stadium in Genoa and I was there to do reports and updates. The access to the press gallery was via an enormous temporary walkway which had been constructed outside the stadium and spiralled its way to the upper tier. Still in my twenties, I negotiated this fairly comfortably in the hot afternoon sunshine, even though I was laden with recording and broadcasting paraphernalia. But quite how some of the older and more corpulent correspondents managed to ascend this rickety structure without keeling over is beyond me. Sherpa Tenzing would have taken one look at it and said, "Fuck that, I'm off."

After a thoroughly dull and goalless first half I was filing live into a news bulletin with the second period only a couple of minutes old:

"A very disappointing 45 minutes for the Scots who've scarcely created a worthwhile chance against the group minnows . . . but Costa Rica are coming forward now . . . it's Juan Cayasso one on one with Jim Leighton . . . he scores . . . and Costa Rica are in front."

As an Englishman who had been largely cold shouldered by the Scottish press pack, I can confess to experiencing a mild delight as I uttered those words. That goal turned out to be every bit as calamitous for Scotland as the failure to score a hatful against Zaire in 1974, Iran's equaliser in 1978 and the draw against Russia which eliminated them in 1982.

Scottish hopes were briefly raised by a 2-1 win against Sweden at the same stadium and qualification was still a possibility as they went into their final group match against Brazil in Turin.

We had decamped to an out of season ski resort called Aosta which was nearer to Mont Blanc than it was to Turin itself and very close to the convergence of the Italian, Swiss and French Alps. As we completed the long coach journey to the stadium on match day, we were greeted by the extraordinary sight of the Brazilian and Scottish pre-match rituals going ahead in full swing simultaneously. Red-faced, kilted Caledonians in Tam O'Shanters were blowing away on bagpipes and dancing highland reels while a few feet away bronzed, yellow-clad Rio beach babes were gyrating along samba style to the accompaniment of percussion and brass. The entire perimeter of the Stadio delle Alpi was a blue and yellow sea of celebration as the most ardent supporters of two entirely disparate nations collided in an extraordinary cultural cocktail that only international sport can mix and serve up.

Shortly before the game got underway there was mass confusion among the press ranks as the official team sheets were handed out in the media tribune. Normally at any match, whether it be a World Cup final or Grimsby v Stockport in the Freight Rover Trophy, the media are given a printed sheet bearing the two line-ups plus substitutes at around 45 minutes before kick-off.

On glancing at the Brazilian team we noticed that the organisers had listed the players under their long and complicated real names rather than the nicknames by which they were universally known. Hence we had, for example:

4. Carlos Caetano Bledorn Verri

15. Luiz Antonio Correira de Costa

We frantically grabbed our World Cup guides to match the shirt number with the players' 'proper' names and eventually got it all sorted out.

4. Dunga

15. Muller

As it happened Luiz Antonio Correira de Costa came on as a sub and scored a scrappy goal eight minutes from time courtesy of a Leighton blunder to leave the Scots in third place in the group with two points.

Now, at that particular tournament, FIFA, in its wisdom, had devised a qualification formula which was so complicated that Professor Stephen Hawking would have considered writing *A Brief History of Time* a far less challenging proposition than trying to determine which four of the third placed teams in the six groups of four would join the 12 winners and runners-up in the last 16 of Italia 90. If you're numerically dyslexic like me, feel free to go and have a sit down.

Ultimately it transpired that Scotland could still qualify for the knockout stages if Uruguay drew 0-0 with South Korea in Udine the following night, as long as Jupiter was in conjunction with Neptune, the 24th of August fell on a Tuesday and the bonus ball number was 17.

Typically for the Scots, they had just started consulting their solar charts when Daniel Fonseca netted deep into stoppage time to ensure the Uruguayans went through and the Tartan Army headed home.

As well as being a long way from Turin, Aosta was also some 30 miles from the Scottish team's HQ. Myself and Press Association reporter Bill Pierce ran into a cab and made the journey across to get a final word on the situation with Scotland manager Andy Roxburgh. When we got to the hotel he was just walking out of a briefing with the Scottish newspapers who were preparing their latest Scotland World Cup obits for the back pages.

We asked him for five minutes of his time so that I could record an interview from which Bill could lift some quotes. His response was: "I spoke to you yesterday after the Brazil game, nothing's changed."

"With respect, quite a lot has changed. Yesterday you were technically still in the World Cup and tonight you're not."

Despite this reasonable and quite logical rejoinder, he steadfastly refused to speak to us and was whisked away into a lift by the press officer who, like so many of these people, appeared to be there to prevent rather than encourage the flow of news. Basically it meant that many Scottish independent radio stations were denied the opportunity to hear the national team manager's reaction to a World Cup exit. It was another example of a very well paid sporting figure utterly abdicating their responsibilities toward the fans and public.

It had been a complete and utter waste of time, not to mention money, since we had the cab waiting outside on the meter to take us all the way back. But I had the consolation of retelling the story so that the listeners would be in no doubt as to what I thought of this dereliction of duty.

Happily England had qualified from the so-called Group of Dearth (a reference to the total lack of footballing entertainment it served up) in Sicily and Sardinia which also included the Republic of Ireland, Holland and Egypt. While some of the England fans disgraced themselves off the field, the team were equally depressing on it, as they limped miserably through the opening phase. The poor standard of play had heaped even more pressure on the habitually beleaguered

Bobby Robson and I think it was David Lacey in the *Guardian* who brilliantly summed up the England boss at that time as a man who continually wore the expression of someone who thinks they've left the gas on. So awful had been the quality of the matches in Group F that, after the opening 1-1 draw with Ireland, one Italian paper came out with the classic headline:

'No Football Please, We're British.'

The Republic of Ireland also qualified, having been awarded second place in the group on the drawing of lots after finishing with an identical record to Holland. The Dutch incidentally also went through from third spot thanks to FIFA's version of the Duckworth-Lewis system. Given that covering England sounded too much like hard work, I was happy to leave that to Andrew, George and Locky as I hooked up with Jack Charlton's Ireland who had now filled the Rapallo hotel rooms vacated by the departing Scots as they prepared for the round of 16 match against Romania in Genoa. Boat rides across gentle, sun dappled waves or baton charges down tear gas filled streets? No contest really.

Once again, I was struck by just how different the Irish fans were to many of their English counterparts. They'd come in hordes from the Emerald Isle to celebrate what was the Republic's first ever taste of a World Cup finals and had already gone further in the tournament than Scotland had in six previous attempts. Having so enjoyed the antics of the Scottish mob, the locals were similarly enchanted by the green-clad Irish contingent, whose presence ensured that the party would rock on amicably in that part of the Ligurian coast for another few days at least.

The whole atmosphere around Jack Charlton's camp was very far removed from the reports we were getting of the increasingly strained relationship between the England team and the media in Sardinia which had developed into a kind of siege mentality. It was open house at the Irish hotel with interviews easy to get and cheerfully conducted.

I had to laugh though at some of the distinctively non-Irish accents liberally sprinkled among Big Jack's cleverly assembled squad, many of whom qualified for Ireland by their grandparents' background. I was joined in Santa Margherita by *Capital Radio* commentator Mick Lowes and we would amuse ourselves by doing absurdly over-the-top impressions of the players' interviews.

"So how are you looking forward to the Romania match?

Mick McCarthy: "Eh oop lad, we're all ready for t'game."

Andy Townsend: "Cor blimey, strike a light guv, it'll be a cracker and make no mistake."

Ray Houghton: "Och aye the noo, ah cannae wait laddie."

Jack Charlton: "Why aye man, it'll be the talk of the toon the morn neet like."

There's a good story (probably apocryphal) about the Republic of Ireland team lining up for the national anthems before an away match in Eastern Europe.

"Blimey, this anthem goes on a bit doesn't it?" says one player to the man next to him.

"Shut up, that's ours," comes the reply.

So I was back to scale the north face of the Luigi Ferraris Stadium once more to see if the Irish could continue their fairytale by beating a very good Romanian side which featured the stylish talents of Gheorghe Hagi and Marius Lacatus. They had finished second in a highly entertaining group, won by the dazzlingly talented but dangerously indisciplined newcomers from Cameroon who had beaten Argentina, to everyone's utter delight, in the opening game of the tournament.

Eastern European teams are often a nightmare to cover because of the difficult name pronunciations. This side for example featured Florin Raducioiu which is pronounced Rad-oo-choi-oo, although later during his unsuccessful spell at West Ham the Upton Park faithful referred to him as That Lay-Zee Fack-in Twat Rad-oo-choi-oo. I always felt the Romanians, who suffered from an unnecessary surplus of vowels, would benefit enormously from a trading treaty with Poland who had a ridiculous overabundance of consonants.

"I'll give you three zeds, a jay and a couple of kays for that o and two of those u's."

What you never stop to consider is how difficult it sometimes is for foreigners to get to grips with our language. Before the game I was approached by a Romanian reporter who asked me for phonetic spellings of the Irish team. To him names like Quinn, Staunton and McLoughlin looked baffling enough but the biggest problem he had was differentiating between Ray Houghton and Chris Hughton which he simply couldn't see as being in any way different.

"How-tern," I mouthed clearly, "Hugh-tern."

Still none the wiser he tried his best to note down the names as I'd said it. I looked down at his notepad and next to both players he'd written H-V-T-N.

A tight, tense and far from entertaining match ended goalless after extra-time and so went to penalties. Irish goalkeeper Packie Bonner saved from Daniel Timofte and David O'Leary scored the decisive penalty in the shootout to send the Republic through to the quarter-finals.

"They're dancing jigs on the terraces, they're dancing jigs on the pitch," I screamed down the microphone, as happy to see the Irish win as I had been to see the Scots lose in that same stadium. It was worth breathing in the petrol fumes from the revving team bus in the bowels of the stadium to capture the mood of euphoria among the players as they emerged from the dressing room after the match and the near disbelief in Niall Quinn's eyes was a sight to behold.

After the match most of the Irish fans headed to the main square in Genoa to watch Italy's game against Uruguay on the giant screen later that evening. The hosts won the game 2-0 with their new national hero Toto Schillaci scoring yet again and setting up a quarter-final date with the Republic in Rome.

It was my first ever trip to the Eternal City and I stayed at a hotel in the Via del Corso with Mick Lowes, who had now been joined by Jonathan Pearce, and *Capital's* expert summariser and all-round good egg Terry Neill. Taking a cue from my taxi ride in Seoul we took to shouting the names of the Italian players in a highly exaggerated Roman accent every time we went out for a beer.

Someone would scream "Schi-laaaaaaaaaaaaaaaa-ci" or "Baaaaaaaaaaa-ggio" or "Mal-deeeeeeeeeeeee-ni", which would elicit great cheers from the soccer mad locals.

Schillaci, by now the tournament's top scorer, had totally eclipsed fellow striker Gianluca Vialli in the hearts and minds of the Italian supporters and had become the country's number one hero. One night we were sitting outside a city centre bar when a beggar with only one leg hobbled past on crutches. After dropping some coins into his tin Mick Lowes got the biggest cheer of all by pointing at the tramp and shouting: "Vi-aaaaaaaaaaaaaaaaa-lli!"

The Irish stayed at a picturesque retreat high in the Roman hills and the daily journey up there to the press conference was as much a joy as the scene which greeted us when we arrived. Reaching the quarter-finals already represented an amazing achievement for the Irish team and the camp had become so relaxed that Jonathan and I interviewed the two heroes from the Romania game, O'Leary and Bonner, over coffee at a table overlooking a deep picturesque valley.

But that wasn't quite the most unusual location that I found myself in while covering the fortunes of the Republic of Ireland team at Italia 90. Pope John Paul II had diplomatically declared himself a joint Italy and Ireland fan since his native country Poland had not qualified, and the Irish players, largely Catholics, were invited to an audience with His Holiness at the Vatican. I followed the squad there and, while they were in the inner sanctum (literally), took the opportunity to mix business and pleasure with a spot of sightseeing while the players were enjoying their tete-a-tete with the pontiff. When they finally emerged from the audience we chatted to them on the steps of the Sistine Chapel in front of hundreds of Irish fans ands some very bemused tourists.

It was a surreal backdrop but we got some brilliant audio with some players saying it was among the greatest moments of their lives (meeting the Pope that is, not being interviewed by me). The golden rule of these occasions is get as much material in the can and cover as many bases as possible; so there I was standing in one of the most famous locations on earth concluding an emotive piece about a once in a lifetime experience, with more prosaic questions like: "Is there a plan to stop Schillaci?" or "how will you breach an Italian defence that hasn't conceded a single goal so far?"

In the end they couldn't stop Schillaci, and the man now known as Toto-Gol scored the winner to end a wonderful Irish adventure which had enriched the tournament no end. I must admit I thought the little Sicilian had ended my adventure too, but after pleading with the news desk I was allowed to head down and join Andrew Gidley, George Matheson and Tony Lockwood with England, who were now in the quarter-finals thanks to David Platt's last gasp winner against Belgium.

I travelled by train to Naples where the team were preparing to face Cameroon, who'd enlivened the whole tournament with their flamboyant football, exotic goal celebrations and the exploits of their 38-year-old striker Roger Milla.

On the day of the game there was a huge security operation to control the England fans who'd blighted the tournament in Sardinia, with the Neapolitans vowing that no such behaviour would be tolerated in their city. When we got to the Stadio San Paolo, a really grim concrete bowl with a moat around the pitch, news came through that a car crash en route to the game had tragically claimed the lives of five people including Bournemouth managing director Brian Tiler and seriously injured the club's then manager Harry Redknapp.

For the first and only time in IRN's history as far as I know, the top of the hour news bulletin that followed contained three different voicers from different reporters at the same stadium. George led with the tragic accident, I followed with details of the fans' arrival and Andrew previewed the match itself.

England, being England, assumed this quarter-final would be a walkover and were given a real scare as Cameroon led twice only for two Gary Lineker penalties, one in extra time, to book a semi-final against West Germany.

After the match Locky and I ran down endless concrete tunnels to the dressing room area so that we could get some interviews. The set-up was very badly laid out with the area shaped like a funnel leading to a small door from which the players would come out. This was where a grounding in independent radio stood us in good stead. Like a couple of rock fans eager to get to the edge of the stage, we pushed, shoved and menaced our way right to the front and waited. Eventually the door opened to reveal a startled Lineker, looking a good deal more unnerved than he had been when running up to take his penalty kicks. He blinked as the cameras and lights clicked on.

Locky and I reacted quickest, firing questions at him as the rest of the world either filmed or recorded the whole thing from behind us. As we struggled back through the mass to file the audio we passed several BBC Radio people sitting on chairs at the back of the room scratching their heads. One of them turned to us.

"This is an absolute nightmare."

"Not for us mate," we cheerily replied and hacked on through the media moshpit.

After a late night celebrating this glorious victory (both footballing and journalistic), Locky and I both overslept and had to dash out of the hotel to get a flight north to Turin, the venue for England's showdown with West Germany. We clambered into a cab and shouted something along the lines of "andiamo, avanti, avanti aeroporto" to the cabbie. Doubtless irked by two English buffoons barking at him in pidgin Italian the driver then embarked upon a death defying white knuckle ride through the back streets as if he was heading for the chequered flag at Monza. We sat terrified in the back hastily scribbling out our last will and testaments on the back of a fag packet.

When we got out, Locky was incensed at what he saw at the driver's recklessness.

"You're a disgrace to your nation," he kept shouting, oblivious to the fact that the driver either had no idea what he was talking about or did and wasn't rising to the bait.

It wasn't the last time we'd fall foul of an Italian taxi driver. Some years later Locky and I were in Genoa covering Arsenal in a European tie against Sampdoria. The hotel was a bit out of town so we booked a cab to take us to a restaurant. Upon arrival Locky, who by now had a pathological mistrust of foreign cabbies, and took great delight in verbal piss-takes of every imaginable variety, said:

"Can I have a very small bill, a very large receipt and can I sleep with your wife?"

The driver didn't flinch. He took the money, wrote out the receipt and handed it to Locky.

"I'm divorced," he replied in perfect English.

Upon arrival in Turin we checked into a horrendous hotel near a town called Alessandria which was about 60 miles away from the city itself. I can only imagine the person who designed this particular pied a terre had done so armed only with a B&Q catalogue and a video of *Crossroads*.

It was a bit like a modern version of that half built Spanish hotel in *Carry On Abroad* and you half expected to be greeted in the lift by a scantily clad Barbara Windsor fluttering her eyelids at a bemused looking Bernard Bresslaw in a cowl. The forecourt featured an exotic collection of JCBs, concrete mixers and large holes. It was as if, instead of Earl's Court, the Ideal Home Exhibition had been staged at the Somme. You needed SAS training to negotiate your way to the reception desk without slipping off a duckboard and drowning in a pool of slurry. The sparsely furnished rooms featured furniture which collapsed at the merest hint of contact and the inside of all the cupboards and wardrobes had been sprayed with some sort of chemical treatment which meant every time you opened a door it was like being maced.

Even worse, the hotel was located absolutely nowhere near any useable amenities so we were pretty much trapped in this flat-pack fortress for two whole days. For reasons I've never understood to this day, the spiky-haired, chart-topping violinist Nigel Kennedy had also chosen to stay in this god-awful dump with his new girlfriend Brix Smith, who used to be in my favourite group The Fall. I was sorely tempted to go up them and say: "Sorry to bother you, but I'm a huge fan of your music," and then, just as Nigel was about to open his mouth, come back with, "Not you, her."

But they looked so lovey-dovey I left them to it.

On the night before England were due to face the Germans, the World Cup was officially pronounced dead and received the last rites from the home nation as Italy lost their semi-final on a penalty shootout to an odious Argentina side who had limped through their group in third place, beaten Brazil by a single goal in the last 16 and had now notched their second successive sudden death success.

You really felt for the Italians, they'd staged a wonderful tournament in which they'd only conceded one goal and in Schillaci had the undoubted star of the show. And yet the manic car tooting and horn blowing which had greeted their every win was replaced by an eerie, funereal silence as the whole nation collectively went into shock.

By contrast England, who'd been awful in their group and squeezed through the knockout stages with two late, late victories, were still in contention. Furthermore they now faced one arch enemy in West Germany for the right to face another, Argentina. We were beginning to feel as if our name was on the cup.

Who were we kidding? Gary Lineker summed it up years later when he said: "Football is a simple game: 22 men chase a ball for 90 minutes and at the end the Germans win."

In this case, of course, it was 120 minutes and as Chris Waddle's penalty sailed high over Bodo Illgner's crossbar, Locky, commentating for LBC, said: "And that's it." When he'd put down his mic he slumped forward onto the desk, head in hands, a position I had adopted some moments before. Eventually we sat up, turned and looked at each other and shook our heads in disbelief. It was one of those moments when words really aren't necessary.

However I did have to get some words from the England camp, although it wasn't a pleasant task. I remember joining a little throng of radio reporters standing by the team buses as Waddle came through. There were still tears in his eyes.

"Which one's our bus?" he mumbled, barely audible above the hubbub.

We pointed silently across, none of us having the heart to put him through a post mortem on what was the worst day of his professional life. David Platt who had established himself as a star during the tournament, not just as a player but in the magnificent way he handled his media responsibilities, spoke eloquently on behalf of his vanquished team. Platty, who I'd often seen playing for Crewe when I was at *Signal Radio*, was an ordinary lad from Oldham who had just turned 24 and yet he was absolutely brilliant towards the press. He was always polite, pleasant, amenable and, above all, interesting to listen to. We knew, even then, that he'd be a great pundit when he retired and I've had the pleasure of working alongside him with *Sky Sports*. Of that Italia 90 squad, Gary Lineker, Terry Butcher, Neil Webb and Tony Dorigo were also what we called 'great talkers'.

The worst ones were Stuart Pearce who would greet almost every request for a post-match interview with, "I'd rather not", and Des Walker who, to all intents and purposes, was completely mute and would probably have reacted to his Mum saying, "would you like a cup of tea, dear?" with a shrug and a blank stare.

We used to amuse ourselves by compiling England XIs based solely on their ability to give good interviews or nightmare line-ups comprising the most monosyllabic or awkward players. I would nominate the following England team based on the relative willingness of players to grant me interviews over the years and the quality of their answers. I've chosen 4-4-2 because, let's face it, it's the only formation they understand:

Tim Flowers
Gary Neville, Terry Butcher, Gareth Southgate, Graeme le Saux
David Beckham, David Platt (c), Neil Webb, John Salako
Gary Lineker, Stan Collymore
Manager: Graham Taylor

Beckham gets a lot of stick in certain quarters for his supposed arrogance and perceived lack of intelligence but I certainly never found this to be the case. Given that he was England's captain and star performer for so long, he would be expected to undertake far more media duties than the other players. Every single time I came across him, and there were many, he was unfailingly polite, pleasant and enthusiastic. When the tapes stopped rolling, some players couldn't wait to dash off but he would stop and talk about how his kids were getting on or what was on the telly and would always happily sign stuff for our children which, of course, they treasured.

When Manchester United took part in their ill fated trip to Brazil for the FIFA World Club Cup in 2000, part of their time was taken up with work as ambassadors for the children's charity UNICEF. One morning a group of kids from one of Rio's slum areas known as favelas were allowed to join in a kickabout with the United players after training. The highlight of this was the sight of a scruffy eight-year-old carrying the ball 30 yards upfield before casually chipping the ball over stand-in goalkeeper Ryan Giggs for a goal which only a Brazilian would dare to score. He then celebrated wildly and enthusiastically with his team-mates as poor Giggsy got absolutely slaughtered by his.

After the session the children performed a samba style drumming session using petrol cans and big plastic bottles as percussion instruments. The players stood in a row behind them as the kids clattered away for what seemed like an eternity. You couldn't fault their enthusiasm, but after ten minutes of this most people's patience had been well and truly tested and many of the players had begun to look decidedly bored. Not Beckham though.

Throughout the entire performance he wiggled his hips and clapped his hands with a fixed grin on his face, utterly captivated by the raw energy and enthusiasm of a bunch of people whose lives could not have been more diametrically opposed to his own.

While Becks deserves his place in the chatty and helpful line-up, the team composed of the misery guts, monosyllabics and wallflowers would have looked a little like this:

David Seaman
Kieron Dyer, Sol Campbell, Des Walker, Stuart Pearce (c)
Lee Bowyer, Nicky Butt, Paul Scholes, Tony Daley
Andy Cole, Darius Vassell
Manager: Steve McClaren

To be fair, it took me an awful lot longer to compile the Silent XI. I honestly can't think of a single non co-operative right-back, so I'm banking on McClaren to play Kieron Dyer out of position. It's also a little harsh on David Seaman since goalkeepers are generally affable types but he was prone to the odd sulk when the press went against him. The same goes for Sol Campbell.

Platty scored his third World Cup goal as England lost 2-1 to Italy in the third place play-off in Bari which, if there had been any justice in the world, would have been the final. But it was Peter Shilton who made all the headlines as he bowed out of international football after winning a record 125th cap in an astonishing career spanning 20 years.

Funnily enough I had seen Shilton's debut against East Germany as a ten-year-old on a birthday treat on my first ever trip to Wembley in November 1970. I thought back to that day and recalled the thrill of travelling up to the famous stadium on the train and tube with my Dad and a school mate, standing at the tunnel end, seeing Bobby Moore, Alan Ball, Geoff Hurst and Martin Peters in the flesh. I can still almost taste the Mars Bars and a Coke at half-time and the celebrations after a 3-1 win, followed by the thrill of finally getting into bed way after midnight on a school day. Nearly 20 years on, the experience of watching international football was just as thrilling as Shilton bowed out in Bari. You may be sitting in a media seat with a microphone doing a job many people would kill for, but take the boyish enthusiasm for the game away and it would be a pretty hollow experience.

Unfortunately it was almost impossible to find anything enthusiastic to say about the final itself. I could hardly believe that less than six years after covering a Surrey Senior Cup tie from the restricted view of the Cherrywood Road tea room I would be broadcasting live from the World Cup Final at the Olympic Stadium in Rome.

In truth Farnborough and Fleet Town would have served up a good deal more entertainment than West Germany and Argentina could muster at Rome's Stadio Olimpico. The cynical South Americans had two players sent off as Andreas Brehme's late penalty put a truly dismal encounter out of its misery to the huge relief of a whole global brotherhood of sofa snoozers. The Germans had the cup, Maradona blubbed like a fat girly and a wonderful tournament finished in a dreadful anticlimax. It was as if the Beatles had reformed and staged the biggest concert in history only to end the final encore with *Octopus's Garden*.

Still, considering the original plan had been for me only to cover Scotland, I'd somehow managed to see the tournament through to the end and now had both an Olympic Games and a World Cup under my belt. Having reported on Johnson's cheating and Gazza's weeping I could have been forgiven for feeling like some sort of herald of 20th century sporting iconoclasm.

In reality I felt like a specky, sweaty, dishevelled little twat in an adidas Italia Novante t-shirt who hadn't seen his girlfriend, downed a decent pint or tasted a proper cup of tea for over a month.

CHAPTER EIGHT

"I own everything that moves around here."

Earlier in 1990 I had travelled with news reporter George Matheson to Auckland in New Zealand to cover the Commonwealth games. The signs that this was going to be a complicated assignment manifested themselves early on. We travelled (economy of course) via Los Angeles and Honolulu, arriving in Auckland some 29 hours after leaving London.

Given the amount of travelling I'd been doing around that time, baggage carousels had begun to lose a little of their attraction. Especially so when you're the last man standing and the monotony of watching the black rubber panels turning endlessly around is punctuated only by the sight of a battered tartan holdall and a cardboard box tied up with string. Neither of these belonged to me and I swear the airport authorities place them deliberately on the conveyor belt simply to try and convince you that your suitcases will eventually arrive. It's not just in New Zealand, you see them all over the world.

Sure enough mine didn't arrive and I was reminded of a particularly amusing piece of graffiti on a 1970s British Airways poster aimed at the international business traveller. The slogan was something like: 'Breakfast in London, lunch in Paris, dinner in New York.' Under which some wag had scrawled: 'Luggage in Tokyo.'

Somehow my socks and undies had made an unscheduled and prolonged stopover at LAX and wouldn't arrive in New Zealand until two days later. George, who fancied himself as a bit of a fashionista, lent me some of his gear which was admittedly more stylish than mine and I bought some other essentials on a shopping spree funded by expenses. This was good as I could splash out on quality stuff I wouldn't normally buy.

Compared to the Olympics, the Commonwealth Games are a cross between a village fete and a school sports day. The anachronistic concept of an imperial collective with England at its hub is increasingly redundant and, with the competition open only to members of this exclusive club, most of the world's top athletes aren't involved. Shorn of the USA, virtually all of Europe, most of the Far East and the Latin American countries, some of the events are utterly devalued. You could hand the bloke next to you at the bus stop a stick of bamboo and he'd have an outside chance of making the pole vault final.

Auckland itself, though a charming city in many, many ways, simply added to this olde worlde feeling. It was a little as you'd imagine Britain to have been in the early 1960s with its quaint buildings, quiet streets, casual way of life, sleepy suburbs and motorways filled with slow moving Vauxhall Vivas.

The volunteers at these Games were largely well-meaning but hopelessly out of touch geriatrics, the stadiums often little more than converted gym halls and the crowds, though cheerful and enthusiastic, were of the nice but dim variety. Many of them seemed more interested in collecting the tournament's commemorative metal pins (that's badges to you and me) than worrying about what was happening in the events themselves. People would station themselves outside the venues with large boards selling these worthless looking trinkets, some of which were produced by the broadcasting organisations covering the Games.

Every time we went anywhere, someone would spot our media accreditation and hordes of people rushed up asking if we had any pins. Given that we were in New Zealand, the local accent rendered this request as:

"Have you got any puns?"

"Yes," we'd reply: "What do you call a man with no arms and no legs in a swimming pool?"

Blank look.

"Bob."

The worst crime of all was when journalists themselves would join in this juvenile pursuit and walk around festooned in tiny, shiny metallic circles and start pestering their fellow reporters. Some seemed aghast that Independent Radio News hadn't commissioned its own Auckland 1990 badge.

"How come you guys don't have any pins?"

"Because we're a serious news operation not a bloody toyshop."

New Zealand had its own version of Independent Radio News (which, I'm willing to bet, probably did have its own pin) and the whole event was a huge story for them given that a major international sporting competition was happening in their back yard. We befriended a couple of their reporters hoping to tap into their local knowledge and pick up some stories.

On one occasion an IRN NZ journalist dashed towards us in a breathless and agitated state.

"Have you heard the news?"

"What news?"

"About one of the members of the organising committee ... "

We waited with bated breath, hoping she'd tell us that he'd been caught on CCTV with his trousers round his ankles in a toilet cubicle entertaining a teenage gymnast. No such luck.

"He's had his car broken into."

As non-stories go this was right up there with the best. You could see the headlines: 'Man No-One's Ever Heard Of Or Cares About Loses Car Stereo In Non-Violent Opportunist Theft'. Even the *Surrey Advertiser* on a slow news day would have stopped short of running this one.

Whereas the World Cup and Olympic Games were EBU events granting us full broadcast rights, the Commonwealth Games saw us assigned non-rights holder status by the organisers in order to protect the interests of the BBC who were the UK broadcast partners. This is also known as news access status and normally means you are forbidden to do any live or off-air commentaries but are permitted to broadcast from venues within a restricted framework such as a maximum of three 30 second updates per hour for example. This was the way things were for us at events like Wimbledon or the Rugby World Cup and we had no problem with it, as long as we could access venues, report into bulletins, collect audio and send down pre-recorded pieces on site.

However, when we arrived in Auckland we discovered that the rules were very different. For some reason our accreditation denied us access to any competition venue and confined us to the Main Press Centre, the central media office which was mainly populated by newspaper journalists. To us, this was a totally unacceptable state of affairs. Basically, it meant that if a terrorist group had blown up the VIP box during the opening ceremony we would have been prevented from reporting from the scene since we weren't allowed in. This, we felt, unfairly prevented a large section of the UK broadcasting fraternity and therefore millions of radio listeners from receiving coverage of a genuine news event. Members of the Royal Family as well as many top politicians were in Auckland for the Games and these occasions are as much about politics as sport.

Back in London, appeals were made to the BBC to help grant us new access rights, but they were trenchant in their insistence that no changes could be made. I got hold of a contact number for the head of BBC Sports Outside Broadcast in Auckland and called hoping to be able to convince him to reconsider. I explained that we simply wanted the right to cover the top stories in the same way that newspapers did and would not impinge in any way upon the BBC's status as the UK rights holders.

In what remains one of the most staggeringly arrogant responses I've ever received to what seemed like a reasonable request, his reaction was: "I own everything that moves around here."

Note the use of the first person singular. This was clearly not a man for whom compromise or conciliation came naturally. I slammed the phone down in disgust and George and I hatched our battle plan. We contacted the venue managers to complain about this ludicrous state of affairs and most were hugely surprised and very supportive. Their attitude was that they wanted the Games to be a success and to have as wide an audience as possible and they couldn't understand why certain organisations were being frozen out.

"No-one tells me who can come into my stadium," was one of the reactions we got. We also tipped off our newspaper colleagues, including James Lawton then of the *Daily Express*, a hugely affable man and a brilliant writer, who was staying at our hotel and included it in his diary column. We became a bit of a *cause celebre* in Auckland and the whole thing culminated with the story making the front page of *The Times* with IRN Managing Director John Perkins eloquently pleading our case, with the BBC insisting they were mystified by the furore while offering little in mitigation.

In the end we won our battle and were handed an accreditation upgrade which entitled us to the normal news access granted to non-rights holders. When we picked up our new passes the lady handing them over stuck a little circular yellow sticker on mine to represent a gold medal, which was really sweet.

Whereas the Seoul Olympics had been a real slog with just two of us to cover such a huge event, Auckland was a piece of piss. The time difference meant there was little pressure on us to deliver material as it happened, since the whole thing was taking place in the middle of the night in the UK. Most of our efforts were geared towards breakfast programmes, allowing plenty of time to put material together which would run throughout the day. Apart from the disqualification of a couple of steroid infused Welsh weightlifters (Anna Bolic and Clem Buterol) and the shocking damage caused to a leading Games official's car there was little in the way of big stories for us to chase.

This gave us plenty of time for socialising in the evening and I discovered a good way of finding out where the best places to go were in Auckland and which I employed on many subsequent foreign trips. If you want a bit of local knowledge, pop into the local unisex salon for a trim. The hairdresser will invariably attempt to engage you in conversation ("so are you planning a holiday this year sir?") and they're generally quite trendy types so you can then pick their brains for useful info.

I got loads of good tips from a girl at a salon in Auckland. She was very into English music so I told her The Stone Roses would be the next big thing and hopefully, for a spell, she was the coolest chick on her block. However, not everyone in this city was quite as hip.

If you learn anything from the Commonwealth Games it is that, in as much as you can generalise, there are plenty of nations in the world that are far more patriotic towards the Royal Family than our own. Canadians, for example, adore the royals as it affords them an air of superiority over their American neighbours. I had a holiday in Ottawa as a 17-year-old in 1978 which coincided (not deliberately you understand) with a state visit by either Prince Edward or Prince Andrew, I can't remember which. The whole place went completely berserk, with crowds lining the streets, flags waving, cameras flashing, wall to wall TV coverage and general pandemonium. I recall donning a Sex Pistols 'God Save The Queen' T-shirt and drawing foul looks from the assembled hordes who got extremely upset at the idea of someone from the mother country dissing Her Maj.

In Auckland we turned up at one of the bars my hairdressing friend had recommended and I was told by the bouncer on the door that I was not welcome. This was about ten o'clock at night, there was no strict dress code, I was well over 21 years old and hadn't consumed a single unit of alcohol.

"Sorry mate, I don't like the look of your shirt."

Horror of horrors, I was wearing a T-shirt bearing the front cover of the Smiths album 'The Queen Is Dead'. I explained to him that it was it was simply a piece of artwork and that I didn't have plans to assassinate any member of the Royal Family or single-handedly bring down the Commonwealth from within. I also questioned his stance on the right to freedom of speech and expression given that New Zealand was supposedly a civilised and tolerant nation.

Unfortunately it was a little like asking a refrigerator to warm up a bit. He steadfastly refused to grant me admission, thus upholding the long and ignoble traditions of nightclub bouncership. Of all the things I loathe and detest in this world and there are many (dinner parties, tinned sardines, 4 x 4s, religious fundamentalism and Phil Collins, to name but a few) bouncers would be pretty high on the list.

These meat-headed, tuxedo-wearing tosspots who couldn't cut it in the army inhabit a tiny sub-species of life on earth one evolutionary step down from the amoeba. In my experience they actually cause far more trouble than they're paid to prevent and if anyone can produce a credible piece of research which establishes beyond doubt the link between violent crime and wearing trainers, I'll stand outside Stringfellow's for a week.

Four years later there were more patriotic outpourings as the Commonwealth Games were staged in the city of Victoria on Vancouver Island just off the south west coast of Canada. This place made Auckland look like downtown New York at rush hour. Imagine if a giant JCB had scooped up a scale model of an archetypal English village made of Lego and plopped it down right into the middle of an amorphous blob of fast food restaurants, motels, tyre shops, Kwik-E Marts and furniture showrooms. The opening ceremony resembled a Walmington-On-Sea wartime village fete with its lacrosse demonstration and maypole dancing.

The centre of the city was so quaint it was almost nauseating. It was full of cake shops and tea rooms and the biggest pub was called the Sticky Wicket, which was a queasy cross between a Wetherspoons and a Harvester. Since preventative costs had whittled the IRN contingent down to a single reporter, I took a stroll downtown to find some English cohorts. You didn't need to be Sherlock Holmes to deduce that the pub, given its close proximity to the Main Press Centre, would quickly attract a host of thirsty hacks. The first person I saw when I walked in was *Sky News* reporter Mark Saggers, who's now a presenter on *talkSPORT*.

Perhaps having learnt their lesson from Auckland, the BBC gave us proper news access accreditation this time, but Saggs was hamstrung by the same restraints I'd had four years earlier. Don't get me wrong, I think the Beeb do a good job in covering these major events but the likes of Saggs and his successors Chris Skudder and Olly Foster are the real broadcasting heroes. With little or no access to venues and therefore the competitors themselves, they manage to satisfy the 24-hour demands of a rolling news operation by sheer force of will, good contacts, shrewd thinking and a bloody-minded refusal to let circumstances prevent them from providing first-class coverage. It was the same at IRN; you lived on your wits and persistence brought its own reward.

There are occasions though when the sheer vastness of the BBC operation can work in your favour. While in Victoria I went along to cover the badminton, but on the way I spotted a discount CD shop with loads of bargains and spent rather too long stocking up with cheap albums which I stuffed into my tape recorder bag before running off to get the bus.

One of the joys of international travel for a saddo music fan like myself is the opportunity to buy cheap, rare or unusual CDs and I would eagerly scour any new location in the hope of snapping up some bargains. I discovered that this was a passion shared by *5Live* Chief Football Correspondent Mike Ingham when en route to Moscow for an England game in 1992. I didn't know Mike that well at the time but we got chatting on the plane about music in general and specifically which was our favourite Beatles album. Later, on one of his sorties into the Russian capital, Mike had found a record shop selling vinyl albums at around 75p a go. By the end of his spree he virtually needed a fork-lift truck to get his purchases back to the hotel, and then had to buy an extra suitcase to get them back home.

"Anything to declare sir?"

"Yes; an entire phonographic library of classic LPs ranging from Hendrix to Patti Smith via the Manic Street Preachers and Leonard Cohen."

I thought nothing more about this until the next international at Wembley a few weeks later when Mike came running up to me in the press lounge and handed me a plastic bag. Inside was a Russian version of the Beatles' 'White Album', complete with Cyrillic lettering, pencil drawings of the Fab Four rather than the normal photos on the inner sleeve and a wonderful lyric sheet all in Russian which was illustrated with weird psychedelic cartoons. It was a fabulous gesture and very typical of a wonderfully thoughtful and generous man.

My self indulgent stopover at the Victoria CD shop meant I'd missed half of the badminton match by the time I arrived at the venue. Luckily I spotted David Oates, a very versatile BBC reporter who's also a good mate, sitting high in the upper section of a temporary stand which was a giant mesh of metal tubes, plastic seats and scaffolding.

"Hi Oatesy, have I missed anything?" I spluttered before sitting down.

As I took my seat I put the tape recorder bag down behind me, only to look round in horror as it plunged thirty or so feet down through a gap in the makeshift stand making a ghastly thud, crash, tinkle sound as it ended its plummet on the concrete floor below.

It was an expensive Marantz cassette machine and I didn't have a spare, so I feared the worst as I descended into the bowels of the arena to assess the damage. My fears were duly confirmed as I picked up the bag and it rattled in the same way as an unopened Christmas present from your auntie used to when you just know it's a bloody jigsaw. The one small consolation was that the CDs had come out of this crash landing relatively unscathed. However the plastic case surrounding my copy of The Cure's live album 'Show' still falls apart whenever I get it off the shelf.

So here I was, charged with single-handedly covering an international sporting event on behalf of over 100 radio stations, but without the means with which to produce any recorded sound. IRN were reluctant to incur the cost of either shipping a new machine 6,000 miles across the world or allowing me to buy a replacement and claim it on expenses.

Armed with this sob story I wandered around the Broadcast Centre, cap in hand, and eventually a local Canadian station very kindly agreed to loan me a machine for a couple of days. For a longer term fix I decided to swallow my pride and see if BBC radio could help me out. Given the scale of their operation they had engineers on site and, in a wonderfully generous gesture, one of the producers Heather Fordham took the tape recorder in for them to examine. Amazingly they managed to coax some life out of it and, although it still sounded as if I was walking around with a packet of cornflakes in my bag, it just about limped its way through the rest of the Games.

I was determined to repay Heather's kindness and, over the years, there have been quite a few occasions when I have been able to help out BBC reporters when they suffered equipment malfunctions, although none of them has ever managed to trash their gear in quite such a spectacular fashion.

The big story in Victoria again involved drugs, with the news breaking during the Games that England's reigning 800m champion Diane Modahl had tested positive for testosterone at a meeting in Lisbon earlier in the season. Again the BOA press officer Caroline Searle, this time in her capacity with the Commonwealth Games Council for England, excelled herself with levels of patience, guidance and indefatigability which put most media liaison types to shame as she helped us piece together this complicated saga.

The IRN newsdesk, previously near oblivious to what was going on in Victoria, suddenly developed a rapacious appetite for this latest 'shame of the nation' story and pestered me for constant updates even when there was patently no new information. This kind of reporting is now commonplace especially in the news 24 arena where the sight of TV correspondents spouting non-committal drivel from outside a dimly lit, non-descript building for no apparent reason is an everyday staple of what is rather pompously termed as 'electronic news gathering'.

"Let's rejoin Dan Smugg who's outside ACAS headquarters now."

"Thanks Fiona, well in the building you can see behind me both sides are currently trying to thrash out an agreement, although it's too early to say what that might be. Talks will continue until that decision is reached but we don't know how long we'll have to wait, how the result will be announced or which side may prevail. Back to you Fiona."

"Thanks Dan. That's Dan Smugg, our Industrial Affairs Correspondent outside ACAS HQ."

To make matters worse there's always a large graphic with the word LIVE in the top left-hand corner and a caption along the bottom of the screen accompanying Dan's appearance which, thanks to the near extinction of professional graphics operators, reads 'Elsie Cavendish – Injured Pensioner'.

Wouldn't it be great if, just once, they were honest about the whole thing.

"I'm Fiona Vain and you're watching 24-7 news. Let's pointlessly try and use up a few more minutes of airtime by needlessly crossing back to Dan Smugg who's standing in the pissing rain outside ACAS headquarters . . . what more can you tell us Dan?"

"Absolutely fuck all, Fiona."

"Thanks, Dan. We'll have more from him in about five minutes time as it's a very slow news day, but first with the latest on Britney Spears' new navel piercing here's our Celebrity Mishap Correspondent Emily Witless."

My method of re-jigging voice pieces to reflect the fact that there was nothing new to report was simply to send down exactly the same piece but with the word 'still' inserted into the opening line.

"We're STILL awaiting news of whether Diane Modahl will be sent home from Victoria."

It actually became a bit of a catchword amongst the British press.

"Hi John, I see you're STILL at the bar."

"Yes, and I'm STILL not going to buy you a drink."

"In which case you're STILL a tight-fisted bastard."

Poor Diane was eventually sent home in disgrace despite the fact that, as was eventually proved, she was completely innocent. Her sample had become contaminated as a result of being incorrectly stored at the laboratory in Portugal after the initial 'positive' test, which explained the abnormally high levels of testosterone.

What the Commonwealth Games may have lacked in sporting relevance it more than made up for in the attractive locations of the host cities. Victoria was a fine example with its close proximity to the Pacific Ocean, the splendid city of Vancouver and the Rocky Mountains which, although more than 500 miles away, were virtually next door in the vastness of Canada itself. My wife Carolyn flew over to join me for a two-week holiday after the Games which she often did at the end of these trips as it offered the prospect of visiting an exotic location with only one air fare to pay.

She arrived on the penultimate day of the competition and we'd agreed to meet at a bar once I'd finished working.

When she walked in I was with a gang of my athletics mates including Ian Chadband, the *Telegraph's* Tom Knight, Duncan McKay of the *Guardian*, Dougie Gillon of the *Glasgow Herald*, Press Association correspondent Stuart Barnes and a reporter whose blushes I will spare by allowing him to remain nameless. This character was quite likeable generally, but had a strange habit of using coarse and graphic shock-factor humour especially when he encountered someone he hadn't met before.

He waited for a lull in the conversation and turned to Carolyn.

"So you're in for a busy night then."

"How do you mean?"

"Well, with seven blokes on top of you."

Carolyn, who'd studied drama at college and now worked in the theatre, kept a deadpan expression, put down her glass, stared him in the eye and with impeccable timing uttered a single word.

"Six."

It was one of the greatest put downs any of us had ever heard and rendered our usually loud and verbose friend totally humiliated and speechless. He was never quite the same after that.

When I arrived in Kuala Lumpur for the next Commonwealths in 1998 I again had to untangle the BBC accreditation pantomime that had dogged us in Auckland, but, with rather less drama this time, I was able to gatecrash the party once more.

This was a far cry from the lace curtains and manicured lawns of Victoria. Everyone referred to the city as KL, although I must admit I've never been a great fan of these Americanised acronyms; let's face it nobody calls Newport Pagnell 'NP'. Another horrible example of this type of thing was US reporters referring to tennis player Andy Roddick as A-Rod (to distinguish him, presumably, from T-Hen, M-Nat or R-Fed). It all seems so humourless and posturing and reminded me of how the inherent difference between the Brits and the Yanks had been encapsulated during the war in Afghanistan. One of the suspected Taliban strongholds was a mountain cave complex known as Tora Bora. The Americans nicknamed it something crass and macho like Hell-Gate, while the British forces referred to it as Tora Bora-Tomkinson.

The first experience I had of Kuala Lumpur was the extraordinary descent to the city's new international airport which had only been inaugurated a week before the Games started. The pilot's announcement of our imminent arrival wakened me from my long-haul haze of tiredness and alcohol and I was keen, as ever, to get a panoramic view of the city out of the window. As we got lower and lower I began to become slightly concerned at the fact that all I could see beneath us was verdant foliage.

"Crew, take your seats for landing," came the captain's voice.

By now I was panic stricken and could see the leaves of trees through the little porthole. Bloody hell we're going to crash in the jungle and have to eat each other, I thought as the horror dawned on me that for all the hundreds and hundreds of flights I'd taken over the years I'd never once paid proper attention to the safety demonstration.

I was just about to adopt the brace position when, through a gap in the greenery, the gleaming, new, state of the art KLIA complex stretched out in front of us like something out of *Star Wars*. I was so relieved I was even prepared to forgive them the acronym. It was similar to the effect you used to get on arriving in the old airport in Hong Kong where the approach was so built up that you fear you're going to crash land in some poor family's living room.

With its landscape-defining Petronas Towers, Singapore-meets-Borneo mix of rainforests and skyscrapers and staggering humidity, this was a wonderfully exotic place. Unlike the New Zealanders and Canadians, the privilege of hosting the first ever Asian Commonwealth Games had prompted the host city to invest in near Olympic standard facilities rather than refurbished scout huts.

Unfortunately the main press accommodation wasn't quite as impressive. It was called the Mint Hotel although clearly not because it had cost a mint to build. It looked like a giant bouncy castle had blown dangerously close to a motorway and been hastily converted into a media venue from its regular function as a giant knocking shop. The rooms were absolutely tiny, not surprising given that they were normally booked by the hour rather than per night. The basement had a gym/health centre which featured subdued lighting, garish internal decoration and large screens showing pornographic images. You'd have got more than you bargained for if you popped in there seeking treatment on your troublesome groin.

Personally, I'm not a big fan of opulent hotels so we soon came to love the absurd minimalism of the Mint with its plastic chairs, near plastic buffet food and nightly musical cabaret in the main bar. This consisted of two tiny Malay girls in tartan mini-skirts crooning along to middle of the road 'classics' like *Islands In The Stream* and *Eye Of The Tiger* accompanied by a backing band who looked like the Western Samoan rugby front row dressed as the Stylistics. They were often led off into impromptu jams by a lovely bloke called Cliff from one of the Welsh regional newspapers who never travelled anywhere without his saxophone and would jump up on stage for a solo every now and then, regardless of whether it fitted in with the song in question or not.

"Ladies and gentlemen, for one night only, please welcome John Coltrane and the Cheeky Girls."

If you put it on ITV on a Saturday night and called it *Crap Factor* it would have drawn a massive crossover audience of chavs, schoolchildren, post-modernists and the sort of idiots who think watching the *Eurovision Song Contest* for its cringe factor represents the last word in irony.

It was a welcome sanctuary from the daily slog of carting heavy equipment around between venues in the oppressive heat and humidity which pushed me to limits of human endurance I had never previously encountered. Even the relatively undemanding activity of standing at a bus stop would result in a profusion of sweat only normally seen when Roy 'Chubby' Brown competes in a triathlon.

This was also a hazard for many of the competitors who weren't used to the oppressive conditions and, of course being British, the weather was a key topic of conversation. I was interviewing England netball star Tracy Neville, who's the sister of footballers Gary and Phil, and, after she smiled politely through the fifteen millionth question that day about her famous siblings, I brought up the subject of the weather.

"So how will you be affected by the hot and humid conditions here in Kuala Lumpur?" I asked.

"We won't, it's an indoor sport."

It was up there with the very best of the many stupid questions I have asked sportspeople during interviews over the years.

Other examples include:

Me: "What particular problems do you think the Swedish strikers will pose tomorrow night?"

Graham Taylor: "None, we're playing Norway."

To Olympic archery competitor Alison Williamson:

Me: "So four years of training and preparation all comes down to that little red circle in the middle of the target."

AW: "It's yellow."

The most embarrassing one of all came during the European Athletics Championships in Helsinki in 1994 when Britain's Rob Denmark won a silver medal in the 5,000 metres. I wasn't commentating on the race and hadn't been paying much attention to be honest. When the race was over I rushed down to trackside to get an interview and immediately spotted a gaggle of athletics writers interrogating an exhausted looking figure in a GB vest. I waited for a convenient pause in the conversation and then thrust forward my microphone.

"Can you tell us how it feels to win a European silver medal?"

"I don't know, you'd better ask Rob Denmark, I was fifth."

It turned out I was talking to another athlete John Nuttall who, quite understandably, looked less than impressed as I gingerly slunk away. My embarrassment was compounded when I finally tracked down the real Rob Denmark and he looked absolutely nothing like John Nuttall so I couldn't even use that as an excuse. Needless to say I have never been allowed to forget that moment by my fellow athletics reporters. Such are the pitfalls of being a football man who occasionally gets parachuted into such a complicated and diverse sport as track and field.

It was in Kuala Lumpur that the true scale of English football's developing world domination first struck me with real force. I recall checking in at the Mint on the first day and getting in a lift to be greeted by a Malaysian girl aged about 14 or 15 wearing a Derby County shirt. I asked her why she was a Derby fan and she said it was considered cool to support an English team and that she liked the shirt. I remember thinking, 'plain white with a cartoon ram on it – you're easily pleased.'

Everywhere you went you saw Premier League shirts and all the bars that had *Sky TV* were packed to the rafters. We watched an Arsenal v Manchester United game in an Irish bar and the locals were going wild. However, this particular Irish bar did have one feature which you don't often see in the hostelries around Galway, Sligo or Clonakilty. Just about the only people not glued to the unfolding action from Highbury on the giant screen were a line of bored looking punters sat on a row of seats at the bar. Each was a blur of massive hair, high heels, garish patterned silk dresses, layers of bright make up and huge silicon enhanced breasts. They had size ten shoes and hands like shovels and looked like the work of a deranged scientist who'd discovered a way of cross-cloning the Harlem Globetrotters and the New York Dolls. These of course were the famed lady-boys of whom I'd been warned prior to the trip.

"You better be careful out there, mate. You can't tell which is which. You might get a nasty surprise."

Actually, most of the women we had encountered in Kuala Lumpur were very slim and petite, well dressed, polite and not in the least bit ostentatious. You would have to be so ignorant, pissed or desperate to actually mistake one of these botox monsters for a woman that, frankly, you'd deserve any surprise that came your way.

There was the odd exception where some confusion might arise. One of the guys was walking along a corridor in a nightclub enjoying the rear view of a curvy looking girl just in front of him who was heading the same way. He overtook her and walked on into the gents toilet. He'd just unzipped his fly when he looked up at the next urinal and saw the object of his desire saunter up, lift 'her' mini skirt, whip out the old man and produce a jet like a fire hose.

It was ironic that in this land of garishly dressed, artificially enhanced weirdos we would end the trip to Kuala Lumpur reporting the death of the woman Simon Turnbull had raised suspicions about in Seoul ten years earlier. On the very last night as we contemplated whether to have just one more beer or go to bed ahead of an early morning flight home, photographer Neil Loft shattered the tranquillity of the Mint hotel bar.

"You're not going to believe this guys. Florence Griffith-Joyner has died."

My reaction won't go down as one of the most sensitive epitaphs of all time: "Fuck me, that's all we need."

Suddenly I was in overdrive, seeking out reactions to the news, filing voice pieces and packages and doing two-ways in which I expressed the widely held suspicion that Flo-Jo (there's another of those annoying acronyms again) had used drugs to enhance her performances and may now have paid the ultimate price. Whether this was true or not may never be known as her autopsy proved only that steroid abuse had not directly caused the seizure which led to her premature death. The Seoul triple gold medallist was only 38 years old and left a seven-year-old girl without a mother. In 20 years no-one has even come close to beating her 100 and 200 metres world records.

While I was able to fairly rapidly bash out enough broadcast material to satisfy the news desk, I felt sympathy for broadsheet writers like Tom Knight and Duncan McKay who had to shake off their tiredness and write thousands of words in compiling their obits, profiles and comment pieces.

I didn't invite Carolyn to join me in Kuala Lumpur as I was desperate to get away from the humidity. I had lost so much weight I was in danger of disappearing altogether. I did, however, hear of one media guy who decided to prolong his stay and visited a tiny, secluded island off the coast of Malaysia for a week of peace and tranquillity. On his first day he went down to the beach to discover that he was completely alone on a deserted stretch. In the far distance he could see a small hut which he presumed to be a snack bar or café. Around lunchtime he made his way up to the building which turned out to be a little round wooden shack with a straw roof onto which hung a painted sign which said 'Massage'.

Peering in, he was greeted by an attractive lady, and adopting the 'it would be rude not to' maxim, accepted her invitation to lie down on the small table in front of her. She began to rub oil into his muscles, allowing the odd stray hand to waver dangerously close to his most sensitive areas. This of course produced the inevitable effect and when she rolled him over, she flashed a smile.

"You want wank?" she asked.

He nodded enthusiastically as she turned and wandered off behind one of those bead curtains and into a back room. He lay there imagining that she was getting changed into a French maid's outfit complete with silk gloves or, better still, fetching one of her friends to join in. A minute passed, then two minutes, then three. When she still hadn't returned after five minutes he began to feel rather like a piece of meat on an abattoir slab and had, understandably, completely lost his urges. Finally, after what seemed like an eternity, the bead curtain rattled and she reappeared.

"Ah, you've finished."

My finest hour in the battle to overcome accreditation restrictions came during the Manchester Commonwealth Games in 2002. Once again we were offered 'Main Press Centre only' status which meant you might as well have covered the event off the television at a Travelodge in Plymouth.

This restrictive policy was bad enough when imposed on us, but it also applied to *Manx Radio*, the only broadcaster based on the Isle of Man, where there isn't even a BBC presence. I'd met their sports editor Tim Glover as part of the Mint Hotel posse in Malaysia four years earlier and he was a lovely bloke who certainly didn't deserve to be left out in the cold.

The Isle of Man competed in its own right at the Commonwealth Games and therefore the event was their biggest sporting story by a mile. As it stood, competitors who Tim knew personally and spoke to every day could only give him interviews if they were conducted outside the accredited venues. At the shooting arena he had to endure the ludicrous charade of phoning the Manx participants and asking them to walk out of the venue, along the access roads through the perimeter fence and onto the edge of a nearby road in order for him to ask his questions as the juggernauts hurtled past. This wasn't just unfair on Tim, it was unfair on the competitors who simply could not understand why they were having to take an unnecessary break in their schedules simply to be allowed to speak to listeners, most of whom were, in all probability, their friends and neighbours.

By now I was a veteran at gaining access to unauthorised areas and boasted that if I wanted to I could gatecrash the MI5 Christmas party. Using contacts I'd developed over years of covering athletics I arranged not only for Tim, my IRN colleague Elliot Cook and myself to get updated accreditations, but also managed to install an ISDN line inside the City of Manchester Stadium and get hold of a batch of the 'authorised equipment' stickers for all our tape recorders and ISDN units which allowed us to get them into the venues. There are several people I'd like to thank for helping me achieve this, but unfortunately I can't as I don't want to dob them in.

The crowning glory of this brazen deception came when English sprinter and local boy Darren Campbell won a bronze medal in the 200 metres. After he had done all his trackside interviews with the rights holders, been dope tested and attended the medal ceremony he finally wandered into a near empty press conference room late at night. I was the only broadcaster there and the only other English journalist in attendance was my old mate Ian Chadband, now chief sports correspondent at the *London Evening Standard*.

Campbell was asked a fairly routine question about what the medal meant to him by an Australian reporter and then launched into one of the most frank, emotional and heart rending speeches I've ever heard from a sportsperson. He told the small but increasingly spellbound gathering how he'd contemplated suicide after suffering bouts of depression following a series of injury problems and the break up of his relationship with his long term girlfriend. The darkest moment came when he travelled home to Cardiff from Manchester on Christmas morning after delivering presents to his young child and contemplated ending his life by driving his expensive sports car at high speed headlong into a wall.

"At Christmas I didn't want to live, let alone run," he solemnly told us. "Here I was with an Olympic silver medal, a beautiful son and girlfriend, a nice car and nice house and feeling like suicide."

A friend of his from Manchester who'd survived several shooting attempts had finally inspired Campbell to get his life back on track, both literally and metaphorically.

This was absolutely extraordinary stuff and it all poured out spontaneously. I filed his entire moving monologue back to the office which they sent out to all the ILR stations and took clips from it which led the bulletins throughout the next day.

It was a fabulous exclusive and all the more satisfying since I'd recorded the whole thing on unauthorised equipment from a room I should have been prevented from accessing under the very noses of rights holders who'd completely missed what was one of the biggest stories of the Games. All they had was the exhausted and sweaty immediate post-race reaction:

"Yes . . . puff pant . . . I'm delighted . . . wheeze . . . it's great to get a medal . . . pant puff . . . on home soil."

Hardly front page stuff.

CHAPTER NINE

"More famous than Julian Golding."

In October 1992 Independent Radio News severed its long standing alliance with LBC and relocated from its relatively new Hammersmith base to join forces with ITN at the television news company's HQ at Grays Inn Road near King's Cross. It made my journey to work from east London a damn sight easier but, to be honest, things were never quite the same again. ITN had previously tried to win over IRN's clients by setting up a rival service, a ploy which spectacularly, and unsurprisingly, failed, given the absurd collection of chancers, dimwits and television rejects they had employed to run the newsroom. But, adopting the adage 'if you can't beat them join them', they persuaded the IRN board to allow them to run the service and many of the existing staff, myself included, were brought across. As a severance gesture we were all handed a cheque for £1 which represented a token settlement of any claims either party may have against the other. They should have checked in my locker first, since I walked away with two tape recorders, several expensive microphones, a couple of pairs of headphones and a library of reference books. All of which were now legally mine.

The problem was that the same ITN personnel who had proved so hopeless as editors, reporters and department heads in their first incarnation were all given the key roles in the new set-up, which meant IRN staff with years of experience were now being led by talentless, shallow, bureaucratic and sometimes plain spiteful people who were hopelessly ill-equipped for running a nationwide radio news agency. It was as if Sir Alex Ferguson had replaced his best strikers at Manchester United with a bunch of Sunday pub team reserves. The evolutionary chaos this heralded meant that each successive news editor became even more extraordinarily inept and vindictive than his or her predecessor. At one point the newsroom was run by a hormonal banshee who decided to save money by not sending a reporter to Paris the day that Princess Diana died, which remains, by some distance, the worst editorial decision I have ever encountered in 25 years as a journalist.

Had I known what was about to come in the summer that preceded the move, I might very well have decided to pack it in and go elsewhere. Inevitably though, the whole thing unfolded with me not only out of the loop, but also out of the country as I went on from Euro 92 to my second Olympic assignment in Barcelona.

I don't know whether the imminent move to ITN influenced the decision, but only one staff member was to be sent to Catalonia and so I was the sole IRN representative at the 1992 Games, although I benefited hugely from the fact that two *Capital Radio* reporters were also on the trip, namely Dave Clark and Julian Waters, who are both now familiar faces as presenters on *Sky Sports*.

Clarky was a relentlessly cheerful and outgoing giant of a man, six feet five inches tall who had played as a second row forward for Scottish Universities at rugby, while Julian was a more thoughtful, introspective figure who I knew well as he'd recently worked alongside me as a freelancer on the IRN sports desk.

This was the first major event we broadcast from using the ISDN system which is now employed by virtually all broadcasters via a very light and easy to use mixer/converter housed in a small plastic case which weighs no more than the average business person's briefcase. The whole thing was in its infancy when we arrived in Barcelona and not nearly as neat and compact. In fact, you needed to be a construction worker with a degree in mechanical engineering just to get it out of the collection of flight cases which were required to transport it across to northern Spain. Once out of its packaging, putting the pieces together to make it work was akin to assembling the Sizewell Reactor and it took a producer and engineer, who *Capital* had thoughtfully flown over, the best part of two days to finally get it up and running. But it was a fantastic resource and made all the colour stuff we sent back so much more vivid and alive than what we'd been used to with Comrex.

By now I considered myself a veteran major event reporter and had learnt quickly how to use the privilege of being at the top table at these tournaments to your advantage. Early on in Barcelona we met some people from MTV who, aside from being persuaded to part with some cool t-shirts, gave us the low-down on what was happening entertainment-wise in the city. They told us that the Australian band Crowded House were playing a low key gig at a small club that night and, although I'm not a huge fan of theirs, we decided to go along.

When we reached the club there was quite a long queue outside, but we walked to the front, flashed our accreditation passes, muttered something about MTV and were ushered in free of charge. Not only did we watch the band from the front row, we also managed to get backstage where we helped them polish off their generous drinks rider. They seemed very generous, genuine, people and I had a lengthy chat with the drummer Paul Hester who was by far the most animated member of the band and seemed to be the life and soul of the party. I scarcely gave him a second thought until I picked up a newspaper many years later and read that he had hanged himself in a park near his home at the age of 46 after years battling with depression.

Barcelona was a wonderful city, a magical fiesta of sound and colour and hosted a wonderful Olympic Games. The stadium at Montjuic was perched atop a hill which overlooked the city and was accessible via a series of outdoor escalators which cut their way rather incongruously through a wooded park but which were filled every day with passionate flag waving fans under an absolutely blazing sun. At the aquatics venue the high diving board lived up to its name, perched way up above the rooftops, giving the impression that the competitors were about to dive into the heart of the city itself.

The Games had opened in spectacular fashion with opera diva Montserrat Caballe belting out an astonishing rendition of the song *Barcelona*, made even more emotive by the fact that her live performance matched perfectly with footage of the late Freddie Mercury, who had died only eight months previously, being projected on the stadium's giant screen. And the sight of the Olympic torch being lit by a flaming arrow fired from an archer's bow was one of the most simple yet striking images I've witnessed at any opening ceremony.

It always helps if the Union Jack flies high during the Games and the sprint victories of Sally Gunnell and Linford Christie proved to be the highlights on the track. I remember later replaying my commentary of Christie's 100 metres win and being almost ashamed at how few times I'd mentioned the other runners in the field. And yet, who now remembers, or much less cares, that it was Frankie Fredericks of Namibia and American Dennis Mitchell who claimed the silver and bronze medals.

Christie being Christie though, there had to be some form of controversy to set against the triumph, although it wasn't quite as dramatic or serious as the drugs inquiry which followed his elevated silver medal in Seoul. The *Sun* newspaper had run a rather crass feature about how well packed the 100 metres champion's skin-tight lycra shorts had been during the competition in Barcelona and had created a new phenomenon known as 'Linford's Lunchbox' complete with speculation on how many bananas, cartons of ribena and cheese sandwiches it would take to recreate the now legendary bulge.

Christie had got hold of a copy of the paper and was incensed, strutting around the stadium waving the article around and complaining loudly that Britain had no respect for its Olympic heroes and berating any journalist who approached him, regardless of whether they were from the *Sun*, *Athletics Weekly* or *Woman's Own*. I did have genuine sympathy with his point of view but not necessarily with the way he was expressing it. I offered him the chance to go on record with his thoughts on the whole episode but he declined. We pointed out that talking to millions back home via radio would have rather more effect in getting his message across than ranting away at a few cynical hacks in the stadium, but he insisted that he would not go on the record to anyone.

Happily we had rather less trouble with the charming and ever helpful Gunnell who would no doubt have consented to an hour long interview with *Furniture Restorer Monthly* if they'd asked her nicely. Just as long as they didn't mention her drawers.

The bigger broadcasters such as the BBC generally have their own earmarked positions close to the trackside and can easily grab the competitors for a few words very soon after the race, just before they make their way back up the tunnel. For the rest of us it's rather more complicated, as we have to take our chances in what is known as the Mixed Zone. This area is usually located inside the tunnel itself and consists of a long row of waist-high barriers which separate the athletes on one side from the media on the other.

The idea is that you can flag down the person you want to speak to and, if they're willing to do an interview, they'll pause for a few moments by the side of the barrier to face the cameras, tape recorders and dictaphones. This all sounds straightforward and civilised enough, but in reality 'war zone' is a more fitting name for this journalistic pressgang. Picture, if you can, a scene in which hundreds of media personnel from hundreds of different countries are all trying to talk simultaneously in every imaginable language to dozens of athletes in a narrow corridor half the width of a residential street. Since the competitors enter this zone in a totally random order you are constantly buffeted by this mass of people every time the Finnish contingent spot a javelin thrower or a gaggle of Kenyan reporters set off in pursuit of a steeplechaser.

The searing heat in Barcelona made this an even more unpleasant experience since everyone was sweating profusely and hot weather generally shortens tempers. At times it was like trying to conduct an interview on a packed tube train which has broken down in a tunnel on the Piccadilly line during an August heatwave. To add to the confusion the whole place is a tangle of trailing wires, cables and other items of technical equipment and so there's the added hazard of trying not to fall arse over tit in the middle of congratulating someone for reaching the long jump final.

Inevitably this leads to flashpoints, arguments and, sometimes, violence. This is usually due to someone who has a prime space at the front refusing to move when an athlete that other people want to get to walks past or people trying to barge their way forward while you're in the middle of an interview.

I remember a particularly trenchant and diminutive Mexican cameraman refusing to step aside so that we could access a British runner. Eventually Dave Clark used his considerable strength to physically lift him, still holding his camera, off the ground and then dump him several feet away before calmly walking through the gap. I've seen punches traded, stand-up rows, threats of violence and heard swear words in a hundred different languages within this most congested and heated convergence of what is optimistically described as 'the Olympic family'.

It is to the eternal credit of most athletes that they are generally happy to stop and have a chat in the Mixed Zone. Big names like Michael Johnson, Denise Lewis, Kelly Holmes, Cathy Freeman, Donovan Bailey and Jonathan Edwards were always very obliging, and not just with broadcasters from their own countries. In most cases, there were TV monitors mounted on the walls within the zone which meant that you could watch the other events while waiting around for the competitors to wander through, although this could sometimes prove to be a distraction. I was interviewing Jonathan Edwards at the Sydney Games in 2000 when he glanced up mid sentence at a monitor showing the closing few moments of the 10,000 metres. Carried away by the unfolding drama he completely forgot what he was talking about and shifted automatically into commentary mode:

"This is incredible . . . Gebrselassie's going to do it . . . go on . . . he's done it . . . unbelievable . . . sorry, what were you saying?"

Of course Edwards is himself now a TV commentator of note, but I believe I was the first person to ever hear him in his current guise.

His fellow triple jumper Ashia Hansen took it a hop, step and a jump further during a chat at the 2002 Commonwealth Games in Manchester. In the midst of a fairly routine explanation of how she felt she'd done in her event, she suddenly became intensely animated as she spotted the English team roaring to victory in the final of the 4 x 100 metres relay on the screen.

"I thought I jumped pretty well today, the conditions weren't great but ... ohhhh...yes, yes ... come on ...oooooooohhh... yes yes yes ... go on go on ... come on... do it do it... aaaaaahhhhhh... yesssssssssssssss!!!!"

It sounded more like the soundtrack to a porn film than an interview with an athlete.

Decathlete Dean Macey, whose promising career was sadly hampered by a series of debilitating injuries, was always good value in the Mixed Zone, although his Canvey Island blokey bonhomie sometimes became a little too prosaic. His breakthrough came at the World Championships in the baking hot August sun of Seville in 1999 when he won a silver medal as a virtually unknown 21-year-old. I remember asking him how he felt, physically, after the opening day's five disciplines had been completed and he replied: "Absolutely fucked, mate."

Once I'd reminded him that his words were intended for broadcast on national radio Dean regained his composure a little and then summed up his schedule in classic style:

"100 metres: bang, whizz, got home quick, nice one.

Long Jump: hit the board well, wheee, bosh, happy enough.

Shot Putt: big heave, wee-ow splat. Not too bad.

High Jump: good spring, got up, slight wobble, stayed on, wa-hey.

400 metres: knackered, dug in, big finish, sorted, well happy."

Occasionally though, you would be greeted by a sulky individual who would walk straight through the Mixed Zone without a word for anyone. Sad to say, several British athletes were guilty of this and generally it was the serial under-achievers who would get the hump after another disappointing display. One such was Julian Golding, a decent sprinter who had won gold medals in the Commonwealth Games and European Championships but had never been a major force in the truly global events.

After failing to give his best at one particular tournament, he persistently rebuffed various attempts by myself and a pack of newspaper reporters to elicit a few words after the race. I followed him right up to the end of the tunnel with the tape recorder running but he simply turned his back and walked on. Frustrated by what I perceived as a wholly unjustified omerta, I turned to face the rest of the pack and shouted: "Bloody hell, he should be begging to talk to us. Who does he think he is? I'm more bloody famous than Julian Golding."

This became another catchphrase and people like Ian Chadband and the *Glasgow Herald's* Doug Gillon would introduce me to people by saying: "This is John Anderson . . . he's apparently more famous than Julian Golding."

Compare this with the dignity and bravery of 400m runner Derek Redmond whose Olympic dreams were shattered in Barcelona after he pulled up with a torn hamstring in the semi-finals but insisted on limping the rest of the way round the track being supported by his father so that he could say he completed the race. Rather than 'throwing a Julian' as it later came to be known, he patiently sat through almost an hour of interviews, withstanding considerable pain, both mental and physical, as he delivered a poignant speech about the real meaning of Olympian ideals which saw at least one seasoned press man reduced to tears.

Kelly Holmes produced a similarly emotive reaction when she pulled up injured halfway round her opening heat at the World Athletics Championships in Athens in 1997, where she was hot favourite to complete the 800m and 1,500m double. It was yet another painful setback for an athlete whose career, at that time, seemed destined to be measured in torn muscles rather than gold medals. No one who watched her pull up in agony that morning would have raised the slightest complaint if she had decided to avoid the post-race interviews and head straight off to the treatment room. But, to her eternal credit, she felt she had a duty to share her emotions with the world. So, wincing with pain, she leant against a metal handrail halfway up the stairs which led to the dressing rooms and spoke at length into a forest of outstretched microphones about her latest injury calamity with frankness, a little bitterness, but above all, great bravery.

"I feel like someone's put a curse on me, I don't know who, but I just wish they would take it away," was the classic line which would be replayed for much of that day.

After we'd thanked her for her time, patience and fortitude, we watched as she went through the glass doors which led to the medical centre. As she got halfway down the corridor, all the pain, desperate disappointment and raw emotion became too much, and she sat down on a small plastic chair and began to sob profusely, remaining inconsolable for several minutes until a member of the GB coaching staff put an arm round her and led her away.

That, Julian Golding, is how a true champion reacts in the face of bitter disappointment.

Of course with a poetic sense of time, place and justice, the curse was well and truly lifted seven years later in the very same city as Kelly sped to glory in the middle distance double at the 2004 Olympics. I am not ashamed to admit that my commentary as she crossed the line in Athens to clinch victory in the 1,500 bordered on the apoplectic and made even my most hysterical moments sound like a discussion about Queen Anne tables on the *Antiques Roadshow*. The voice got more and more emotive and agitated, like a cross between David Coleman and Bruce Dickinson of Iron Maiden, until it finally exploded as Kelly crossed the line in first place:

"Kelly Holmes becomes a British Olympic legend. She's the first Brit to win the middle distance double since Albert Hill in Antwerp way back in 1920. Steve Ovett couldn't do it! Seb Coe couldn't do it! Steve Cram couldn't do it! But Kelly can! And that's why Kelly's the queen of the track in Athens."

The commentary was praised by *Daily Mail* columnist Charlie Sale who said it was the best description of the race he had heard and captured the moment perfectly. A few weeks later it was broadcast over the top of the video footage at the British Athletics Writers' Awards dinner and brought the house down. Even Kelly herself was in stitches as the polite tinkle of cutlery was interrupted by this near psychotic eulogy. Sadly, I was not able to deliver such a stirring accompaniment to Chris Boardman's gold medal triumph in the 4,000 metres individual pursuit cycling in Barcelona. The hitherto unknown 24-year-old from the Wirral burst into the public consciousness with his revolutionary new bicycle which was built by Lotus and cost £4,000 but weighed just 20 pounds. However, the company's marketing department must have been on holiday when the company issued the following snappy description of this new space age machine:

'An advanced composite monocoque with minimum drag aerodynamic cross sections, formed with unidirectional and stitched high-strength carbon fibre in an epoxy resin matrix.'

Clearly this was never destined to sit comfortably on the back page of the *Daily Star* or, indeed, within the confines of a 25-second radio report, and so it became known as Chris Boardman's Superbike.

Although cycling is now an Olympic sport at which Britain regularly excels, in 1992 it barely warranted a mention. Prior to Boardman's success, the last time the country had celebrated a gold medal victory on two wheels was when a couple of blokes on a tandem won a two kilometre race more than 70 years before. This of course was in the early developmental stages of the modern Olympics and represented a far more gentle and innocent Olympic Age.

It was a time when the United States of America were rugby champions, the Tug Of War was a centrepiece of the track and field schedule and Leon de Lunden of Belgium won a gold medal for blasting 21 birds out of the sky in the live pigeon shooting competition. This totally unique instance of living creatures being slaughtered in pursuit of Olympic glory was to prove a mercifully short-lived event (certainly for the 300 or so birds who twittered their last) as the skies above the venue in the host city Paris rained blood, feathers and mangled poultry down onto competitors and spectators alike. Imagine the scene if the London Games organisers had decided to revive the discipline in Trafalgar Square in 2012.

So, when the British press contingent clambered aboard a bus to take us to the velodrome for the climax of Boardman's golden quest, a straw poll revealed that nobody among the nation's finest scribblers, broadcasters and snappers had the faintest idea what the 4,000 metres individual pursuit actually entailed. What we did know was that, whatever happened, this was going to be one of the stories of the Games especially since, with a dash of dramatic irony, Boardman's opponent in the gold medal race was from traditional rivals Germany. His name, incidentally, was Jens Lehmann, although not of course the one who later played in goal for Arsenal.

The media bus think-tank finally managed to ascertain that the event consisted of two riders stationed 180 degrees apart on the track pedalling round the circuit simultaneously, the winner being the one who made up the most ground on his opponent at the end of the 4,000 metres, hence the word 'pursuit'.

Given that the baffling world of track cycling includes an event in which riders chase a man on a sort of motorised scooter once favoured by the more adventurous breed of 1960s shopping pensioners and another in which a group of cyclists ride up and down a steep bank in unfathomable patterns and positional changes which can only be compared to Morris Dancing on wheels; this pursuit event seemed relatively straightforward.

Dave Clark and I were not providing actual live coverage of the race but wanted to capture the closing stages on tape so that it could be replayed in forthcoming news bulletins. We stationed ourselves close to the finish line and prepared to launch into the commentary just as the riders were entering the final circuit. There we were, with our pause buttons upright on our recorders waiting to deliver the kind of high octane, over the top hyperbolic and jingoistic rants which we were pioneering as the staple diet of independent radio sports coverage at the time.

It was clear, even to us cycling neophytes, that Boardman was going to win as he was almost on Lehman's shoulder as the last lap loomed and that, barring a stray cat or a Spanish lollipop lady wandering across the track in front of him, the gold medal was as good as his.

The bell rang for the final lap and we took a deep breath.

"It's Chris Boardman for Great Britain . . . legs pumping furiously in pursuit of golden glory . . ."

We'd barely got through our first sentence when Boardman whizzed past Lehmann, raised his arms in the air and freewheeled for a hundred metres or so before dismounting and punching the air in triumph. Dave and I looked at each other in utter bewilderment and our tape recorders, still running, captured the following exchange:

"What's happened Clarky, why's he stopped?"

"Dunno mate, I think he's won, though."

"How can he have done? There's still half a lap to go."

"Search me, perhaps Lehmann's been disqualified."

"Bloody stupid event."

What eventually dawned on us was that once a rider overtakes his opponent he has won the race, since the pursuit has been successfully completed. In our defence, it has to be said that this outcome is extremely rare and had never before occurred in an Olympic final.

Boardman's pride and excitement at winning gold gave us some wonderful interview material, which made up for the fact that our planned commentary of the final lap had been rendered completely unusable. It turned out that Lehmann the cyclist was of the same grumpy demeanour as his goalkeeping namesake and insisted he'd been beaten by Boardman's futuristic bike rather than the rider himself. We gleefully reported his fit of sour grapes in the finest tabloid radio traditions: "On yer bike, Jens."

It's not just the competitors themselves who are prone to the odd hissy fit when things don't go their way. I've always found Australians to be wonderful company, tremendous drinking partners and great sports enthusiasts and have always had a wonderful time in their country but there are times when I can't believe they have the gall to refer to us Brits as 'whingeing Poms'.

They excel at many sports, notably cricket, swimming and rugby as well as that silly game with too many posts, too many players, too many refs and too many tight pairs of shorts.

Although I wouldn't call myself a swimming fan as such, one of the most amazing occasions I have ever witnessed at a sports venue was the final of the 4 x 100 metres freestyle relay at the Sydney Olympics in 2000. The discipline was very much the preserve of the Americans who had never lost an Olympic final, but the Aussies, with wonder boy Ian Thorpe in his pomp, believed they could end that dominance. It was a claim which the Americans' brash anchor man Gary Hall Jr (who was part fish, part town crier) dismissed out of hand, suggesting that his team would smash the Australians "like guitars" in the final. A peculiar analogy which gave the impression that they were about to stick a pair of goggles and a rubber all-in-one on The Who's Pete Townshend and unleash him as their lead-off man.

As Hall and Thorpe dived into the pool for the final leg, the Americans held a strong lead, but with every single Australian voice in the Aquatics Centre screaming with a ferocity which could probably be heard 15 miles away at the sailing regatta, the Thorpedo launched his counter attack. With 20 metres to go he left Hall trailing in his wake to claim an astonishing victory. Even better was the celebration, as the Australians lined up and played air guitars as a riposte to Hall's boast.

While the Aussies love nothing better than hearing the strains of 'Advance Australia Fair' echoing around a stadium, the flipside is that, in my experience, they don't take quite as kindly to losing against the odds. Another of my top ten 'hair on the back of the neck' moments came at Newlands in Cape Town in 1995 when Rob Andrew landed a mighty drop goal to clinch a dramatic late quarter-final win for England at the expense of Australia at the Rugby World Cup.

I was among a group of English media who boarded a bus outside the press centre after the game, to be greeted by the morose faces of a much larger group of ageing Aussie hacks who spent the whole journey moaning and griping about how English rugby was an affront to the game and that the victory had been achieved in a negative manner which ran against the spirit of the code. On and on it went until we could take no more. Well versed on the football terraces of England we launched into a loud vocal counter attack:

"Sing when you're winning . . . you only sing when you're winning."

"You're shit and you know you are. You're shit and you know you are."

"Stand up if you're in the cup, stand up if you're in the cup."

By this time we were standing on our chairs, clapping our hands in the air and laughing directly in the puffy, red faces of the now apoplectic antipodeans.

The euphoria didn't last long of course. England faced New Zealand at the same stadium in the semi-finals where Jonah Lomu smashed the English rear-guard like . . . well, like guitars.

The 1995 Rugby World Cup in South Africa was a wonderful tournament set in fascinating and varied venues from the majesty and splendour of Cape Town, to the warm coastal climes of Durban to the chaotic, cosmopolitan clutter of Johannesburg. I was lucky that I had a wonderful group of travelling companions with whom we shared some brilliant times including Dave Clark and his new *Capital* cohort Jim Proudfoot, and the LBC duo of Andrew Parkinson and the legendary rugby broadcaster Andrew Titheridge, known to all and sundry as Tits. Our tour guide on the Johannesburg stretch of this trip was David O'Sullivan, a presenter on the popular talk radio station 702 *Eyewitness News*, whose local knowledge and boundless enthusiasm when it came to eating and drinking ensured that we would never be stuck for a decent night out.

The group matches were staged in Durban where the hotel had magnificent views out across the Indian Ocean, the weather was glorious, the beach was yards away and there were some fantastic bars along the strip, most notably Joe Cool's which became a favourite not just for us but for certain members of the England team who would sneak out occasionally for a crafty pint. If this had been the national football team, the sight of a group of players in a crowded bar during a tournament would have probably made unnecessarily sensational front page headlines. But rugby seems to have a much more integrated spirit between competitors, the media and the fans and so we never once thought of filing an 'England stars in drunken shame' type story.

After winning their group comfortably, England relocated to the less picturesque high altitude environment of Johannesburg. We occupied a string of rooms on the top floor of the Parktonian Hotel, a cylindrical high-rise in the heart of Johannesburg's Braamfontein district. This was an all-suite hotel and the rooms were huge but it quickly became known as The Kraptonian because of the completely haphazard standards of service on offer. You could order a beer in the bar and, 15 minutes later be presented with a plate of spaghetti bolognese, and if you needed room service it was better to order from the breakfast menu at midnight as it would generally arrive in your room at about 7am.

Just to add to the 5-star feel, we heard that someone had been shot dead in the foyer a couple of days before we arrived. A reminder if any were needed that Johannesburg is not the safest place on the planet.

And it was in this city that I came the closest I ever have to fearing that my days were about to end quickly and unexpectedly in a foreign location. Jim Proudfoot and I decided to try and blag our way into a Mike and the Mechanics concert at a large hall on the outskirts of Johannesburg, assuming that our World Cup accreditation passes would get us in. Christ only knows what possessed us to go along in the first place, since the Genesis guitarist's side-project peddled the kind of sentimental, middle-of-the-road drivel which would normally have me reaching for a revolver. Luckily my credibility remained intact as we were bluntly refused admission to the venue by a bouncer the size of the entire All Blacks front row.

We knew that Parky, Tits and the others had gone to a club even further out of town, so we got in a cab and went over there instead. It was a journey of around half an hour and the place itself seemed to be completely in the middle of nowhere. After a good few beers with my press colleagues and some very friendly locals, we decided to head back at about 1am. Wisely, given the location of the venue, the others had pre-booked a taxi which duly arrived to whisk them away but there was no room for Jim and me. We joined a very long queue of people who were waiting for further cabs to arrive although they were turning up at a frustratingly slow rate of around one every 15 minutes.

Eventually a group of youngish guys wearing baseball caps came up and offered us a lift back to Johannesburg. We were very grateful and jumped into the back of one of two very flash cars which were parked nearby. Once onto the freeway we became concerned that the speedometers were registering speeds well in excess of 100 miles per hour and that the two drivers appeared to be engaged in some sort of impromptu road race. As the cars changed lanes continually and overtook each other at will like something out of a Hollywood high speed chase, we huddled terrified in the back seat, our protestations about the over use of the accelerator completely drowned out by the roar of high performance engines. Worse was to follow.

At one point, with the cars occupying the two outside lanes, they drew alongside each other and the two guys in the passenger seats wound down their windows and appeared to be gesticulating at each other. Within seconds we heard the first of a very loud series of sharp cracking sounds which pierced even the noise of the revving motors. We quickly realised that they were firing guns out of the windows into the air, both howling with laughter.

Jim and I, panic stricken by now, said nothing for fear that any ill-advised comment might be met with a loaded barrel. Eventually they stopped shooting and the car pulled up outside a drab and dirty concrete building on a dark street corner.

"Where are we?" I finally plucked up the courage to ask.

"This is Hillbrow," one of them replied. "Would you like to come in for a drink?"

Prior to leaving for South Africa I had, as was my custom, been reading up about the country in various travel guides and remembered mention of this suburb in a chapter about Johannesburg. This was a high poverty, high crime district which, though pleasant enough during the day with its street markets and cosmopolitan residents, was very much to be avoided at night time. With this in mind I felt obliged to politely decline his offer:

"Er, no thanks. It's very kind of you but it's getting on a bit and we have a busy day tomorrow. Thanks all the same."

"I said 'do you want to come in for a drink?'," he repeated loudly in a manner which suggested that his original question had been of the rhetorical variety.

"Y-y-yes okay," we meekly agreed.

We were ushered through a huge reinforced door with one of those sliding metal criss-cross devices behind it. Once inside, a security guard type who made Jonah Lomu look like John Inman, slid the doors to, fastened a couple of enormous bolts and finally locked them from the inside. The scene which greeted us was a squalid space, rather like a decaying gym changing room in which various dodgy looking blokes were hanging around chatting away conspiratorially while sipping beer from bottles. One of them showed us around a network of little rooms off the main area in which a series of wretched looking, drugged up women were sitting around looking utterly bored. We assumed they were not gathered here for a Tupperware party.

By now the panic had been replaced by sheer naked terror. Here we were at two o'clock in the morning, locked inside a grim-looking brothel in the worst district of the most dangerous city on earth, surrounded by a group of heroin-ravaged whores and their gun-toting associates.

Jim leaned towards me, his face ashen, and whispered, "Get me out of here."

Eventually somebody handed us a beer and we clenched our buttocks while keeping up the pretence of chatting away amiably with the guys who'd driven us back from the nightclub. Once I'd emptied my bottle I looked at my watch and eventually plucked up enough courage to suggest that it might be time we were off.

One of them then wandered away and we could see him in the distance having a chat in what looked like hushed tones with the gargantuan bouncer and we stood there dreading what their discussion entailed. A short while later he returned:

"OK guys, nice to meet you. There's a cab booked for you and it'll be here in five minutes. Enjoy the rest of your trip."

Incredibly, true to his word, the door soon slid open and a taxi driver poked his head round. We thanked them for their kind hospitality, leapt into the cab and headed towards the comfort and security of The Kraptonian.

To this day I have no idea why they decided to scare the living daylights out of us with a car chase from hell followed by a visit to one of Johannesburg's sleaziest inner-city knocking shops. The only moral I can offer from this tale is that even gun wielding, petrol-crazed ghetto-dwelling, brothel keepers must have a compassionate side.

On the day before South Africa met New Zealand in the final, David O'Sullivan took us to a little bar known as a shebeen in the heart of Soweto, where we drank to the prospect of a home victory with the locals. This was astonishing in itself, given that rugby had long been the preferred sport of the apartheid regime. Yet, here we were surrounded by a group of black South Africans of all ages, who 24 hours later would be glued to the TV set in their homely little pub cheering on their new heroes in what traditionally was the white man's game.

On the morning of the final, we were being driven to the ground by a lovely guy called Sarel who Jim had befriended earlier in the trip and who had been happy to act as our driver. At one point he found himself behind a pick-up truck in the back of which a guy was proudly waving the old South African flag which still carried the hideous connotations of apartheid. To our amusement he lost grip of the flagpole and it dropped into the road in front of us. Sarel put his foot down and accelerated over it in a symbolic gesture of defiance against those who saw the emergence of a new Rainbow Nation as a challenge to their ghastly, Neanderthal prejudices.

From the Soweto shebeens to the vineyards of the Cape, South Africa celebrated long and hard as their side won the World Cup for the first time and the Webb Ellis trophy was handed over to skipper Francois Pienaar by President Nelson Mandela, both men wearing the Springbok number six shirt. It was a moment that Pienaar summed up brilliantly during a post-match interview in the middle of the pitch. He was asked what it was like to have 45,000 South Africans behind him, roaring his side to victory.

"We had 45 million South Africans behind us today."

The Welsh comedian and singer Max Boyce made a rather irritating career out of it, but there's no denying the special feeling you get from being able to say 'I was there' at a moment of great historical or sporting significance.

On the day Princess Diana died in 1997, my wife and I were preparing to host a barbecue at our garden flat in north London and feared the trauma of the whole affair might dissuade people from turning up. As it happened, everyone duly arrived and wandered around stuffing their faces, quaffing ale and saying: "It's what she would have wanted."

We still try and host a similar event at the end of August each year and it remains lovingly known as: 'The Princess Diana Memorial Barbecue.'

This was just at the time when radio station owners in their infinite lack of wisdom had decided that speech content was an unnecessarily costly burden on their resources and would best serve their listeners not by offering an entertaining and informative mix of local news and sports programming but by battering them into submission with the constant, monotonous rotation of the new Spice Girls single with such alarming regularity that the temptation to pour superglue into your earholes became overwhelming.

Preferring to give in cravenly to its clients rather than set its own agenda, IRN had cut back dramatically on the number of news reporters they employed and limited their role to little more than that of desk-bound pen pushers. However, the Diana story was so huge that even programme controllers who considered *Spice Up Your Life* to be the absolute zenith of 20th century culture, were forced to concede that they had to give over their regular schedule to carry live coverage of the funeral.

IRN took on the job of producing extended coverage of the event but few of the news reporters had any real experience of live broadcasting or the ability to commentate on unfolding events. Fortunately, in political editor Peter Murphy they had a hugely capable anchorman but it was we sports reporters who were charged with the task of providing live commentary from the proceedings. I was stationed on the roof of a public toilet on the fringes of St James' Park overlooking the exact spot where the young Princes William and Harry along with their father, grandfather and Diana's brother emerged to walk behind the cortege on its slow journey towards Westminster Abbey. It was a very strange experience for me, as I whispered solemnly in hushed tones, trying to adopt a reverential style of commentating which was a million miles from the screaming pandemonium of England penalty defeats or Olympic 100 metres finals. It was hard at times not to refer to the route as the course or produce the kind of lapse the legendary cricket commentator Brian Johnson fell into when describing the wedding of the Queen and Prince Philip: "The happy couple preparing to climb the steps up to the pavilion . . . er . . . er . . . palace."

Now I am no royalist, indeed I counted myself among the many people who felt that the whole situation had developed into a kind of mawkish pantomime in which the entire nation had taken leave of its senses and dissolved into a rather absurd carnival of protracted blubbing. But, as a human being, it was hard not to be moved by the sight of two young lads who, in the midst of their blackest days, had to try and hold it together in front of hundreds of thousands of gawping onlookers and a worldwide television audience of 2.5 billion.

Once I had whispered my last, I jumped down onto the pavement to join the throng in listening to the funeral service being broadcast from the Abbey via giant speakers along the route. As a fan of the post punk miserablism of bands like The Fall, Joy Division and The Smiths, I can honestly say that, even though he's a fellow Watford supporter, I am not a huge lover of Sir Elton John's music, particularly the soppy, slow numbers he'd begun to make his speciality in recent years. I must say though, that his specially rewritten version of *Candle In The Wind*, though virtually unlistenable today, brought a shiver to the spine as it drifted out of the speakers and hung in the air above a hushed audience. I did, however, take exception to Viscount Althorp's suggestion during his speech that his sister had been hounded to her death by the unwanted intrusions of the press.

Five years later when the Queen Mother died, I resumed my alter ego as royal funeral correspondent as I peered out from the windows of the Mansion House at the passing cortege, by now much more at home with the process of describing a slow moving gun carriage being escorted sedately through the streets of London accompanied by members of the Queen's Guard. As the procession wound its way past I couldn't help but think, I bet Nicholas Witchell or Jennie Bond couldn't do West Brom against Hull.

CHAPTER TEN

"Such a typically American name."

Having sampled the contrasting but equally alluring charms of Seoul and Barcelona, I must confess the prospect of the Games of the XXVI Olympiad being staged in Atlanta, Georgia, the Bible-Belt home of Coca-Cola and CNN, didn't fill me with quite as much enthusiasm. And yet, when I look back, those 16 days in the American Deep South provided perhaps more memorable incidents and sheer absurdities than any other event I have ever covered.

Nobody, with the possible exception of the city's half a million inhabitants, wanted Atlanta to have the Games in the first place. This was, after all, 1996 and surely the rightful place to stage the Olympics in the centenary year of its modern incarnation was its original and spiritual home in Athens. Indeed there were dark rumours circulating sections of the press that romance and tradition had been thrown aside like a misplaced javelin by the International Olympic Committee in favour of the more prosaic lures of business and high finance. One newspaper in the Greek capital went as far as to suggest that, 'the Olympic flame will not be lit with oil, but with Coca-Cola.'

Another ominous sign was the choice of the mascot. Generally these marketing devices at least point to some kind of connection with the host city or country. Montreal had a beaver, Moscow had a bear, Los Angeles an eagle and so on. The geniuses that worked for the Atlanta marketing department came up with 'Izzy', a computer generated fantasy figure which looked like one of those dreadful cuddly toys you win by knocking over three tin cans with a bean bag at a small town fun-fair. It said nothing about America, nothing about Atlanta and nothing about the Olympic Games. I can only imagine that his name derived from this conversation:

"Izzy any good?"

"Izzy fuck!"

None of which seemed to bother the locals who insisted that the Games had finally found their home in God's country and that the rest of the world could kiss their asses and go to hell. One English journalist was chatting to a taxi driver in the city and ventured to suggest that the Games should have gone to Athens rather than Atlanta. The cabbie was absolutely incensed: "No way, no way man," he spluttered. "If there's one place in this state the goddam Games should never be held, it's Athens."

Unburdened by even the most cursory knowledge of geography, he was refer-ring to the small university town of Athens, Georgia, which is 60 miles to the east of Atlanta and famous primarily for being the home of rock band REM. It has never, as far as I am aware, ever been touted as a prospective Olympic venue. Another classic example of the locals' blissful ignorance of the wider parameters of this global extravaganza was the euphoric outbreak of cheering, hooting, whistling and whooping which greeted the team from Georgia at the opening ceremony. The competitors from the recently independent former Soviet nation looked somewhat bemused at the reception they got as the home crowd gave a standing ovation to what, they thought, was their local team. It reminded me of a news item I saw in the run-up to the 1994 World Cup, when an interviewer was asking New Yorkers who they thought would win the tournament. One truck driver paused thoughtfully for a second, scratched his chin and said:

"Wisconsin."

My travelling companions on my third Olympic excursion were Barcelona buddy Dave Clark and his *Capital* partner in crime Steve Wilson (now a top BBC football commentator), and my IRN sports desk colleague Guy Swindells, a hugely likeable, knowledgeable and affable fellow with whom I got on famously well. At the time, like a lot of British people, I think we might have naïvely viewed the United States as some sort of idyllic land of good organisation, hard work and efficiency where everything runs smoothly all the time. That's how the Americans would like us to feel, but of course, as anyone who's crossed the Atlantic knows, the reality is rather different.

The early signs were not good. When we arrived at Atlanta airport, we were greeted with the sort of queue you'd only normally expect to see if a topless

Cheryl Cole was handing out wads of £50 notes in the middle of Oxford Street. As we joined the tail end of it we realised that this was the line for receiving accreditation, a process which in Seoul and Barcelona had taken only a matter of minutes. Two hours later we were still in the queue as a thinly staffed and ill-prepared group of Atlanta volunteers struggled to cope with the influx. Guy turned round to me at one point and said:

"I bet the competitors don't have to put up with this."

Whereupon I pointed to two tall figures in tracksuits even further back than us. Both reigning 100 metres champion Linford Christie and French sprint sensation Marie-Jose Perec were looking at their watches, shaking their heads and tut-tutting like everyone else.

When we finally got through the accreditation process around three and a half hours after landing, we checked in at our hotel, the Ramada Clarion in downtown Atlanta. The talk was that you didn't want to be billeted in this part of town as it was crawling with low-lifes, druggies, prostitutes and criminals. We laughed off the obvious gags about how we'd therefore fit in pretty well and actually found the area to be slightly shabby but reassuringly quiet, certainly no worse than Hackney, where I was living at the time. We later discovered that Atlanta civic officials, who were worried that the city could be presented in a bad light, had actually paid many of the junkies, tramps and undesirables to take a one-way ticket out of town.

The Ramada was shaped like a giant multi-storey Polo mint with a swimming pool at the base of the hole. The *Capital* boys had to present a daily programme live from the hotel, which was a mix of chat about the Olympics and the latest football news ahead of the new Premiership season. Given the heat, they broadcast from a balcony overlooking the pool and would startle sun-bathing American guests by speculating loudly on whether managerless Arsenal could mount a realistic title challenge or if rookie Ruud Gullit could fill the gap at Chelsea left by Glenn Hoddle's appointment as England boss.

Given the scare stories about the area, I decided, in the absence of a room safe, to leave my valuables in the main safe in the hotel's administration office. A very nice, helpful lady arranged to keep my belongings secure and I thanked her for her time and trouble. As I turned to leave she said: "You know I just can't place your accent. Which part of the United States are you from?"

"I'm not. I'm from London, England," I spluttered, a little taken aback.

"Well that's incredible," she replied.

"Why?"

She pointed to my accreditation badge.

"Because you're called John Anderson, it's such a typically American name."

I was at once equally stunned and annoyed at the absurd conclusion she had jumped to and my reaction seethed with righteous indignation.

"A typically American name?" I screamed back at her, barely concealing my anger. "A typically American name? Listen lady, I'll have you know there were people called John Anderson running around the Highlands of Scotland several hundred years before America was even discovered. I'll give you a typically American name: Sitting Bull."

"Thank you sir, have a nice day," she curtly responded as she quickly ushered me almost physically out of the door. It's interesting to note how even the most innocuous and fleeting reference to the genocide of its indigenous population by early American settlers brings about a state of apoplexy among their ancestors.

In the weeks that followed, Steve Wilson and myself in particular would take great pleasure in annoying the Americans by refusing to kowtow to their irritatingly bland style of 'have a nice day' type politeness. On one occasion we got into the hotel lift at the end of a particularly hard day to be greeted by a stranger saying:

"How are you guys doin' today?"

"Thank you for asking. As it happens we're tired, frustrated and utterly pissed off."

On another occasion we were asked:

"So what do you make of the USA so far?"

"Well we knew it was shit, but we didn't realise it was Third World." This resulted in our fellow guest embarking on several levels of floor-staring before rushing out of the lift quicker than Michael Johnson leaving his starting blocks.

The Atlantan Yanks made up for what they lacked in knowledge of the event with a patriotic fervour which bordered on the psychotic. Thousands of locals filled the stadia at every event and cheered enthusiastically, regardless of whether they had the faintest idea about what they were watching. Frankly, you could have put an American vest on a wheelie bin, entered it in the 400 metres, and the partizan crowd would have cheered ecstatically as it trundled around the track. But, although the cynical amongst us may view this kind of thing with a queasy discomfort, many of the competitors thrived on the high octane atmosphere the Americans generated within the stadium. Jonathan Edwards told me in an interview that he had never in his life lined up for the qualifying round of the triple jump with a 70,000-strong crowd baying its approval. Normally there would be more track officials in the stadium than spectators for these opening events, but Edwards and his fellow competitors found the atmosphere truly inspirational.

On the subject of track officials, I have watched many athletics events over the years and these stewards and marshals who wander around athletics arenas in matching blazers and white slacks carrying little flags have always held a kind of strange fascination for me, one breed in particular standing out. In events like the long jump and triple jump, it's often impossible for the crowd to know whether the competitor has overstepped the take-off board and thus registered a no-jump. It is therefore useful to have someone sitting in line with the board who can scrutinise the jump at close quarters and then raise either a white flag for a legal attempt or a red one for a foul. This also goes for the throwing events where similar issues need to be resolved. But can anyone explain to me why it is necessary to have an official performing a similar function during the high jump? The athlete runs up, leaps into the air and either clears the bar and celebrates wildly on landing, or knocks it over and beats his fists into the mat in frustration. There are no grey areas and the whole thing is completely visible to everyone in the stadium. In some instances a competitor can get his run-up completely wrong and crash through the bar like a ram-raider through a shop front, accompanied by the sharp clang of the aluminium barrier hitting the ground. And yet, in the blur of flailing limbs and flashing metal, a little man in a cap raises a red flag in the air just to clarify that it was a non-clearance. For those about to adjudicate in the high jump, we salute you.

The time between our arrival in Atlanta and the Games actually getting underway was spent making sure everything was in place, producing stories and features and gathering interviews with key figures, snippets of which can be liberally sprinkled around throughout the coming days.

Our first mission in Atlanta, as it is in every major event, was to check that all the lines of communication are in place. Steve Wilson and I went along to the Olympic Stadium which, aside from workmen making final adjustments, dancers rehearsing their opening ceremony routines and people testing the Tannoy, was huge and empty.

Tradition seems to dictate that once you've plugged in your equipment and tried to call London you're to be greeted with the eerie silence of technical problems, and so it was here. We found some telecommunications people who seemed spectacularly disinterested in helping us but grudgingly agreed to and so we resigned ourselves to a long wait. To kill the time we wandered around the stadium, accessing VIP areas, dressing rooms, sponsors' lounges, athletes' warm-up areas and even the podium from which president Bill Clinton would officially declare the Games open. The organising committee had been at great pains in the run-up to the event to boast about how security was their number one priority and that these Games would be the tightest ever in ensuring there'd be no threat from terrorists. And yet here we were, swanning about inside the stadium a couple of days before the grand opening, our bags unchecked, our movements undetected, our motives unchallenged.

When the audio links with London were finally established, the first story we filed was about how we'd uncovered appalling security lapses within the principal Olympic venue, as the hosts singularly failed in their promise to throw an impenetrable cordon around the stadium.

This sort of thing did not go down well with the locals who took umbrage at the mildest forms of criticism but were soon having to run the gauntlet of disgruntled journalists from all over the world who were reporting, with total justification, the dreadful lack of proper organisation in respect of transport, accommodation, volunteers and just about everything else. The local radio shock-jocks were aghast at the flak they were getting; one even suggested that, "any foreigner who dares to criticise our Games should be put up against a wall and shot." This was not a liberal town. The State of Georgia still has capital punishment and you could detect racist undercurrents among many of its citizens. For example, the local rail transport system goes by the acronym MARTA which stands for Metropolitan Atlanta Rapid Transit Authority, but locals 'joked' that it really meant Moving Africans Rapidly Through Atlanta.

But it was the transport system which had been set up to ferry competitors, officials and the media around the venues which was Atlanta's most spectacular and crowning failure. There is nothing worse when you're chasing stories and facing deadlines than running late, especially if it's through no fault of your own. The relatively straightforward process of getting people from A to B was rendered completely haphazard by the fact that the volunteer bus drivers in Atlanta were poorly selected, poorly trained and, worst of all, in many cases not even from the city.

On one occasion I was on a crowded bus trying to get to the cycling venue when the driver hurtled past what was clearly the correct exit on a freeway. We pointed out that he needed to turn around and go back, only to be greeted with the shrugging response:

"Sorry, but I'm from Oregon, I only got into town two days ago."

Eventually we got there (the cycling venue not Oregon) but only after the equivalent of going from Waterloo Station to Wembley via Milton Keynes.

You could almost forgive these poor drivers for not knowing where they were going given their unfamiliarity with the locale in these pre sat-nav days, but what constantly irritated was their unswerving adherence to rules and regulations and total inability to use anything remotely approaching common sense or initiative when things went wrong.

As in most events of this type, there is a transport hub from which buses would radiate outwards towards the venues; the map looked like a giant spider with the routes as its legs. Generally if you had to get from one event to another it would be via this central location which, luckily for us, was a short walk from our hotel. The problem was that drivers had been told not to drop people off en route. I was on a bus coming back from the Aquatic Centre which got stuck in heavy traffic and eventually ground to a complete halt outside a hotel. A couple of Aussie journos walked to the front of the bus and politely asked the driver: "Excuse me, could you drop us off here please mate, this is our hotel."

"Sorry sirs, I'm not permitted to open the doors during transit."

A flaming row ensued in which the pair understandably became quite irate, pointing out that since the bus wasn't moving it technically wasn't in transit and therefore they should be let off. Other passengers called for the driver to open the doors but to no avail as he stood his ground and insisted they remain steadfastly shut. This went on for several minutes with the bus still anchored, motionless in the gridlock. Finally, one of the Aussies took out a cigarette and lit it inches from the driver's face, blowing a puff of smoke into his cab.

"Hey you!" the driver screamed, "no smoking on the bus. If you don't put that out I'll have to throw you off the bus."

"Suits me, mate," replied the Aussie as the doors opened and he and his friend stepped onto the pavement.

This was as nothing compared to a bus ride that Guy Swindells, Dave Clark and the Press Association's Martin Lipton embarked upon. They were heading out to the rowing venue at Lake Lanier which was some 55 miles from the city centre, a journey which would ordinarily take just over an hour. It was the opening heat of Steve Redgrave and Matthew Pinsent's title defence in the coxless pairs; Redgrave was starting his bid for a fourth consecutive gold medal and so this was a massive story back home. After 45 minutes or so it began to dawn on the predominantly British passengers that they might be heading in the wrong direction. The driver was a young woman in her twenties, accompanied by an older steward. Eventually questions started to be asked about the route but both volunteers insisted they were heading the right way. The press party remained unconvinced but amused themselves nonetheless by every five minutes or so shouting at the driver:

"Are we nearly there yet?"

However when another half an hour passed without spotting a single signpost for the venue, the mood turned to anger and frustration. The British contingent, who'd previously settled for good natured teasing, were now on the verge of plotting a hijacking. Oblivious to all of this, the driver trundled determinedly on as if she was Sandra Bullock in a sequel to the film *Speed* which was called *Slow*. Eventually a full scale mutiny broke out on board with furious hacks demanding to know what was going on. Finally, the driver found a slip road, pulled off and dissolved into a flood of tears.

"I told them I didn't want to go on the freeway," she sobbed. "It's scary and I don't like it."

Even the coldest of hearts could not fail to be moved by the pitiful sight of this poor out of town girl, hopelessly miscast as an Atlanta bus driver who had, almost literally, reached the point of no return.

But, after much consoling and handing out of tissues, she did regain her composure sufficiently to turn the bus around and somehow eventually managed to negotiate her way to Lake Lanier, albeit a good two hours after the race had finished and with Redgrave and Pinsent long since gone. As the disgruntled press party filed off the bus the steward called out cheerfully: "You all have a nice day."

At which point the diminutive Martin Lipton had to be physically restrained from decking him on the spot in a scene resembling Norman Wisdom squaring up to Mr Grimsdale in one of those 1950s black and white comedy films.

However, one place we thankfully didn't need a bus to successfully find our way to was the bar at the Ramada Hotel. With the average day finishing at around ten or eleven o'clock at night, there was little time to explore the wider environs of Atlanta, although we did occasionally visit a nearby club called Mumbo Jumbo's which we immediately re-christened Mungo Jerry's for no apparent reason. It was one of these impossibly trendy hang-outs, an explosion of chrome and leather, full of well-off and well-dressed young people with a cumulative IQ of around 25, gyrating to the in-house DJ who played techno and house music at ear split-ting volume. IRN had just recently set up an entertainments desk and were keen to put out something with an Olympic flavour; so they asked me to file a report on Atlanta's nightlife and club scene. Unwilling to waste more than a couple of minutes on an assignment which I considered to be rather beneath me, I grabbed a 'What's On In Atlanta' brochure from the hotel foyer and walked across to Mungo Jerry's. I then sat under the main speaker with a tape running and used the list of nightclubs as a guide as I improvised an in-depth review of the hip and happening places to be:

"I'm here at Bell Bottoms, the numero uno club for celebrity spotting in Atlanta's fashionable district just north of Midtown. Over the road is the

Fandango where you can dance 'til dawn to the latest hip hop sounds or if you're in the mood for romance, Dante's is the hot place for cool lovers . . ."

Compared to these exotic-sounding locations, the Ramada Hotel bar resembled Moe's in *The Simpsons*; it was sparsely populated, plain, functional and yet strangely magnetic. It was staffed by wonderfully friendly people with marvellous Southern accents who would greet you with a huge smile and say, "What can aaah git y'all?" The only window looked out onto a grubby, nondescript warehouse building which reminded me of the Dallas book depository from which Lee Harvey Oswald shot John F Kennedy. You wouldn't have given it a second glance were it not for the fact that every half hour or so a giant stretch limousine would pull up, whereupon a couple of huge security men in sharp suits and dark glasses would usher the passengers up a rickety metal staircase and into a small door at the side. With our imaginations racing, we assumed it must be some sort of cover for a drugs or money laundering operation run by the local mafia.

In fact, the reality was even more exciting than that. The bar staff, who were full of useful local knowledge, explained that the inside of the building had been converted into four ultra-luxurious apartments which were rented out to A-list celebrities who wanted to attend the Olympics. The shabby outer facade remained unchanged in order to protect privacy and anonymity. Over three nights we saw basketball star Shaquille O'Neal, comedy actor Dan Ackroyd and the Godfather of Soul himself, James Brown, emerging from limos. Aside from a small group of in-the-know autograph hunters who gathered nightly outside the building, and the Ramada bar staff, it seemed that no-one else was in on the secret. Although soon enough radio listeners in the UK were, as I excitedly filed this celebrity exclusive to the entertainment desk who were now hungry for more stories after my fabulous piece about the nightclubs.

One night Guy, Dave, Steve and I were enjoying a beer with an LBC radio reporter we'd met called Dan Miodownik, when the barmaid casually dropped into the conversation that the latest occupant of the place across the street was none other than Jack Nicholson. He, of course, was an LA Lakers fanatic who was in town to watch the American Dream Team in the basketball. We bagged the table nearest the window and waited for the limo to arrive. Sure enough an hour later there it was and out of it stepped the unmistakable figure of the Hollywood legend, wearing dark glasses and puffing casually on a cigarette. Dan decided that he was going to get the scoop of a lifetime. He grabbed his tape recorder, ran out of the hotel and joined a line of fans who were queuing up to get Nicholson's signature, to which he was happily obliging. At last Dan came face to face with the movie legend.

"Hi Mr Nicholson, my name's Dan Miodownik, I'm from LBC Radio in London. I was wondering whether you'd be willing to spare just a couple of minutes to tell all your fans back in England how you're enjoying the Olympic Games?"

In a scene which could have come straight out of one of his films, Nicholson tilted his head, lowered his sunglasses slightly, removed the cigarette from between his lips, blew out a puff of smoke, raised his eyebrows and flashed that classic Nicholson smile.

"I don't think so."

With that, he turned and walked up the stairs as Dan trudged back towards the bar.

Guy Swindells also had a brush with greatness when we were waiting to get into a Chinese restaurant a couple of blocks away. It was late, there was a long queue and we were very hungry. Being the sort who can survive on one half decent meal a day I was quite happy to bide my time but Guy is one of those people who gets very irritable on an empty stomach. He hadn't eaten since breakfast and was becoming more and more frustrated.

"How much bloody longer? I'm starving, where's the waiter? Why's it taking so long?" he grumbled repeatedly to the increasing annoyance of some of the other, more patient members of the line. On and on he went, until finally a guy turned round and hissed "sssshhhh" at him. Guy was just about to counter this with, "oh piss off you twat", but was glad he didn't when, on closer inspection, the angry customer turned out to be Stevie Wonder. As he turned away, I whispered to Guy: "Don't be so uptight (everything's alright)."

It wasn't just celebrities who caused us amusement in what was turning out to be the worst but, in a strange way, best Olympics I'd ever covered. On another night we walked into the bar to find it packed with Nike employees who, we later discovered, were manning the company's giant exhibition stand at the Centennial Park expo which was located about a mile from the hotel. Every single one of these people was wearing a Nike shirt, Nike shorts, Nike socks, Nike shoes, a Nike baseball cap and, in all probability, Nike underwear too. In the spirit of bonhomie I got chatting to a couple of them. They seemed very earnest and intense so I attempted to inject a little levity and humour into the proceedings:

"So what are you guys doing in Atlanta? Obviously you all work for adidas."

At this point, all of them got to their feet in unison pointing indignantly at the world famous swoosh logos on their clothes.

"No, no no," they exclaimed in horrified tones. "We're Nike."

Struck dumb by this astonishing mass inability to grasp even the simplest dose of irony I turned and left them to it. I'm willing to bet they sometimes retell the same story but with a slightly different last line.

"And, get this, the dumb limey actually thought we worked for adidas."

Another way that the big sporting goods companies such as Nike and adidas promoted their wares during the Olympics was by hosting specially arranged media conferences in which they paraded the star names with whom they had equipment deals. It was often the only opportunity we'd get to interview the likes of Michael Johnson, Linford Christie or Donovan Bailey prior to their events. But, quite apart from the business of gathering material, these get-togethers were also hugely popular with the press as they generally provided a splendid lunch and lots of 'freebies' in the form of shirts, kit-bags, hats and other desirable items which were given away to journalists like party bags at the end of a five-year-old's birthday celebrations.

Sometimes we would attend press conferences with absolutely no news value at all, simply so we could get our grubby hands on some free gear. Generally, the city which was next in line to host a major tournament would organise an introductory party to promote themselves, and their keenness to impress meant there were generally rich pickings on offer. It didn't always work out that way though. In Gothenburg while covering the 1995 World Athletics Championships, a few of us attended a function thrown by the organisers of the Athens event two years hence. After sitting through an interminable series of long and dull speeches, virtual tours and travel agent style videos, we were finally invited to collect a bag full of stuff on the way out. An unseemly scrum ensued in the rush to grab the loot and head off to something rather more newsworthy. We got outside the conference room and opened the bag in a frenzy of anticipation only to find a CD of traditional Greek folk music, a video of ancient Hellenic dancing and a T-shirt bearing a winged horse logo which was so twee it would have been deemed unwearable by a three-year-old My Little Pony fan.

Early on in Atlanta, Reebok hosted a big promotion which was primarily a showcase for the French sprint star Marie-Jose Perec who would go on to win an unprecedented 200m and 400m double in Atlanta. I went along because two of Britain's top names, 400m man Roger Black and high jumper Dalton Grant, were also in attendance. Having got the interviews we wanted, myself and *Sunday Times* athletics correspondent Ian Chadband were lining up for the buffet when we noticed a small table from which a woman was handing out some classy looking polo shirts. On joining the queue we heard her asking people what nationality they were before handing out the shirts.

"I'm sorry I had to ask," she explained to a guy two or three in front of us, "but these items are only for French journalists and we have to make sure you are French."

We turned our accreditation badges back to front so that we couldn't be identified and waited until we got to the front of the queue. When we were duly challenged I affected a ridiculous accent pitched somewhere between Jean-Paul Gaultier and Rene in 'Allo 'Allo and told her: "My name is Jean-Marc, I work for *Canal Plus* and my friend Serge is from *L'Equipe*."

"Okay that's fine," she replied. "Apologies for asking, but there are some non-French journalists trying to get their hands on these shirts."

Quick as a flash Chad cut in: "Zat ees ze English. So tee-pee-curl of zem."

I was proudly wearing my brand new and illicitly acquired Reebok polo shirt the night before what was set to be the biggest day of the Olympics from a British perspective. In the morning, Redgrave and Pinsent were competing in the coxless pairs final with Redgrave aiming to complete the remarkable feat of winning a gold medal at four successive Games. Guy and Dave Clark had gone to bed early for a crack of dawn start, since previous bus escapades en route to Lake Lanier had taught them to leave nothing to chance. Steve Wilson and I were enjoying a final beer in the bar before turning in ourselves. We were facing a massive day too with not only the blue riband 100 metres final, in which Linford Christie was defending his title, but also the triple jump final featuring Jonathan Edwards who'd smashed the world record in Gothenburg at the World Championships the year before.

We were chatting away to a couple of Irish TV guys who were also staying at the Ramada when one of their mobile phones went off. We instantly knew something was up given the alarmed and amazed expression on his face as he took the call.

"Something's happened in Centennial Park, some kind of explosion."

Steve and I jumped off our bar stools, picked up our tape recorders and ran out of the hotel towards the Park. We saw people rushing away from the site, some looking panic stricken and could hear the blaring sirens of what sounded like a thousand emergency vehicles. As I hurried down towards the Park I kept the tape rolling and did a running commentary (literally), describing the scene unfolding in front of me. Steve and I were the only ones heading downhill towards the incident and had to battle against a human tide of people moving in the other direction. Eventually I reached a police cordon tape which I ducked under. I was met by a sulphurous smell and could see plumes of smoke rising up into the night sky above now deserted exhibition stands.

Suddenly I felt someone grab my shoulder. It was an armed police officer. I still had the tape running to record him threatening to arrest me unless I moved back to the other side of the tape. I saw two young guys sitting on a bench, out of breath and gazing despairingly across at the scene of chaos in front of them. I sat down next to them and they gave me a moving first-hand account of what had happened.

Along with thousands of others they had been enjoying a rock concert in the centre of the Park when there was a loud bang. One of them had been in the armed forces and instantly recognised it as the sound of a bomb going off. He'd seen people injured by flying glass and shrapnel and helped evacuate the area. None of the police officers were willing to go on record but we did manage to interview some other eyewitnesses including ambulance staff and paramedics.

Once back in my hotel room I filed all the audio plus voicers and features. This was obviously going to be one of the stories of the year and arguably the biggest single incident at an Olympics since the terrorist attack on Munich in 1972. It was the early hours of the morning in London and so there would be a massive breakfast impact and we made sure radio would be leading the way. I finally got to sleep around 5am at the end of what must have been a 22-hour day. Steve had got into bed at around the same time but was woken up an hour later by a frenzied hammering on his door. It was Clarky.

"Steve, Steve, you've got to wake up . . . there's been a bomb."

I spent the next day following up the bomb story. We learned that, although over one hundred people had been injured in the blast, mercifully only two had died. The explosion would have caused much greater devastation had the rucksack containing the pipe bomb not been tipped over shortly after being planted by the bomber, causing the force of the explosion to be exerted downwards. Sadly one of the victims was a Turkish cameraman who was staying at our hotel and, like us, had run out of the Ramada to report the event. He died of a heart attack as he rushed to the scene.

True to form, the Americans were blaming everyone but themselves in the immediate aftermath with a myriad of conspiracy theories. Fingers were pointed at various enemies of the state but four days later suspicion fell upon a security guard called Richard Jewell who'd originally been hailed a hero for helping people to safety as the bomb went off. Despite the fact that he hadn't even been arrested, never mind charged, he became the subject of an appalling trial by media as cameras filmed his house being searched and followed his every move. I was amazed at how far the American media went in condemning this man. It seemed they'd decided that he was guilty until proven innocent and cared little about the fact that every single piece of evidence against him was utterly circumstantial.

Of course they had got it horribly wrong; Jewell was completely innocent and, I'm pleased to say, later successfully sued several news organisations for libel. The real bomber was an American white supremacist called Eric Rudolph, who in 2005 pleaded guilty to four separate bombings, including Atlanta, and was imprisoned for life without parole.

Despite this awful episode it was decided, rightly in my opinion, that the show must go on and the morning after the bombing Steve Redgrave duly won his fourth gold medal in consecutive Olympic Games. This was a fact which went totally unreported on the hideously biased and jingoistic US TV coverage who only seemed interested in home successes and stories. When Carl Lewis later won the long jump for the fourth successive time they went into overdrive, hailing this extraordinary run of Olympic dominance and eulogising the American for his astonishing achievement. In fact he was the first man to win four gold medals at successive Olympics since the day before yesterday.

American TV did Atlanta no favours at all with their nationalistic approach; American competitors finishing way down the field in events would be given three times as much airtime as champions from other nations. Events without any American participants were largely ignored, regardless of how newsworthy they were in general terms. Even the fact that some of these programmes were specifically intended for foreign broadcast made little difference to the moronic triumphal chest beating, but of course simply added to the increasing criticism from all quarters for the poor organisation, oppressive commercialism and lack of warmth and spirit at these Games.

The organising committee went under the acronym ACOG which stood for Atlanta Committee for the Olympic Games. But badges, T-shirts and stickers were soon appearing with the logo accompanied by the slogan: 'Atlanta Can't Organise Games'.

The ACOG motto was 'The Celebration of the Century' although most of us were now referring to it as 'The Cock Up of the Century'. A small but fitting example of how bad it had all become was the story of an enterprising Downtown fast food restaurant owner who was offering a side order of five onion rings arranged in the shape of the Olympic logo. He was threatened with legal action for breach of copyright.

After the rowing success, we sensed this could be one of the biggest days in British Olympic history and I was back in the stadium commentary posi-tion less than 24 hours after the bombing to see if Christie or Edwards could strike more gold. I had to cope with the fact that the two events were going on simultaneously, with the triple jump in full swing as the competitors lined up on the start line for the sprint final. Whereas most 100 metres are over in a matter of seconds, this one dragged on and on with a succession of false starts. I would start the commentary and have to stop as the second gun brought the runners back and then, almost without taking breath, launch into a description of Edwards or his American rival Kenny Harrison making their latest hop, step and jump into the sand pit.

Things became even more chaotic when Christie false-started for a second time and was duly disqualified. Rather than accept his fate with dignity, he proceeded to spend several minutes remonstrating with officials before finally disappearing down the tunnel in a right old strop.

Back in the triple jump Edwards was misfiring too with a couple of opening no-jumps. I think in all the confusion of having to switch between the two events I may have referred to his first legal jump as: "A disappointing third attempt for Edwards – only 17 metres and 13 seconds."

Back on the track the 100 metres finally got away cleanly with Donovan Bailey coming from nowhere to claim the gold medal and a new world record. I don't think I'd mentioned his name at all in the commentary until he actually crossed the line, such was the astonishing nature of his late burst. With none of the three medals going to American runners I had visions of NBC executives calling an emergency meeting to discuss whether it was actually worth screening the race in their highlights programme.

The drama didn't end there. As we stood to acclaim the hugely likeable Bailey as the new Olympic champion, Christie reappeared, stripped to the waist, and strutted his way alongside the track still furious at his disqualification. It was an appalling piece of sulky attention-grabbing which would have embarrassed even the most precocious of five-year-olds and we said so.

Edwards compounded the feeling of anti-climax by losing out to Harrison for the triple jump gold, but unlike Christie, was fair minded and gracious in defeat. Bailey, incidentally, went on to lead the Canadian sprint relay team to triumph, further enraging Americans. Most of the press contingent, myself included, were on their feet cheering when he raised his finger in a 'number one' gesture as he crossed the line.

As I headed away from the stadium I felt a little like I did in Seoul after the whole Ben Johnson saga was over. The Centennial Park bomb had gone off only 22 hours previously and yet so much had happened in that single day that, to me, it felt like it belonged to another Olympics.

Given that I'd only spent about four hours of that day actually asleep, it would probably have been prudent to head straight for bed. But it's hard to wind down when your head is spinning with the adrenalin of it all, and good sense rarely gets a look in. After a good few beers and much animated chat I eventually retired upstairs. I threw off my clothes and, given that it was so hot in Atlanta, jumped naked into bed for a much needed and well earned sleep.

A couple of hours later I woke up feeling desperately uncomfortable; there was a scratching sensation on my bare skin and as I groped around for my glasses my arm hit a concrete wall. I squinted through bleary eyes and the light seemed unnaturally harsh. When they finally opened fully I realised that I was standing, as nature intended, in the corridor outside my room with the door locked behind me. I had somehow, in my exhausted and drunken state, sleep-walked out of the room and fallen asleep again on the grubby, beige corridor carpet.

In a sprint every bit as determined as Bailey's a few hours before, I hurtled down the corridor to the fire escape clutching my tackle and climbed the four storeys up to Guy's room. I hammered on his door with one hand as the other still struggled desperately to cling on to my dignity. After what seemed to me like hours rather than mere seconds, it opened.

"Oh my God what's happened?" he enquired, blinking through the light himself. "Has there been another bomb?"

Then he lowered his gaze and the full horror of the pitiful sight which stood before him was revealed. He dissolved into a fit of hysterics before throwing me a pair of shorts and a T-shirt so I could go down to reception and get a replacement room key.

The episode summed up the whole surreal nature of the Atlanta experience, a combination of cock-ups, chaos and calamities. It wasn't just me who felt this Games had fallen well short of the standards of previous ones. All Olympics are officially declared over with a speech at the closing ceremony by the president of the International Olympic Committee. In the past, every Games had been successively described as being the best ever. But, in a break with tradition, Juan Antonio Samaranch described Atlanta merely as "most exceptional". It was damning with faint praise on a grand and global scale. What he might as well have said but was forbidden to by protocol, was: "Well frankly that was a pile of old shit."

Incidentally, the only other time I have gone for an impromptu, nocturnal streak was a few years later in a hotel in Leeds after a Champions League game at Elland Road. This time I was woken by one of the concierges who kindly opened up my room for me. I was gushing with apologies and embarrassment but he was fine about it.

"Don't worry mate, happens all the time."

CHAPTER ELEVEN

*"F****** Krauts!"*

1996 was something of an *annus mirabilis* for me, quite apart from the fact that my first daughter Becky was born on Halloween that year, arriving the day before my own 36th birthday.

In March I travelled to Las Vegas to report on Frank Bruno's WBC heavy-weight title showdown again Mike Tyson at the MGM Grand hotel. I arrived three days before the fight in order to get plenty of preview and colour material from the world's glitz and gambling capital. However, as someone whose entire annual betting outlay consists of a once a year punt on the Grand National, I was pretty impervious to its ostentatious charms.

Thousands of British fans also made the trip to cheer Bruno on and I made friends with a couple of lads from Gillingham who were on my flight and staying at the same hotel. This being Vegas, I was met at the airport by a stretch limousine and offered them a ride.

We sipped Budweisers from the fridge in the back as we were taken along the strip to the Excalibur Hotel, a ludicrous attempt at a recreation of King Arthur's Camelot. My younger daughter, Katie, once had a plastic, multicoloured, Disney princess castle which closely resembled this architectural monstrosity. It was a gaudy fusion of multi-coloured towers and turrets wedged incongruously between the giant black pyramid of the Luxor hotel and the fake Manhattan façade of New York, New York. Were it not for the 800,000 slot machines, whir-ring air conditioning and gleaming escalators you really did get the impression of being transported back nearly 1,500 years in time.

All the hotel staff were absurdly liveried in period costumes. I was checked in by Lady Guinevere, and my bags were carried to my room by Sir Gawain. On another occasion Merlin ushered me to my seat in the restaurant and the toilets were cleaned by people wearing jesters' outfits which merely compounded their indignity.

The bars all had strange forest themes, with plastic dragons' heads poking out from the fake ivy, and the furniture was rendered unnecessarily uncomfortable by its attempted adherence to sixth century carpentry designs. I wondered, as I walked through this anachronistic den of iniquity, whether the hotel manager sat at a large round table, wearing a jewelled crown and interrupted important meetings every now and again to engage in secret trysts with a mysterious, sword-wielding showgirl by an artificial lake.

Not wanting to spend more time than was absolutely necessary in this absurd kingdom, I decided to head to the press centre at the MGM Grand to find out who was around and what was going on. The two hotels were literally across the road from each other so I assumed it would take a mere three minutes or so to get there. Indeed the journey over the bridge which spanned the two sides of the strip had been made easier by the fact that there was an escalator at each side and a travelator in the middle.

Given that Las Vegas is home to the largest population of grossly overweight, lard arses on the planet, this seemed unnecessarily indulgent. I can only assume that the cynical hotel and casino owners had a vested interest in ensuring that their guests' vital statistics remained on the elephantine side of obese by sparing them even the most rudimentary forms of exercise. The logic, presumably, being that any pounds shed might compromise the inability to lift themselves out of their seats at the roulette tables and slot machines without needing oxygen, and thus they would spend more time witlessly frittering away their cash. They needn't have worried, most of the visitors were so fat they qualified for their own postcodes and none of them remotely entertained the idea of actually putting one flabby leg in front of another. Indeed the only movement you could detect on the travelator was the faint oscillations of quivering blubber beneath the inappropriate shorts and ghastly, lurid T-shirts. Trying to overtake someone on the pavement was like attempting to break through the entire defensive roster of a leading NFL team.

Outside the hotel, looking impossibly thin in this carnival of corpulence was a beggar holding out a plastic cup, into which I dropped all my loose change. You couldn't help but feel so sorry for him. Living rough on the streets must be bad enough anywhere in the world, but here he was in a town where greed and opulence reigns and every spare nickel and dime is shoved into a slot machine. I filled his cup every time I walked past and didn't gamble away a single penny in the week I was there.

On entering the Grand, via its giant, golden lion portico I discovered that the media zone was located in a tented area right at the opposite side of the hotel. Like many of its residents, the MGM was absolutely vast and the journey from one end of the building to the other took the best part of half an hour. The sheer scale of the building took my breath away; if you added up the guests, staff and punters, there were probably about 50,000 people inside at any one time. It was as if a town the size of Margate had been given a complete makeover and placed under one giant roof.

When I finally made my way through this extraordinary micro-city of bars, restaurants, shops, concert venues, bowling alleys, exhibition centres, theatres and cinemas and found the press centre, I was pleased to see my former IRN colleague Brett Spencer who was now working for whatever ITV's breakfast programme was called in those days (I always thought *Crap, Prattle and Shop* would have been a good name). After a brief chat about when we'd arrived and where we were staying I asked Brett what he'd been filing.

"Well not a lot, given the news from back home."

Since I'd spent most of the last 24 hours either airborne or changing planes I had no idea what he was talking about. He solemnly explained that a gunman had burst into a primary school in the small Scottish town of Dunblane and murdered 16 children and a teacher before shooting himself. To compound my sense of horror, the following morning ITN sports correspondent Graham Miller arrived in town and showed me a copy of the *Daily Mirror,* which carried the heartbreaking class photo with the kids who'd died circled. There were journalists from all over the world covering the Tyson–Bruno fight but, on that day, there was only one topic of conversation.

The pre-fight weigh-in took place in one of the large halls inside the hotel and hundreds of Bruno's fans managed to get in to add their support. As Tyson made his grand entrance, flanked by his ridiculous entourage of hangers-on and minders, the macho posturing was rapidly cut short by the Brits who gleefully launched into a football style chant: "You're supposed to, you're supposed to, you're supposed to be at home."

It was highly amusing to watch the greatest heavyweight of his generation being utterly upstaged by a mass of interlopers in Wolves, Burnley and Tranmere tops. Bruno's arrival was greeted with euphoria from the noisy visiting contingent, causing Tyson's main cheerleader, Steve 'Crocodile' Fitch to snap and snarl at them from the front of the stage. This of course provided further ammunition for the baying Brits:

"Who the fuck, who the fuck, who the fucking hell are you? Who the fucking hell are you?" they sang deafeningly.

By the end he should have been renamed Steve 'Pussycat' Fitch.

Among those who'd gone along to support Bruno were David Baddiel and Frank Skinner who were enjoying huge success at the time with their *Fantasy Football League* TV show which would hit new heights later in the year during Euro 96. I gained an interesting insight into the persona of comedians when I approached them to ask if they'd be willing to do a short interview. Baddiel quickly agreed and I suggested we move to a quieter spot to do the piece. He was all smiles as we walked out of the arena, chatting amiably about Chelsea's season and the absurdities of the whole Vegas scene. All the while Skinner walked a couple of paces behind us, head down and not uttering a word, but when we finally settled down and the tape was running he immediately burst into his stage persona delivering brilliant lines and quick-fire wit as he jousted with his comedy partner. Once I'd finished he went back to his quiet normal self just as quickly. Funnily enough, I often see Skinner at Fall gigs; like me he's a huge fan of the group and is always polite and tolerant of the people who come up and pester him.

Unfortunately the Americans had the last laugh as Tyson pummelled Bruno into submission in the third round of what was to be the last fight of the British boxer's career. I left Vegas with an overriding desire never to return to this city of fat, chain-smoking slobs mindlessly pouring coins into gaming machines in the ghastly environs of a fake Arthurian castle. Happily it remains my one and only visit.

Fortunately my next big boxing trip took me to the altogether more agreeable ambience of New York to watch Lennox Lewis's first heavyweight unification contest against Evander Holyfield at Madison Square Garden three years later. The fight itself was an absolute travesty with Lewis winning handsomely on everyone's cards except the judges' who, inexplicably, rated the contest as a draw. My attempts at a celebrity interview fell flat this time though. I approached rock star Paul Weller who was queuing up to get into the arena but received a similar response to the one Jack Nicholson gave Dan Miodownik in Atlanta, albeit without the accompanying style or charisma.

After the fight was over and the interviews had been filed, I got into a lift and, just as the doors were about to close, spotted a tall woman trying to get in. I pressed the open doors button so she could enter and looked up to see none other than movie sex symbol Bo Derek, older now than in her Hollywood heyday but still impossibly glamorous and immaculately dressed in a shimmering silver coat and expensive leather boots.

"Thank you," she said.

"That's okay," I replied. "What floor do you want ... 10?"

She flashed a faint, knowing smile: "Ground please," she whispered before turning her back on me for the remainder of our short journeys downwards.

Back home everyone was looking forward to the summer with more relish than usual. England was preparing to host Euro 96 and football was coming home as Baddiel and Skinner kept reminding us in their number one hit, *Three Lions*. It was the first major football tournament to be staged on home soil since the World Cup triumph of 1966.

On that day when Geoff Hurst scored his hat-trick, Bobby Moore received the Jules Rimet trophy and Nobby Stiles danced his joyfully insane, toothless jig across the Wembley turf I was 5 years and 271 days old and had just completed my first year at primary school. Like millions of others I was glued to the television all afternoon and celebrated the greatest day in our nation's sporting history by emulating Nobby's jig around our back garden. Or so I'm told. The depressing truth is, I have no recollection whatsoever of English football's finest two hours. This colossal gap in my memory banks is made even harder to bear by the fact I can vividly remember watching Sir Winston Churchill's funeral the previous year. No disrespect to one of our greatest historical figures, but how on earth can the image of a coffin being borne through London on a gun carriage be more memorable to me than the agonising wait for a Russian linesman's flag to signal the validity of Geoff Hurst's controversial goal? I can remember exactly what I had for lunch on my first ever day at primary school (two slices of spam with mashed potatoes and baked beans, since you ask) and yet the memory of some people on the pitch thinking it was all over was somehow consigned to the out-tray of my hippocampus.

It's a cruel, cruel state of affairs because, like everyone else, I am still bloody waiting for another opportunity to savour such an ecstatic feeling. If I'd have been born German it wouldn't have mattered as I'd have enjoyed two World Cup victories, three European Championship successes and no fewer than 11 major international finals since they were beaten at Wembley in 1966. It is little wonder that the Germans, a wonderful nation of people and a great place to visit in my experience, bear the brunt of such footballing resentment amongst English fans.

When Euro 96 started, it was a strange feeling to be covering a major international tournament via the North Circular Road to Wembley or the M40 to

England's training camp at Bisham Abbey. There was none of the on-tour cama-raderie of the hotel breakfast and saloon bars or the coach journeys to and from matches and training sessions. But there was no denying that this was a superbly organised and hugely atmospheric event which showcased the very best of the English sporting public. My wife Carolyn, by then six months pregnant, went to every game at Wembley and encountered only courtesy and companionship among enthusiastic fans enjoying the occasion for all the right reasons.

There was increasing optimism too that England might finally end the 30 years of hurt, such was the momentum of Terry Venables' team. I gushed, eulogised and hyperbolised my way through the group stage as Paul Gascoigne's audacious goal against Scotland and the mesmeric 4-1 dismantling of Holland provided indelible memories.

We were even getting that large dollop of luck that all champions need when, in the quarter-final against Spain, two Spanish goals were controversially disal-lowed and, horror of horrors, England actually won a penalty shootout. Stuart Pearce came to symbolise the spirit and ambitions of a nation as he ran towards the crowd, his fists pumping and his face contorted after smashing his spot kick into the net.

"He's buried the penalty and he's buried the ghosts of Italia 90 with it," I screamed from the gantry.

Two days before that game we'd been granted a rare interview with Pearce, who was never the most media friendly of players. I knew that, like myself, he was a huge fan of punk rock music and, after we'd dealt with all the footballing ques-tions, I asked him whether he would be allowed to attend the Sex Pistols reunion concert which was taking place at Finsbury Park in north London the day after the Spain game. He said he was hoping to since he was a close friend of Jake Burns, the front man of Stiff Little Fingers, who were also on the bill, but wasn't sure if Venables would let him go. It was a nice alternative angle which tied the week-end's big sporting and entertainment stories neatly together.

I had scored press tickets for the gig via our entertainment desk and went along with Guy Swindells who was also a fan and a mate of mine known universally as 'Bash' who now travels the world as part of Coldplay's road crew. The passes we had granted us access to various backstage areas and, more importantly, the media bar. This was brilliant since we could go out and enjoy the acts we wanted to see like Iggy Pop and the Buzzcocks, but avoid the likes of Fluffy and the Wildhearts by nipping back into the bar for a few beers as we cheered on Croatia against Germany in the match which would determine England's semi-final opponents. Inevitably the Germans won.

During one of these breaks we spotted Pearce and Gareth Southgate sipping mineral water and chatting in a corner so we went across to say hello. The normally taciturn Pearce was having trouble containing his excitement at being given permission to come and see his favourite band but expressed a little disappointment that Southgate had been the only other member of the England squad who showed any interest at all in going to the gig with him. Southgate celebrated his seventh birthday during the summer of punk in 1977 and I very much doubt that a copy of the *Never Mind the Bollocks* album was among his presents. He is, however, one of an increasingly rare breed of footballers who seeks to actively broaden his horizons beyond the game. He explained that he was fascinated to see what all the fuss was about as he'd never been to a concert of this nature before.

Just before the Pistols were due to come on, the crowd were treated to an unexpected surprise as the two England stars shuffled rather awkwardly onto the stage to absolutely thunderous applause. With considerably less confidence than he'd shown from the penalty spot the previous day Pearce mumbled into the microphone:

"Ladies and gentlemen, the Sex Pistols."

At which point the headliners launched into *Bodies* and proceeded to enthral the crowd with a performance which was a good deal more polished than any they had achieved during their initial years of infamy 20 years previously. At the end of it all Johnny Rotten introduced the final song of the encore with the words:

"This is what Stuart Pearce is going to give the Germans on Wednesday night. No fucking fun."

As Guy and I walked out of Finsbury Park at the end of an absolutely amazing weekend, we both felt utterly convinced that this was to be England's time and that even Germany couldn't stand in the way of a nation and its destiny. And we weren't alone; everywhere we looked there were St George crosses fluttering, horns beeping and thousands of voices singing about how 30 years of hurt had never stopped them dreaming.

The whole nation was by now so gripped in Euro 96 fervour that pretty much every news organisation had virtually given up covering any other stories. IRN took the decision that, rather than producing updates from the Germany semi-final every ten minutes as was customary, we would provide full live commentary from Wembley which the individual stations could opt into and broadcast on their own frequencies. The broadcast would begin with what was known as a clockstart, which meant that I would introduce the coverage from Wembley on the exact stroke of 7.30pm. This enabled individual presenters to back-time their introductions so it sounded like I was part of their programme. Given that the conclusion of the broadcast would depend on the length of the match itself, with extra time and penalties a possibility, it was agreed that my last words would be "and now back to you in the studio" at which point the local host would cut the feed from London and pick up.

I was to share commentary duties with Stuart Pyke, an unreconstructed northerner and St Helens rugby league obsessive whose speciality was cricket coverage, but was also a very good football man. Although trips south of the M62 generally brought him out in a rash, we got on famously. The basis of our friendship was the pretence of a mutual disrespect based along north/south regional lines. To him I was a "soft southern Jessie" and he referred to me exclusively as FP. A harmless enough epithet you would think, except when you consider that the P stood for pig. I, in turn, harangued him for a supposed love of pies, flat caps and whippets and called him FNB which stood for 'Fat Northern Bastard', although he was known as Spyke to everyone else.

The broadcast went very well, although I was slightly annoyed that it was the fat northerner rather than the slim southerner who got to describe both Alan Shearer's early goal and Germany's equaliser scored by the aptly named Stefan Kuntz. The rest, of course, is painful history as Gareth Southgate missed the penalty which sent the Germans through and ensured that the 30 years of hurt would go on. And on.

As planned, I finished the broadcast with a rather doleful "and now back to you in the studio" thus handing back to the stations who had carried our coverage of the game. I then threw off my headphones and looked across at Spyke; we were wearing the exact same expressions I'd exchanged with Tony Lockwood in Turin six years previously. Here we were again, denied in the cruellest possible fashion by arch enemies, and this time on our own home soil. We felt the pain of every other England fan filing almost silently out of the stadium as a million white vans prepared to fly their St George crosses at half mast.

At last I found the only words I could to convey my sense of misery and frustration:

"Fucking Krauts!"

Unfortunately, amid all the drama and disappointment, someone at IRN had forgotten to cut the feed from Wembley to the stations and, although the vast majority of them had opted out at the right time and resumed their own programmes, one small station in the north east failed to do so. This meant that my handover of "and now back to you in the studio" was followed by 20 seconds of silence, followed by the words "fucking Krauts" being broadcast into the homes and cars of every listener in their region. I admit it had been very unprofessional of me to swear with the on air red light still showing on the mixer, even if I did truly believe I was off air at the time. On the other hand, I think it pretty much summed up the feelings of the entire nation. I'm sure if they could have got away with it the *Sun* would have loved to put that very phrase on their back page.

Southgate, the villain of the piece in so many eyes, went up even further in my estimation as he bravely faced the cameras and microphones in the tunnel afterwards. Oddly he was forced to stand on a slightly raised podium surrounded by bright TV lamps as he spoke courageously and eloquently of his misfortune. This had the effect of thrusting him, quite literally, into the spotlight. I've seen plenty of lesser men who, having suffered much lesser sporting calamities, duck meekly out of such situations. But he stood tall in his lowest professional hour and merits our deepest respect for that.

Of course, England being England, I only had to wait two years for the next dose of penalty shootout heartache. Glenn Hoddle's team had qualified for the France 98 World Cup in the most nail-biting fashion with a 0-0 draw against Italy in Rome amid chaotic scenes on and off the pitch. The hideous over-reactions of Italian police contributed hugely to violent episodes on the terraces while Christian Vieri's header in the dying seconds of stoppage time provided one of those 'suspended animation' moments when time appeared to stand still for a brief second. As fans, players, commentators and millions of television viewers drew breath, their mouths agape, the ball flashed wide and England were through. It had been a heroic display evocative of the one in Sweden eight years before, even to the point where we had a blood-soaked hero à la Terry Butcher, with skipper Paul Ince ending the game with his white shirt stained red, causing Paul Gascoigne to famously quip that his head looked like a pint of Guinness.

Just before their departure for France, England held a training camp at the golfing resort of La Manga, a beautiful verdant green complex, framed by mountains on the south eastern coast of Spain. The media were invited along and our punishing schedule consisted of a daily press conference in which Hoddle and a couple of his players would be available for interview and we would file any relevant stories which came out of it. I spent the rest of the time lounging around by the pool listening to music and reading while others played golf. The evenings were generally spent at the main hotel where the England squad were staying. With the players segregated from the general populous under heavy security in a kind of five star Alcatraz environment, we would congregate for a drunken sing song in the piano bar which would later gain infamy during two separate visits by Leicester City. In the first Stan Collymore allegedly let off a fire extinguisher and in the second three players were wrongly accused of sexual assault.

We were also allowed to use the immaculately manicured training pitches to stage our own matches when no-one else was using them. For someone whose apex of achievement in competitive football consisted of pub fixtures in the Surrey and Hants Border League Division Five (South) and the Potteries and District Sunday League, I had generally been used to playing on the kind of surfaces that necessitated the packing of crampons, fishing waders and pot holing equipment into your kit bag, so this was a pure joy. In one particular game I was enjoying the lush grass, even surface and clement weather when a cynical hack from behind from a cynical hack from the *Daily Mirror* flipped me up in the air and back down to earth with the full impact borne by my left shoulder and I lay on the manicured pitch fearing that I'd suffered a break or dislocation. Fortunately there were medical people on hand to take me to the nearest hospital in Cartagena. My old *Signal Radio* pal Rob Beasley, who was now working for the *News of the World*, kindly offered to follow the little ambulance to offer me some moral support but got lost on the way.

I was dropped off at the casualty department and left there. Although a near fluent French speaker, I was able to do little more than order a beer in Spanish, so I cut a dismal figure as I sat on a chair in the waiting room for a depressing couple of hours still wearing my Brazil number ten shirt and harbouring dark thoughts of spending the entire World Cup in a hospital bed with a broken shoulder. The people at La Manga were kind enough to send one of their bilingual staff out to assist me and happily the X-rays revealed no serious damage although the pain was agonising. News of my injury had got back to England quicker than I expected, since a *Sky News* crew had filmed the training ground incident and used it in one of their packages that afternoon.

Games of football on foreign fields are generally more enjoyable than this one and, running parallel to the England national team is a less heralded but no less enthusiastic band of sporting brothers known as the England Media XI, who generally play matches against their foreign counterparts on the afternoon of the senior game. Sadly I have only managed to win a handful of caps thanks to a combination of not being available due to the constant on-demand nature of radio work and, frankly, being a crap player. I did score on my debut in a 3-2 win against Sweden in 1989, in a side which featured Ray Clemence and Trevor Brooking who qualified through their work as radio summarisers. Clemence played at left-back rather than in goal and sent a late penalty flying high over the crossbar. It was, he explained later, a deliberate ploy to waste time as the opposing keeper was forced to run back a long away to retrieve the ball, using up a few more vital seconds. I did once score a hat-trick past Ray in a match in Rotterdam, although I don't like to boast about it. Mainly because it was at table football. Quite a few ex-pros have stooped to the turgid depths of representing the press team including Terry Butcher, Tony Gale and even Bobby Charlton. I'm told that one frustrated journalist turned striker who'd become rather carried away with his own self importance actually complained to the England World Cup winner about the service he was receiving from midfield.

"Come on Bobby, play it to feet. Play it to feet."

The foreign teams were just as canny in using ex-players turned media pundits to strengthen their sides. England were thrashed by France in a game during Euro 92, which was not surprising given that one of their midfielders was World Cup legend Jean Tigana who had only stopped playing for Marseille the year before. Years later I was in Katowice yet again for England's seemingly annual group game against Poland. We were invited to play a game at a nearby town called Tychy, which is famous for producing the brand of beer which bears its name; discarded cans of which are an increasingly unwanted feature of the part of north London I live in. The town was unveiling its new sports ground and we were to feature in the first ever game to be held there against a Polish Select XI. The whole occasion was taken very seriously by the locals. We were marched out onto the pitch by the referee and lined up as the Tannoy announcer went through the squad list mispronouncing most of our names. This was followed by the two national anthems and handshakes before the captains exchanged pennants.

I was on the subs' bench and, looking on, it was clear that England were in for a tough afternoon. By half-time the Poles were 5-0 up, with their suspiciously gifted number ten having bagged a hat-trick. I came on for the second half but barely touched the ball as the home side, fitter, stronger and much, much more talented, ran rings around us although, to our credit, we only conceded a further three goals.

Afterwards we learned a little more about the hosts' talented number ten. Admittedly he was a local lad, although he'd come through the ranks to play professionally for GKS Katowice before spending several seasons as a prolific goal scorer in the German Bundesliga with Hamburg and Eintracht Frankfurt. His name was Jan Furtok and he scored ten goals in 36 appearances for Poland who he represented in the 1986 World Cup. At the time of the media game he was only 41 years old. To add to the odds stacked against us, most of his team-mates had also been professional players in the Polish first division. Given that we, by contrast, were a bunch of ageing, overweight pub players with hangovers, an 8-0 defeat on that day goes down as one of the finest results in English footballing history.

My cricketing career is even less auspicious since my CV reads 'can't bat, can't bowl, fields a little', but I did once turn out for an LBC XI in a charity match against a celebrity team led by an amazing old chap called Bertie Joel, who was still playing cricket well into his nineties. I recall making a handful of runs before being clean bowled, which is not, in itself, worthy of much attention and went onto the scorecard thus:

J.M. Anderson b D.J. Gilmour   8

I only bring this to your attention since the bowler in question was Pink Floyd guitarist David Gilmour. Good job it wasn't lbw or he'd probably have claimed it was comfortably plum.

The big story of the La Manga trip was Hoddle's decision to leave Paul Gascoigne out of the World Cup squad amid question marks over not only the midfielder's fitness or lack of it but also his increasingly erratic behaviour. On hearing the news Gascoigne trashed a hotel room and had to be physically restrained. England held a press conference to officially unveil the squad on a large terrace overlooking the resort at which Hoddle shifted nervously in his seat as he was grilled about the Gascoigne story. The whole scene was given a surreal air by a bizarre publicity stunt in which somebody who was dressed as a giant spicy sausage Peperami had managed to not only gain access to the conference but grab a prime seat in the front row just a couple of feet from the England manager. Given the security measures put in place by the FA to protect the national team and its entourage, it seemed a little strange that a six foot high, purple, savoury snack, could breach the cordon without raising even the slightest suspicion that he may not have been a bona fide member of the English press corps. Only when he began to ask ridiculous questions about Peperami did the security men finally twig that he was an interloper and he was manhandled out of the area by a couple of England minders in a scene reminiscent of Dom Joly's *Trigger Happy TV* show.

France 98 was a wonderful competition to cover. England were based at La Baule, a glorious, upmarket seaside town in Brittany which we knew well as we had also stayed there during the previous year's Tournoi de France.

It was in a bar in this friendly place that I met the only person who came closest to a genuine challenge at Lolita Baby's 'absurd name' title. As we were introducing ourselves to a group of locals, I held out a hand to one of the girls.

"Hi, I'm John from London. Pleased to meet you."

"Hi, I'm Fanny from Brest."

The Tournoi had been a mini tournament aimed at means-testing some of the venues, training facilities and accommodation ahead of the World Cup itself. The four-team round-robin contest also featured France, Italy and Brazil. In their opening game against Italy at the Stade de le Beaujoire in Nantes England played superbly and won 2-0. The star of the show was Manchester United's Paul Scholes who, in only his second international appearance, scored a superb goal and set up the other in a man of the match performance.

The problem was that he instantly became the centre of attention with everyone clamouring for quotes and interviews. Now, to say that Scholesy is publicity shy and unhappy in the spotlight is akin to saying that Keith Richards may at some stage in his life have experimented with drugs. The area inside the stadium where the post-match interviews were to take place was extremely confined and narrow and television, with its need to accommodate lights, cameras, monitors and microphones took up most of the space. We radio reporters were nudged aside with little or no room in which to work and, in the end, the only place we could find that was big enough and quiet enough to do the job properly was the gents toilets. This was no great hardship for myself and *Capital Radio's* Rob Wotton, but *Radio Five* producer Charlotte Nicol was understandably less enthusiastic. It was, however, a case of any port in a storm and so in she went.

When the FA's Adrian Bevington arrived he had both Scholes and David Beckham with him. Apparently Scholes was so nervous about facing the press that Becks, to his credit, volunteered to go along as well to offer moral support rather like a father with his nervous 11-year-old on the first day of school. So, standing sheepishly in front of a row of urinals with the smell of anything but success in his nostrils, Paul Scholes began his first major radio interview.

Now this particular face to face encounter won't go down alongside Nixon and Frost, Parkinson and Ali or even Wogan and Best as the most memorable of all time. Mumbling, stumbling and stuttering, our new hero muttered monosyllabically into the trio of microphones under his nose. The whole thing was over in about three minutes and each question was a good deal longer than its subsequent answer. Once the ordeal was over you could feel his relief as he raised his stare from the white tiled floor for the first time.

"You didn't enjoy that very much did you?" said Charlotte in an attempt to break the stony silence.

"I'd be less nervous walking out onto the pitch for a World Cup final," Scholes replied, which was, by far, the most interesting and cogent sentence he'd uttered all evening but, sod's law, came when the tape machines were turned off.

Given that all of Scholes's answers edited together would have barely made 30 seconds of usable audio, Beckham saved our bacon as he eulogised at length about his team-mate. After he'd done his bit we thanked them both for their time and wished them well.

"Thanks," said Beckham, "that's the first time I've ever been interviewed by a woman in a gents toilet."

"And hopefully the last," replied Charlotte as she ran towards the door for some fresh air.

England went on to beat France in Montpellier and emerged victorious from Le Tournoi despite losing their final game to the Brazilians at the Parc des Princes in Paris. The prize for this morale-boosting success was probably the crappest trophy ever to (dis)grace an international football tournament. It was as if the organisers had lost or broken the original piece of silverware and had to somehow get hold of a new one at short notice just minutes before the final kicked off.

So when Alan Shearer stepped up to receive the spoils of his nation's triumph he was handed what looked like one of those cheap, plastic black and white footballs you can buy at seaside petrol stations, glued onto a breadboard which had been sawn in half and hastily splashed with a coat of Dulux satin black. Frankly a seven-year-old could have done better with a few detergent bottles and some sticky back plastic. There's a brilliant photo of Shearer holding the trophy aloft looking utterly ashamed at having to parade this hideous artefact in front of a packed stadium. In an interview afterwards, Ian Wright told me the players were embarrassed at having to do a lap of honour carrying the wretched thing.

"You hold it."

"No, you hold it."

"I don't want it, you hold it."

Of course the trophy they really wanted to get their hands on was a far more glittering prize and the following summer England went into France 98 with all the usual hope, hype and hyperbole from the media. After covering the opening game in which Scotland were beaten by Brazil amid the usual tartan/samba backdrop and, of course, the usual Scottish defeat, I travelled from Paris to La Baule by train and joined up with the England press party. Our base for the duration of England's campaign was the wonderful L'Hermitage hotel, a lovely old building which was right on the main beach. We would fly out for each match from the quaint little airport at nearby St Nazaire which, with its small, curved terminal building and picket fence, looked not unlike the one where Humphrey Bogart says cheerio to Ingrid Bergman in *Casablanca*. On non match days a coach would ferry us through this beautifully manicured little town with its invitingly high density of excellent bars and restaurants, to watch training and attend the ensuing press conference.

Generally the press would be allowed to spend half an hour at the training session itself, so that the TV cameras and photographers could get enough shots of the players. During this time, the squad would do little else than a few stretching exercises and a little light ball work. The more interesting tactical stuff in which the team would work in formation was conducted after we had gone and behind closed doors.

The training ground had a tall, thick hedge surrounding it and passing locals would look on with bemused expressions at the group of English reporters battling it out to try and find a gap in the foliage through which the more enterprising amongst us would try and spy on the session to glean bits of information about what the starting line-up and shape of the team might be. I've even heard of journalists buying stepladders or climbing onto rooftops in a bid to stay one step ahead of their rivals in the circulation war.

The tented area where the interviews took place was the work of the FA's wonderful media liaison officer Joanne Budd who, at every tournament I attended, excelled herself by ensuring that we had comfortable surroundings to work in. In La Baule there was always plenty of tea, coffee, baguettes and croissants on offer which could be enjoyed on a decking area at the front, adorned with café style tables and colourful potted plants. Joanne also ensured that we got copies of all the English papers on a daily basis and, if you asked her nicely, would keep aside a couple of the goodie bags which the players handed out to local children, for us to give our own kids.

The conferences were split into three sections in three separate rooms with newspapers, television and radio all being granted around 15 or 20 minutes each with Hoddle and whichever players had drawn the short straw at breakfast and been forced to face the media. Some players enjoy this experience more than others and so we saw quite a lot of Gareth Southgate, Graeme Le Saux, Rob Lee, Tony Adams and Gary Neville. Adams told us that he felt these sessions helped break the monotony of life cooped up in the hotel where he had a room adjoining that of his former Arsenal team-mate Paul Merson. The two were battling with their respective addictions to alcohol and gambling at the time and would offer comfort to each other when the demons would resurface. I had been at the press conference two years earlier when Merson had broken down in tears in front of the nation's media and, like most who were there, felt desperately sorry for him while being struck by the courage it took to make this public admission of his problems.

Others, like Teddy Sheringham, Alan Shearer and Michael Owen clearly didn't particularly relish the prospect of facing the press but saw it as part of the job and were always polite and co-operative. Then there were those including Paul Scholes, Sol Campbell and David Batty who were happy to keep the whole thing at arm's length.

After the first few days we started to notice that the players had devised a subtle method of amusing themselves during their media appearances. When we listened back to our interviews we became aware that some of them were surrepticiously slipping song titles into their answers. Adams described La Baule as a "Ghost Town" while Southgate trumped that with "it's not exactly Club Tropicana." When asked about the increasing number of foreign players coming into the Premiership another player referred to it as a "Sign O' The Times" and there were also references to "Heroes", "I'm A Believer" and "Always On My Mind".

I'm sure bets were being placed at the team hotel as to who could come out with the most ridiculous title and this was clearly becoming quite competitive, to the point at which Le Saux answered the very first question of one interview by saying: "Never mind about that, did you know that I've Got A Brand New Combine Harvester?"

Unable to resist a challenge as absurd as this one, I concocted my own hideously contrived radio report to reflect the fact that we'd sussed them out. To borrow a musical phrase myself, it went something like this: "Don't Get Me Wrong there's no Shame Shame Shame in the Three Lions having some Fun Fun Fun but Enough Is Enough. Only Yesterday they were playing Silly Games but We Can Work It Out, and To Cut A Long Story Short, That Joke Isn't Funny Anymore so we Won't Get Fooled Again. Now Get Back and Play The Game because you're Simply The Best and Nothing's Gonna Stop Us Now."

I also started putting song titles into my questions. I asked Hoddle's assistant John Gorman how awful it would be if we "Lost In France", to which he not only laughed but proceeded to belt out the Bonnie Tyler hit in a off key Scottish baritone.

ITV were a little slower on the uptake than most of us on this, but eventually sent a reporter to ask Alan Shearer to explain what was going on. Keeping a straight face, the England skipper teased his interrogator by denying all knowledge of it and insisting he had no idea what he was talking about. Eventually, after being virtually begged to give a response, Shearer admitted: "Well we did used to put song titles into our interviews, but It's All Over Now . . ."

Unfortunately, with the opening game victory over Tunisia in Marseille soured by serious crowd trouble, the mood was far less relaxed when the team returned. Hoddle was never very easy with press conferences, especially the newspaper ones in which questions were fired in from all sides and were often quite challenging and aggressive. Most of the national papers would also send a news reporter to these events to cover the non-footballing stories that came up. We always referred to them as "the rotters" and their presence did nothing to help matters as they pushed the England boss for a quote on the hooligan aspect which he was unwilling to offer.

I think Hoddle saw our radio conferences as a bit of light relief and, on one occasion, walked into our room saying: "At last some sensible questions." This enabled me to chance my arm and throw in a few inquiries about the disorder in Marseille which got a far more lengthy and lucid response than the few crumbs he'd tossed out for the rotters to fight over just minutes earlier. These so-called supporters were not fit to follow the England team, he insisted, and couldn't call themselves football fans.

Hoddle didn't enjoy the post-match press conference in Toulouse much either, as England were beaten by Romania thanks to Dan Petrescu's last-minute winner. But qualification was ensured with a very one sided 2-0 win over Colombia in which David Beckham belatedly opened his England goal scoring account with a stunning free kick. I'm a little ashamed to admit that I had been rehearsing for this one: "Beckhhhaaaaaaaaaaaam!!! C'est magnifique."

All of which took us to another of the matches which has been woven into the very fabric of English football folklore. 30 June 1998 at the unprepossessing Stade Geoffroy Guichard in the equally nondescript town of St Etienne, and a last 16 encounter with Argentina.

Shortly after arriving at the ground, someone came up to me and said that a local TV crew were looking to interview an English journalist about the game in French. My mother is French and the first words I ever uttered were in her native language and, although not completely bilingual, I was pretty confident that I could make sense. Having said that, it is very difficult to undergo an interview in a foreign language as you don't have much thinking time and there will inevitably be moments when you are groping for a word and it just doesn't come. This particular interview was rendered all the more complicated by the preposterous nature of the opening question which I could easily translate as: "Of course whenever there's a game between England against Argentina everyone automatically thinks of the Falklands War. Is that how you see it?"

I was completely taken aback and managed to cobble together a few sentences to the effect that I most certainly did not see it that way. This was a football match not a war and to compare the two was utterly absurd. It seemed to get the message across as his next question was rather more relevant.

"Erm, okay. So how do you think England will line up?"

In the 150 or so England matches I covered for IRN, I don't think there was ever one as exciting and compelling as this. My voice reached opera soprano levels when Michael Owen scored his wonder goal, I railed at David Beckham for his sending off, shrieked at the referee when Sol Campbell's header was disallowed and then, of course, was forced to endure another penalty shootout disaster. By the time Carlos Roa saved David Batty's spot kick I'd virtually lost the ability to speak due to a combination of 120 minutes of apoplectic shouting and the fact that the cigarette I lit up after the final whistle was about my 40th of a very long day. As I filed my post-match reports I sounded like a cross between Des Lynam and Leonard Cohen.

It was a pretty sombre journey back to the airport as we digested the reality of yet another cruel, cruel exit from a major tournament. I remember being rudely awakened from a deep sleep by a shove from FA press officer Adrian Bevington.

"Bloody hell, Bevo, I'm trying to get some kip here. Have we taken off yet?"

"No mate, we've arrived at St Nazaire."

Back in La Baule we faced the inevitable anti-climax of England's exit, although for those of us that were to stay on for the rest of the tournament the workload decreased dramatically and we could relax accordingly. Four days after the Argentina game our spirits were lifted as we watched the Germany v Croatia quarter-final in a bar with a giant screen along with a large group of French locals. Despite my Franco-Britannic background I am only too well aware that the English and the French have never been the most comfortable of bedfellows. That night though we were united against a common foe as we stood shoulder to shoulder cheering an epic Croatian win.

The ever cheerful Martin Lipton, now Press Association football correspondent, came up with a brilliant opening line to his report which summed up the feelings on both sides of the Channel. "The Germans have their own word for it: schadenfreude."

CHAPTER TWELVE

"That was rubbish."

When I had answered the newspaper ad for my job at IRN in 1987 I remember being particularly struck by the phrase 'must be prepared to travel abroad as part of the job.' It seemed an oddly worded sentence to me; as if the idea of a profession which allows you to visit foreign countries as a matter of routine was somehow a matter for grave deliberation. To be honest, I couldn't have been more excited if they had put 'must be prepared to lie in a hammock being fed grapes by a posse of Nubian slaves'.

It wasn't just the prospect of discovering glamorous new places that fired my imagination but also the totally indeterminable methods by which those destinations would be chosen. Most families face the annual holiday dilemma of 'where shall we go this year', a matter which is usually resolved after much discussion of location, weather, affordability, ease of access and so on. The venues for many of my trips were determined by FIFA or the International Olympic Committee or the International Association of Athletics Federations.

It has been, perhaps harshly, suggested that the deliberations which precede the bestowal of the privilege of staging the Olympics or the World Cup is decided not so much on sporting grounds but rather on the shopping plans and restaurant choices of the delegates' wives. The fact is though that there aren't that many nations on the planet capable of staging such extravaganzas and therefore, by definition, the venue is generally a glamorous, modern and upbeat location packed with history, culture and state of the art facilities. Barcelona, Sydney, Rome, Paris, London, Cape Town and Lisbon have all provided wonderful backdrops to events which I have covered.

But the really interesting and alluring aspect of this global travel lottery comes when the destinations are not at the whim of an IOC or FIFA member but the result of a random draw, as in the qualification matches for major football tournaments. Here, there is no concession to comfort, luxury or aesthetics; frankly you could end up in any old dump and often do. I was lucky enough to be following England home and away and so would sit with my fingers tightly crossed as the draw was made for the latest World Cup or European Championships group and ponder the best and worst case scenarios within the parameters of the seeding system.

The sort of draw I wanted would be based not so much on football considerations but rather the desirability of the locations from a social or cultural perspective. The dream ticket, given the restrictions imposed by the seeding system, would be something like:

Spain (Barcelona or Madrid, both are magnificent cities)
Czech Republic (history, beer, nightlife and the president likes The Velvet Underground)
Finland (never tire of Helsinki, mad people, great bars)
Latvia (never been to the Baltics, very lively and cheap I'm told)
Cyprus (sunshine, sea and a guaranteed three points)
The flip side of the coin was the fear of being handed five holidays in hell:
Germany (we'll end up somewhere drab like Cologne or Dortmund and probably lose)
Norway (dull, expensive and bloody freezing)
Poland (oh no, not again)
Georgia (harsh, grim, no chance of ISDN working)
Luxembourg (boring place full of eurocrats and bureaucrats)

Generally you ended up somewhere between the two with the inevitable trip to some grim part of Eastern Europe counterbalanced by the prospect of a nice visit to Malta or Italy.

I later discovered that I wasn't alone in harbouring wholly selfish reasons for wanting certain opponents to pop up in the group. I was in Oporto for the Euro 2004 qualification draw and had gone to a restaurant with Bill Leslie, who was then working for *Capital Gold* and is now a *Sky Sports* football commentator. Seated at the next table were a group of representatives from the Lithuanian FA. We got talking to them and the discussion inevitably turned to the draw itself the following day. They told us Lithuania were absolutely desperate to play England who they'd never faced before at international level.

We nodded sagely and ventured that that was perfectly understandable given the prestige attached to facing the nation who brought football to the world and had such a rich sporting tradition.

"No, no," laughed the Lithuanian FA president. "It's because you pay the most TV money, we always pray to be drawn with either England or Germany because it means more cash for us."

He then ventured a further enticement without a hint of levity: "You would have a wonderful time in Vilnius, our women are most accommodating. The Italians were very active."

Sadly we weren't paired with Lithuania, but Scotland were and, from what I gather, their fans had a very nice time there.

Prior to joining IRN I had had a fairly limited first hand knowledge of the world at large. I had been to the USA, Canada and Trinidad on holiday but hadn't got further than France, Spain, Italy and Ireland as far as Europe was concerned. Suddenly the qualification draws took on a magical significance and offered tantalising opportunities.

It took me back to the days of my childhood when I would listen in rapt attention as the draw for the FA Cup was broadcast to the nation on Monday lunchtimes. Like millions of others I would wait for my team to be drawn, fingers crossed for a favourable home draw, already dreaming of Wembley's fabled twin towers.

"Number 23 . . . Manchester United" (please God, please God, no).

"Will play number 48 . . . Watford" (well there's always next year).

The entire process was conducted with what seemed, even to a primary school student like me, to be an admirable minimum of fuss and nonsense. This was gripping entertainment brought to you courtesy of two blokes, 64 numbered balls, a velvet bag and an announcer. The draw process and its unfolding drama had absolutely no need for any diversions or distractions; every ball drawn out of the bag had a story attached to it and every pairing of clubs would reignite memories of some dim and distant triumph or disaster. To be seated in front of a crackly wireless at a sandwich-laden table on a freezing December day was to be transported into the very folklore of the world's most famous knockout competition.

Of course, as with so many things nowadays, some idiot decided that these occasions would benefit from being transformed into a showbiz extravaganza which could be stretched out into several hours of pointless light entertainment razzmatazz. I imagine the same person to be responsible for the advent of such life changing innovations as personalised Donny Osmond singing birthday cards,

High School Musical themed advent calendars and chilli and chocolate flavoured crisps.

I have sat through various draw ceremonies over the years, with increasing desperation as the relatively simple task of arranging 48 football teams into eight group of six has evolved into a cross between the *National Lottery Show* and the *X-Factor*. Seemingly the simple fact that Iceland will meet Kazakhstan in Group 4 can't possibly be determined without the aid of a tawdry selection of miming pop groups, vacuous models and bored looking former players gyrating, sashaying and shuffling their way respectively across the stage. There's also, of course, the unintentional comedy moment when the ever more elaborate ball-plucking device breaks down and it takes several minutes of embarrassed to-ing and fro-ing before we finally learn that Finland's final Group F opponents will be Estonia.

England and Poland seem to be drawn together like star crossed lovers across a crowded dance floor every time anyone gets anywhere near one of those clear plastic pots full of coloured balls from which the teams are picked. There have long been rumours of these draws being fixed, with suggestions that some heated up balls are tipped into the pot so that they can be distinguished from the others by touch. If this sort of thing really did go on I would suggest that, once England had been pulled out, all the other balls except Poland's had been doctored to administer a sharp electric shock to the hand of whoever was entrusted with carrying out the lucky dip.

"And the second team in Group D along with England will be . . . aaarrrggghhhh . . . Poland."

This meant that I was to become so well acquainted with the Polish city of Katowice (pronounced Cat-Oh-Vit-Sir) over the next few years that I was almost toying with the idea of buying a flat there to make life easier. It's located in the south of the country in Upper Silesia; an unapologetically working class town which has long since thrived on the coal mining and steel production industries. These days it is rapidly developing as a cosmopolitan city with art galleries, modern shopping centres and a thriving business district.

When I accompanied England there for the first time in a World Cup qualifier under Graham Taylor in 1993, it was like the setting for some immense gothic novel or a painting by LS Lowry. The whole city was relentlessly and depressingly grey. Grey streets were fringed by tall grey buildings nestled under resolutely grey skies. Even the people seemed grey as they went about their daily business in grey clothes to the soundtrack of state radio being broadcast from the tops of grey lamp posts out of old fashioned grey loudspeakers. In fact the only things that weren't grey were the rivers and canals which cut through this bleak metropolis;

they were what might be described as effluent yellow. It was late May but the monochrome uniformity of this place made it feel bitterly cold.

The one thing Katowice did offer was the opportunity to visit the Auschwitz concentration camp and Holocaust Museum which is about 25 miles away from the city. On my first trip to Poland I went there with *Capital Radio's* Jonathan Pearce and Steve Wilson and from the moment we passed through the entrance gate, bearing the sickeningly inappropriate motto *Arbeit Macht Frei* (Work Makes One Free), three normally garrulous and outspoken football commentators shuffled around in numb silence, almost unable to truly grasp the scale of the atrocities which had occurred in this dreadful place. Nothing really prepares you for the sheer, relentless horror of this Nazi death factory and everyone, I'm sure, takes their own personal memories from Auschwitz, whether it be the gas chambers, the execution yard, the empty cans of Zyklon B or the piles of shoes, glasses, false teeth and other personal artefacts the million victims left behind.

For me, two things remain in the mind above all others. Firstly, there's a long hall inside the camp on the walls of which are hung the head and shoulders photographs of hundreds and hundreds of the inmates, wearing those demeaning striped uniforms with their heads shaven. As l walked along the corridor, I would pause from time to time to examine more closely this extraordinary gallery of human suffering. But although these wholly innocent people found themselves at the epicentre of the most grotesque example of man's inhumanity to man, none of these faces betrayed any fear, belittlement or sorrow. Pair upon pair of steely grey eyes stared back at me from these black and white images and their message spoke only of pride, dignity and, above all, defiance.

My other most indelible memory of Auschwitz is a single sheet of paper encased in a glass frame at the museum upon which had been typed a list of names, nationalities and dates of birth. It reminded me a little of the pension scheme membership schedules that I would routinely scan through in boredom as part of my insurance job at Crown Life. Yet this list, signed and dated by an official, carried the names of those people who had been executed at the camp on that particular day. The deaths of real human beings had been itemised and processed, like car parts, sacks of rice or rolls of carpet, by typists, filing and ledger clerks, managers and secretaries. In this sense the offices at Auschwitz differed from any other office in only one respect; whereas others dealt with insurance, accountancy or banking, here the line of business was genocide. I still have a horrible mental image of an Auschwitz middle management figure in a neat suit and hat leaving the breakfast table, grabbing his briefcase and kissing his wife and children goodbye before setting off for another day playing a small but significant part in the systematic destruction of hundreds of thousands of human lives.

As Jonathan, Steve and I made the return journey to our day job, hardly a word was exchanged as we sat, our heads bowed, lost in thought. Football is only a game.

Many of the other journalists on the trip complained endlessly about the grim surroundings and almost total lack of nightlife on offer in this bleak industrial landscape, and it is true that Katowice didn't offer much in the way of international cuisine, glitzy nightclubs or bohemian cafes. The bar at our hotel, the Warszawa, which was generally accustomed to serving no more than half a dozen customers at any one time, suddenly became crammed with thirsty English journalists vying for the space in which to raise their elbows within its tiny confines.

None of which bothered me in the slightest. I was absolutely thrilled to be staying in a place that most people would either have never heard of or avoided like the plague. It was fascinating to be thrust into a culture so totally removed from my own and be offered a first hand glimpse of the realities of life in the Upper Silesian coalfields. The restaurant at the Warszawa was never going to earn any Michelin stars but, while some pulled faces and bemoaned the lack of burgers and chips, I happily threw myself into a diet of red cabbage, potato dumplings and borscht.

One of the great pleasures of random international travel is that you're never quite sure what is going to end up on your plate, a situation which I have always viewed as a challenge rather than a dilemma. Since enjoying the global breakfast in the Press Willie-Gee dining hall at the Seoul Olympics, I have (and I would advise all vegetarians to skip the rest of this paragraph) sampled the delights of ostrich, crocodile, reindeer, springbok, octopus and monkey gland sauce. I did, however, draw the line at one item on the menu at a restaurant in Beijing: tiger penis soup.

That trip to Katowice instilled a desire in me to savour every moment of every venture into an unfamiliar or unusual environment. I used to spend the whole of every journey from the airport to the hotel with my face pressed against the window of the coach, simply absorbing the everyday scenes which flashed past in tiny fragments of time and space. My mind would fill with images and scenarios. What was it like to be a construction worker in Skopje? How would the children from that school in Coimbra turn out? Why was there a queue outside that roadside cafe in Sofia? What were the strange concrete pillbox-like structures dotted along the road from Tirana airport for? Why were so many of the tree trunks on the outskirts of Chisinau painted white? I would probably never learn the answer to the majority of these questions and yet it was so fascinating to speculate.

As well as covering all the team news, groin strains and general gossip from the England camp, I always felt it my duty to incorporate some of the colour and flavour of the host country into my reports. For example, if you were in a very poor nation like Albania, you could illustrate a voice piece by observing that it would take the average local worker more than 80 years to earn what Alan Shearer makes in a week. Or, when in Macedonia, suggest that England might face stern opposition from a nation whose history was forged on the military exploits of Alexander the Great. There were more light hearted opportunities to be had too; you could go to a place like Luxembourg, a country of financial power brokers but part-time footballers, and suggest that it would be embarrassing for England to lose to a bunch of bankers.

I did however take umbrage at a BBC reporter at the World Athletics Championships in Athens in 1997 who proudly told me that he'd signed off a report with the following line:

"It's a great place this, you can get a meal for a fiver, a beer for 50p and a taxi anywhere in the city for less than two quid."

While applauding his attempt to add some colour to his piece, I did venture to suggest that such information could severely compromise his position when submitting his expenses. It's never a good idea to be too specific about the cost of food, drink and cabs.

Of course the references you could throw into reports didn't have to be cultural or historical. Around the time that coverage of Sven-Göran Eriksson's alleged affair with the Swedish TV presenter Ulrika Jonsson became headline news, the urge to have some fun at the England coach's expense was simply too great to resist. Hence, I concluded one match preview with the words: "Hopefully England will win and, at the end of another long night, a breathless Eriksson will be screaming 'eureka' rather than 'Ulrika'."

Eriksson had been in a rather better mood when England won 5-1 against Germany on that unforgettable night in Munich during the 2002 World Cup qualification campaign. The press are often accused of relishing the opportunity to write critical pieces when things are going wrong but less enthusiastic about delivering eulogies in times of triumph. I must admit I have a good deal of sympathy with this as, in my experience, it is far more fun to have a right old rant about something than it is to go all gooey- eyed about how great everything is. You go into any pub in the country and you'll find bar room conversations are more often fuelled by angst, bitterness and injustice than love, peace and harmony.

As I pondered how to start my recorded report for the next morning's breakfast bulletins, it struck me that millions of England fans would be waking up in a state of near disbelief at what they had seen at the Olympic Stadium the night before and so I began my piece: "Wake up, splash your face with cold water, throw back the curtains and take a deep breath. Yes, it really did happen."

Clever though I thought that was at the time, the moment which best summed up that wonderful night came afterwards at the hotel bar where one overworked, stressed and mercilessly taunted German barman was attempting to administer to the considerable drinking requirements of a room full of celebrating England fans. He inquired what one supporter would like to drink and was greeted by a raised right hand with all the fingers spread.

"I'll have FIVE beers," he said, emphasising the number. Then, pointing his index finger skywards, "and have ONE for yourself."

Five years earlier Glenn Hoddle's first game as England boss and David Beckham's international debut had both taken place in one of the backwaters of European football which had you reaching for the atlas as soon as the draw was made. Although it sounds like the kind of made-up place that might feature in a Marx Brothers comedy, the tiny former Soviet republic of Moldova actually occupies a less than desirable piece of real estate sandwiched rather uncomfortably between Ukraine and Romania. This five-year-old nation had been the vineyard of the former USSR and had high hopes that the export of wine would play a big part in securing their economic future. Many of the country's four million or so inhabitants had little vineyards on the smallholdings from which they led a largely self-sufficient existence.

While the pleasant summer weather was highly conducive to the production and cultivation of grapes, the winters were harsh and long. With no natural reserves of oil, gas or coal within its borders, Moldova's energy supplies had to be imported from Russia. Unfortunately, if the mother country was running short, supplies to this southern outpost would be severely reduced or even cut completely.

And so I am able to provide the solution to my query about the white painted Moldovan trees. Faced with energy shortages on an annual basis, priorities had to be assessed and tough decisions made. They simply couldn't afford the luxury of street lighting beyond the centres of towns and cities and so the trunks of the trees which lined the roads in outlying areas were painted white so as to reflect car headlights and thus keep the routes a little safer. Such hardships would render many people bitter and miserable and with good reason, but the Moldovans couldn't have been more warm and welcoming. The day we arrived coincided with a national holiday in the country and the little parks round and about were thronged with people in brightly coloured traditional dress enjoying the sunshine as if they didn't have a care in the world.

At the time there was only one decent hotel in the capital Chisinau and the days of the media flying on the same plane and staying in the same accommodation as the players had long since gone. So, while the squad settled down in a relatively modern hotel complete with swimming pool and casino, we checked into the equivalent of a 1950s Borstal. The catering facilities consisted of a single hatch in a gloomy refectory through which a wizened old lady who looked as if she'd survived the Russian revolution would pass cups of thick, stewed tea and a very limited supply of biscuits and cakes. At least she had wisely decided to invest in a few crates of local beer which were quickly and avidly snapped up.

The rooms were musty and dank, there were no locks on the doors and the furniture wouldn't have looked out of place on the set of *One Flew Over The Cuckoo's Nest*. But discomfort is an occupational hazard on jaunts such as these and, since they generally lasted only a couple of nights, grinning and bearing it was the only option. The real problem in Moldova was that mobile phone reception was an absolute lottery and there were only about two telephone lines out of the hotel. I spent the first evening dialling out over and over again for what seemed like several hours before I was finally able to file any material.

Happily, we didn't have to dine in the hotel that night as the Moldovan FA very generously laid on a meal for us at a nearby restaurant where the food was plentiful and very good. We were also able to sample the fabled Moldovan wine, earthenware pots of which were plonked onto the wooden table tops in a seemingly endless stream and duly emptied with increasing gusto. The quality, I have to say, was excellent and we talked excitedly about how we would help boost our generous hosts' economy by buying Moldovan wine from English supermarkets on our return. The enthusiasm was slightly dampened however when someone decided to coax the last few drops out of the remaining jugs before we headed home. When he upturned the very last one, he was greeted with a large splash as red wine splattered onto his white shirt and a cockroach about the size of a walnut plopped upside down into his glass, furiously kicking its legs in the air as it battled to avoid the twin threats of death by either drowning or alcohol poisoning.

One of the standard jokes about visits to places like this which offered little in the way of genuine nightlife and entertainment was:

"It's so boring here I might even go and watch the Under 21s tonight."

Generally the senior squad were accompanied by their junior counterparts who would play their match on the night before the main game, often in tiny stadiums in out of town locations. With so much to file on the eve of the big game it wasn't usually practical to travel any distance to watch the young players in action and we would rely on the venerable services of Press Association reporter John Curtis whose job it was to cover these junior games and whose dispatches would form the basis for a great many of the newspaper and radio copy stories on the game.

JC as he was known, is an affable Midlander with an encyclopaedic knowledge of pop music and county cricket who cut a rather incongruous figure among the press corps with his resolutely non-trendy wardrobe and distinct lack of interest in boozing or partying. I was with him during a lull in the frenzy of England activity at the 1998 World Cup when we decided to go along to see the Norway players who were also based in La Baule. Among them were a sizeable contingent of Premiership players including Henning Berg, Ronny Johnsen, Tore Andre Flo and Ole Gunnar Solskjaer who all spoke excellent English and were very relaxed, patient and approachable.

After I'd finished interviewing Solskjaer, JC stepped up and introduced himself. At the time there was a Manchester United defender called John Curtis, who later played at Blackburn and Nottingham Forest and his reporter namesake sensed an opportunity to ingratiate himself: "Hi Ole, I'm John Curtis," he cheerfully ventured, "the one from the Press Association, not the Manchester United player."

Solskjaer looked up at the rotund, forty-something figure standing before him in a pair of uncomfortably tight maroon shorts and a Dick Dastardly and Muttley T-shirt.

"No," he replied, betraying a faint smile, "different shape."

But JC's finest hour came during the World Cup in 2002 which I sadly had to cover from a television screen in London due to the prohibitive cost of the broadcast rights. The day after England's 1-0 group win over Argentina he wandered out of his hotel to get onto the coach for the journey back to the airport. He climbed aboard and sat down, looking at his notes from the previous night and considering what his follow-up piece would be. After a few minutes the realisation dawned on him that he may just have got onto the wrong bus. As he glanced up at the figure next to whom he'd plonked himself, he clocked the rugged, bearded features of Argentine super striker Gabriel Batistuta who flashed him a look which would have melted concrete.

In Moldova, the Under 21 game was played in the same stadium as the England team were due to kick off their World Cup 1998 qualification campaign the following night so we decided to go along and get our bearings.

Beckham had of course been the focus of attention during the day with his debut looming and was put up for interview in the afternoon. At the time he was 21 years old and had made headlines just weeks before with an audacious goal from the halfway line for Manchester United against Wimbledon. It was the first real personal exposure any of us had had to him and we were struck by his soft spoken shyness and polite, almost embarrassed demeanour. He fielded our questions respectfully albeit without saying a great deal and there was very little to suggest that this handsome and personable yet timid young man would eventually become football's biggest global name. In fact, I remember being more excited by the interview I'd done with the erudite and confident Everton defender Andy Hinchcliffe who, as all pub quiz regulars will know, was the other England player making his debut that day.

I subsequently spoke to Beckham many times when he was on England duty and once met his father Ted who used to go to every game to watch his son play. Beckham senior went to great pains to stress the importance and influence of Sir Alex Ferguson on his son's career and the family atmosphere which he engendered amongst his generation of fledglings at Old Trafford which also included the Neville brothers, Paul Scholes, Ryan Giggs and Nicky Butt. Sunday dinners chez Fergie were a regular treat for the families of the young players and as a result they became very close.

Sadly the Manchester United manager's bonhomie didn't often extend to the media. I myself was once thrown out of a press conference by him because he didn't want his comments recorded and re-broadcast, and I've often seen him turn on a newspaper reporter for trying to earwig one of the radio-only sessions or vice versa. Just about every member of the so-called Manchester mafia of football reporters and broadcasters had been banned from the club's training ground by Fergie at some point, although he almost always allowed them back once he'd made his point. The local ILR stations in Manchester were rarely allowed to talk to the players themselves before matches and so the interviews I would send down with Beckham and his clubmates from the England get-togethers were the only proper opportunity that our north west IRN clients such as Piccadilly Radio would get to air feature-length pieces with the United stars.

I did once get a brief glimpse into the more personable side of Sir Alex, who many say is fascinating and very amusing company with people he likes and trusts. He was promoting his autobiography *Managing My Life*, which is among the most interesting of soccer related books, and I was invited to interview him at his publishers' office in central London. Thoroughly relaxed in a pristine short sleeve checked shirt and sipping tea from a bone china cup, he was charm personified as I was granted a 20-minute audience in which he happily discussed everything from the Glasgow shipyards to Posh Spice and back again.

It was the same with Brian Clough. I was at the City Ground when Nottingham Forest were relegated in Clough's very last game in charge in 1993. In the latter part of his career he had been notoriously standoffish with the press and rarely spoke to anyone in post-match situations. However, I spotted him in a corridor after that match and politely asked if he would be willing to give us a few words.

"I'm afraid not young man," came the inevitable response.

The sheer excitement of being referred to in those terms by the legendary figure meant that it remains the proudest I've ever been after failing to get an interview. I did get one with him a year later though, when Clough published his autobiography and, like Fergie, he was charm personified as we sat down to chat about it for 20 minutes or so in a posh London hotel.

However the biggest thrill I ever got out of doing an interview was the time when Pelé arrived at Old Trafford on an Umbro promotional visit. Like so many people of my age, the Brazilian became a hero of mine when I watched the 1970 World Cup as a nine-year-old, crying tears of anguish as England lost to West Gemany in the quarter-finals but then jumping for joy as Pelé, Jairzinho, Tostao, Rivelino, Gerson and Carlos Alberto ran the Italians a merry dance in the final. I'm not usually star struck in the slightest, but just being in the same room as the great man was enough to set my heart a-flutter. Eventually a gathering of radio reporters huddled around the immaculately dressed figure in the press room as he gave us a little private audience in rather broken English. He was asked which of the current Manchester United players he particularly enjoyed watching.

"Manamac and Oven," came his rather mystifying response.

He had not only mispronounced the names of the players but also got the wrong club. He meant to say McManaman and Owen who were, of course, at Liverpool at the time. But such was his lustre and aura that we just carried on without questioning what he meant or daring to correct him. Frankly, he could have recited the nine times table and we'd have simply looked up at him in awe and wonder.

When the interviews had been completed, there followed a scene which I have never witnessed before or since in a media conference. One by one, seasoned sports journalists got up and went across to the top table and formed an orderly queue, standing patiently in line like schoolchildren, holding out little bits of paper for Pelé to sign.

Back in Moldova, having decided that a night out with the Under 21s was the best (indeed only) chance of some evening entertainment, we duly arrived at the stadium. Well, stadium is perhaps too grandiose a word to describe the dilapidated collection of farm outhouse buildings surrounding a patch of meadowland which Emmerdale's finest would have dismissed as unfit for growing kale. The grass was about a foot long and the pitch underneath it had more craters than the Sea of Tranquility. It was surrounded by a four lane running track which was so cracked and rutted that tufts of greenery poked out at regular intervals from the depths of vast fissures which criss-crossed the surface. You could imagine the thrilling finale of the Moldovan national 400 metres final, as the favourite rounded the final bend in first place only to plunge headlong into a ravine, never to be seen again. It's the only stadium in the world capable of staging a 100 metres steeplechase.

The senior England side obviously held similar views to us as to the entertainment value of this part of the world and arrived to watch the game themselves, only to find there was nowhere for them to sit. Rather than risking serious injury by negotiating the crumbling terraces, they filed up the stairs and towards our little wooden shed of a press box, which was already fit to burst. It was at this point that Paul Gascoigne decided to enliven the proceedings by whipping down Paul Ince's tracksuit bottoms and exposing him to the world. As if the sight of Ince's bare arse wasn't enough, the extra influx of people saw us battling with the players for space and we all ended up wedged in shoulder to shoulder (or cheek to cheek in Ince's case).

My attempts to file updates on the match were seriously hampered by the giant presence of David Seaman to my immediate left. After each update I delivered he turned around with a huge grin and said something like: "That was rubbish."

Happily the grass was cut the next day and England won 3-0, with Hoddle and Beckham making their respective international debuts comfortably enough. They might not have done had they, like us, been forced to use the toilet facilities alongside the press seats in Chisinau.

It has long been an occupational hazard of the international football reporter that the facilities in many foreign arenas do not come anywhere near the standard of even the most rudimentary ones back home and I feel that the bravery shown by these noble souls in the face of often unbearable sanitary squalor and dilapidation deserves wider recognition. And so (cue drum roll) I bring you my nominations for the prestigious category of Worst Toilet At European Football Venues or, as I'm sure they'll eventually become known, the Golden Khazis:

1.   Republican Stadium, Chisinau, Moldova, 1996
Walk down the rickety wooden steps and across the cracked, weed strewn, four lane running track and you will find a dilapidated hut surrounded by a

swamp of human effluent. Make sure you cover your face with a handker-chief, then tread very carefully and attempt to piss into the cracked bowl from as far away as possible (at least it doesn't matter if you miss). It was comparative luxury for us blokes, but Charlotte Nicol of *Radio Five* still rates it as one of the most depressing experiences of her life.

2.   Tofig Bakhramov Stadium, Baku, Azerbaijan, 2004

Tofig Bakhramov was the famous Russian linesman who awarded Geoff Hurst's controversial goal in the 1966 World Cup final. He went on to become general secretary of the Azerbaijan FA and the stadium is named in his honour. But gratitude can only go so far. If only he'd had a brother who was a plumber. This was a concrete encased single facility with an attractive non-flush feature which didn't have a toilet roll holder never mind any paper. Armed soldiers would unlock it for you if you were des-perate enough to go or had suffered a violent reaction to eating at one of the food stalls outside the stadium. The downside was that you had to then provide them with a bribe before they'd let you out.

3.   Atatürk Stadium, Izmir, Turkey, 1991

One of those awful hole in the ground jobs at the basement of a baking stairwell which at least had a holder, but still no paper. The lock had fallen off in 1927 and not been replaced so if you were unlucky enough to need a 'crouch' you had to adopt an uncomfortable stance like a sprinter in the 'set' position but with your arms pressed up against the door. The only saving grace was the fact that the dank, thick stench of cigarette smoke blocked out the other, even more unpleasant odours. A final word of warning, never enter one of these type of toilets with anything in your back pockets as things tend to fall out. Someone once told me of a holidaying mate who had to stick his hand down the hole and fish around to retrieve his passport.

4.   Qemel Stafa Stadium, Tirana, Albania, 2001

To be fair I never actually went into this one. That was the problem, nobody did. It was the only toilet in the whole stadium and was rendered impenetrable by a huge padlock which remained fastened throughout. At half-time I had no option but to join a line of locals pissing up against a wall. I was feeling a little guilty but then looked up to see the half the British press corps queuing up behind me. When in Rome.

5. Olympic Stadium, Moscow, 1992

Nothing much in this stadium worked, least of all the toilets. They stank to high heaven and had all the usual no flush, no paper, no lock, no seat features so popular in Eastern Europe at the time. It was incredible to think the Olympic Games had been staged in this dump just 12 years previously.

CHAPTER THIRTEEN

"Have we scored?"

They say that smell is the most profound of the senses for evoking memories, but luckily I haven't encountered anything quite as hideous as these five insanitary cesspits in the years since and so I'm happy to say my recollections are very much all in the mind.

Albania, for example, is not the sort of place where you expect to find state of the art facilities anywhere. In the half a century since the end of the Second World War the country had, even by the standards of other former communist states within Europe, run a gruesomely hard-line regime. Under the country's authoritarian leader Enver Hoxha, freedom of speech, religion and movement were denied to the population and Albania, socially and politically, became almost completely isolated from the rest of the continent.

When England went to the capital Tirana for the first time in 1989 it was only four years after Hoxha's death and I'm told very little had changed. The people were desperately poor and many technological advances had yet to reach this outpost of mainland Europe. For example, if you hailed a taxi, a horse and cart would pull up and beckon you in.

I had actually visited Albania on a day trip from the Greek island of Corfu during a holiday in 1991, the first year that visitors from abroad had been allowed into the country as tourists. As we approached the coastal town of Sarande by ferry we noticed two tall turrets protruding out of the sea, each topped by a small crow's nest. These, we were told, had been manned by armed soldiers who would shoot dead anyone who strayed a certain distance away from the shore to stop them attempting to swim the two miles across the Ionian Sea to Corfu and from there flee to political asylum in southern Italy. The streets of the town were dusty, potholed and without a car in sight, there were only the most basic of shops and hordes of grubby young kids would surround anyone who stepped off the ferry in the hope of bagging some sweets, chewing gum or other forbidden fruit. Depressingly they also asked us for pens, since the local school didn't have any.

These kids represented the country's immediate post-Stalinist future and there were already signs of a cultural emergence. Many could speak short sentences of English and told us which English teams they supported (Liverpool were very much in favour at the time) and how they idolised the likes of Gary Lineker, Peter Beardsley and Paul Gascoigne. Given what we knew about Albania's isolationist past we wondered how they had become so well versed in the ways of the West.

"Eurosport," they cheerfully explained.

"Have you heard of Watford?" I asked, expecting puzzled stares.

"Yes, yes. Former club of John Bar-Nez."

A decade later I went with England to Tirana for a World Cup qualifier and the globalisation was even more pronounced. The horses and carts had been replaced by proper motorised cabs and there were many more private cars in use. Every now and then the usual, miserable convoy of clapped out rust buckets would be punctuated by the sight of a brand new, top of the range Mercedes or BMW with tinted windows. Communist rule, it seemed, had been replaced by mobster rule as ruthless individuals had quickly pounced into this nascent economy for their own ends. Bars, restaurants and nightclubs had begun to spring up all over the capital, but they were far beyond the grasp of the average citizen who still led a largely hand-to-mouth existence. Our hotel had a large balcony which looked out over one of the main squares, in the middle of which was a depressing gathering of beggars, whores and hustlers who wouldn't have looked out of place in an engraving by Hogarth.

In the dark days of the Hoxha regime, before Eurosport had brought British superstar footballers to the attention of Albanian schoolchildren, any form of foreign entertainment was totally banned by the government. That is, with one notable and surreal exception. The communist leaders decided that it would be instructive to give the population a glimpse of just how decadent and unequal life was in the consumerist and capitalist West. As a result, there were weekly screenings of Norman Wisdom films on state TV. The veteran comedy actor's repressed and yet defiant character of Norman Pitkin, who was forever at odds with his so-called superiors, was held up as the living embodiment of how the free economy spawned a society where spoils were unjustly divided and the toil of the workers went unrewarded.

And so 'Pitkin', as Norman Wisdom was universally known in Albania, became a national hero and was invited to visit the country in 1995, whereupon he received the kind of welcome The Beatles encountered on their first tour of America. Indeed he enjoyed a brief spell of pop stardom himself after releasing a single called *Big In Albania*, which made the national charts.

On the day before the game in 2001, large crowds had formed at the England training camp in Tirana as Sven-Göran Eriksson's team made their final preparations for the match. As the likes of David Beckham, Michael Owen, Rio Ferdinand and Ashley Cole stepped off the team bus a huge gasp came up from the supporters. But their eyes and cameras were trained not on the millionaire, global superstar players in their smart blazers but on a small man in his mid eighties clowning around on the touchline.

"Fucking 'ell it's Norman Wisdom."

In this part of the world Beckham could happily walk unmolested through the streets whenever Norman was in town.

He turned up at the match itself wearing a red and white halved shirt bearing the badges of both nations and entertained the crowd by doing his famous falling over routine in one of the penalty areas. It was one of those occasions when, to use a phrase which is too often employed without genuine justification, you really couldn't make it up.

England won 3-1 with Andy Cole scoring his first and, as it turned out, only international goal. After the game we were lurking around outside the players' entrance hunting suitable interview victims when Cole walked past and gave us a few words on how delighted he was to have finally broken his duck. Just as he was about to get on the coach, one of the fans who was standing a few yards behind us shouted out:

"Hey Andy, congratulations on your first goal for England."

"Cheers," shouted back the happy striker, thumbs aloft.

"Yeah, it makes up for all the other chances you fucking missed in your career."

To be fair, when you've come all the way across to a place like Tirana to support England you're entitled to make your feelings known.

My sorties into post-Stalinist landscapes had begun in earnest on my first trip to Moscow in 1992 when England played a friendly against what was briefly known as the Commonwealth of Independent States during the interregnum between the break-up of the USSR and the establishment of its former members as individual nations. As ever, at that time, I formed an Independent Radio alliance with *Capital*

Radio's Jonathan Pearce who was beginning to make a real name for himself as broadcasting's loudest and most passionate football commentator.

Jonathan's co-commentator in the late eighties and early nineties was Bobby Moore who commanded respect and admiration in equal measure anywhere he went in the world. Given that he had led England to its finest sporting hour at Wembley in 1966 he was almost impossibly humble and self-effacing with a calm air of authority which never once slipped into anything remotely approaching arrogance.

While in Moscow we spent an afternoon doing the tourist trail and I ended up following Bobby down the steps into Lenin's tomb in Red Square. As I reached the foot of the staircase in reverential silence I was confronted by a Russian guard who looked at me, shook his head and raised his hand, the palm facing outward. I was puzzled as to what the problem was and shrugged my shoulders, whereupon Bobby immediately aimed a discreetly pointed finger towards my hip area. He was indicating that I still had my hands in my pockets and I quickly removed them, realising that it was being construed as a rather casual and disrespectful attitude. Bobby gave me one of those stern 'young people of today' kind of looks, having instantly understood the situation and calmly and politely dealt with it leaving me in no doubt that I would never again repeat it. For me it summed up the presence and bearing of a man whose first thought on climbing the Wembley steps to receive the Jules Rimet trophy was to wipe the mud and grass from his hands lest he despoil the Queen's gleaming white gloves.

On the day of the game, Jonathan, Bobby and I were sharing a scruffy little broadcast booth high up and behind thick glass at the back of the main stand in the crumbling Olympic Stadium, which was by now a pale shadow of the gleaming arena in which Steve Ovett and Seb Coe won epic middle distance victories in the 1980 Olympics. None of the lifts were working which meant we had to ascend a grim, concrete staircase several flights up from the written press area to our position and when we got there, like the lifts, our broadcast lines weren't working and there were no telephones either.

Jonathan sent Bobby back down the staircase to call the London studio from one of the newspaper guys' phones to see if they could sort things out and get us on air. We could see him way below chatting away and, eventually, with the game around five minutes old, the red lights flashed on, the lines sprang into life and we were in business. Jonathan picked up his commentary, as I gave the thumbs-up and beckoned for Bobby to come up and rejoin us. As fate would have it, England went ahead within seconds and, as the World Cup winning captain negotiated the gloomy stairwell for the third time that evening, Jonathan was in overdrive:

"Cross from the right, up goes Linekaaaaaaaaaaaaaaahhhhhhhh!!!! England lead 1-0 in Moscow. Gary Lineker up at the near post to head home his 48th international goal putting him just one short of Bobby Charlton's all time record. Just six minutes played, it's CIS nil England one."

Moments later Bobby finally reappeared and sat down.

"Well, what a start for Graham Taylor's men. Bobby Moore is alongside me."

Unruffled, unperturbed and utterly relaxed, Bobby sat down and delivered his reaction:

"Have we scored Pearce-o?"

Tragically, of course, Bobby died the following year and I remember being shocked by his gaunt appearance as he sat alongside Jonathan at Wembley on his last visit to the venue whose name will always be inextricably linked with his. I can't pretend I knew him well, but even a few days in his company demonstrated why his memory will never be lost by football fans as long as the game is played anywhere in the world.

It was around that time that I first ventured into Turkey which almost turned out to be my last trip anywhere. We were headed for Izmir, a populous port city on the Aegean coast for a Euro 92 qualifier, aboard a charter plane which had the media representatives occupying the front seats with the players and coaching staff at the rear. I was sitting just behind one of the wings and could see huge droplets of rain splashing against the window as we were making our final descent into the airport. It was early evening and I was peering through a rapidly gathering storm to try and gain some impression of the city whose blurred, twinkling lights were just about visible below us. All of a sudden I saw a green flash at the window and a sudden lurch as the plane shuddered dramatically as if it had hit a huge divot in the sky, tossing it up then down before, thankfully, regaining an even keel.

It turned out that the engine on one of the wings had been clipped by a bolt of lightning causing the aircraft to wobble in the air causing a brief but awful heart in mouth moment when you fear the very worst. It was an ashen-faced and very relieved press corps who finally disembarked, although the players seemed remarkably unshaken by the experience. I spoke to Ian Wright about it and he said: "Didn't notice mate, I was asleep with the headphones on."

That reaction is not quite as surprising as it sounds. The players often drift through these excursions in a state of near total oblivion, which is understandable given the regime imposed on them when representing their country abroad. While we journalists can sample the history, culture, nightlife, restaurants and bars on these trips, for the players it's akin to being sequestered in a particularly hardline cloister of Franciscan monks.

A visit to a fascinating location such as Istanbul, Rio de Janeiro or Casablanca consists of little more than airports, coaches, hotel rooms, training grounds and the game itself. Their diet is strictly monitored, obviously there's no room for alcohol and most while away the hours watching DVDs, listening to music or playing cards. The overriding emotion appears to be boredom and all the apparent glitz and glamour of life as an international footballer is counterbalanced by the often very humdrum nature of their everyday existence. How they must envy the ex-players who have turned pundits and can happily join the press gang in sampling the delights of a few days off the leash in an unusual setting. As well as Bobby Moore, other travelling companions I've had the pleasure of spending time with are Terry Butcher, Tony Gale, Neil Webb, Alan Smith, Terry Neill, Clive Allen and David Speedie.

Terry Butcher, through sheer force of personality, looms large in many of these adventures. Some players, understandably, are a little reticent when it comes to mixing with the supporters as they often get pestered and, occasionally, abused by some of the travelling fans. Butch though was universally loved by the England faithful for his passionate, never-say-die style of play and the unquenchable pride and passion he demonstrated in his 77 matches wearing the Three Lions on his chest. He liked nothing better than to get amongst the fans who treated him with awe and reverence. I remember a night in Malta when he heard an AC/DC song blaring out of the speakers at a lively bar and waded straight into the centre of the dance floor and began moshing with the best of them.

He loved heavy metal music and even had Guns'n'Roses' *Sweet Child Of Mine* as his mobile ring-tone. Aside from his footballing achievements, he told me his proudest moment was when he and former Ipswich team-mate Paul Mariner were invited to sing backing vocals at an Iron Maiden concert. Even now I am still reminded of him every time I hear *Pretty Fly (For A White Guy)* by the Offspring. In the course of a drunken night out in the Bulgarian capital Sofia, the song was played repeatedly at one of the bars we visited and thereafter became a theme tune. For days afterwards we would greet each other by screaming: "Give it to me baby. A-ha A-haaaaaaah!"

Which would prompt quite a few strange looks from the other guests at the hotel.

On another sortie into the wastelands of Eastern Europe, Butch almost caused permanent damage to my eardrums in a rather different way. We were in Macedonia for a Euro 2004 qualifier in the capital Skopje. By this time, we radio reporters were benefiting from the introduction of a wonderful new piece of kit called a sat-phone which worked in the same way as an ISDN, but without the need to pre-book a broadcast line. You could set it up in any outdoor location and by pointing a little satellite dish at the sky and, via some transmitting device orbiting the planet, contact the newsroom and send back studio quality audio from virtually anywhere. Unfortunately they didn't work indoors or in stadiums as the signal would break up if anything got between the dish and the heavens.

It was early September and gloriously sunny in the historic old town and we would set up our dishes on a daily basis in a little car park just outside the hotel and file away in our shirtsleeves to our hearts' content. The afternoon before the game I was sending down a voice piece when I saw Butch wandering towards me. As I was in full flow he came up and stood right in front of the dish causing the signal to break up and send a hideous screech of hiss and feedback into my headphones. The guys in London who were diligently recording the piece would have been a little surprised at its content:

". . . Wayne Rooney hopes to become England's youngest ever goalscoraaaaaaaaaaaaaaaaaaaaaaaaaaahhhhh . . . Butch get out of the fucking way . . . aaaaahhhh . . . Jesus you nearly blew my fucking head off."

"Sorry mate, just wondered what you were up to," he replied and strolled off again, hands in pockets, as if nothing had happened.

Rooney did become England's youngest ever scorer and England won the game thanks to his goal and a David Beckham penalty. Just before the spot kick was awarded a Macedonian journalist decided to get up off his seat and leave the press box. As he did so he kicked the plug out of the mains socket from which Dominic McGuinness from *talkSPORT* and I were powering our ISDN units and took us both off air. We were doing 'as live' commentary which was being recorded back home so that the goal clips could later be sent out, but by the time we'd re-established contact the goal had gone in and the moment had passed. So, during a lull in the game soon afterwards we both had to do a pretend commentary on the whole penalty incident, which puzzled a section of the crowd nearby who wondered why these two Englishmen were loudly and enthusiastically describing a goal which had been scored a couple of minutes earlier.

* * * * *

My journey as the senior sports reporter at Independent Radio News ended in a suitably surreal location as I found myself in Baku, the capital city of Azerbaijan, a country I had scarcely even heard of when it popped out of the draw alongside England in the qualification group for the 2006 World Cup.

It was one of those places that you have to pay an admission fee to get into, so I went to the Azerbaijani embassy in west London to get a visa which, in truth, was a blatant piece of chicanery designed to extort fifty quid from you in return for a rather pointless stamp in your passport. I had to tell the almost impossibly laid back bureaucrats at the embassy to hurry up as I'd been summoned to a meeting that afternoon which would feature a 'major announcement' about the future of IRN. I'd been in the industry long enough to know that this was unlikely to feature plans for across the board pay rises, free health care and the construction of a giant go-kart track for the staff to use between shifts.

Inevitably, the very management dickheads who probably couldn't even spell brewery let alone organise a piss-up in one, uttered glib phrases like 'core services', 'downscaling' and 'market forces' while informing us that the service was to be drastically slashed, with departments pared down and jobs lost. Strangely these job losses did not include any in management positions, despite the fact that thousands of pounds would have been saved, productivity trebled and morale incalculably boosted by replacing the Editor in Chief and his News Editor with a wastepaper basket and a pot plant.

Under this proud new regime there was to be a reduction in sports output, which meant major events would no longer be covered as the majority of the material would be generated from a desk at the ITN HQ at Grays Inn Road rather than by reporters in the field. By the time all the bullshit about how this had been a very difficult decision to take but that the output wouldn't be affected had been spouted by these vanguards of the later global recession, I had already decided to move on.

But first I had my final mission; three days in a former Soviet gas and petroleum centre on the shores of the Caspian Sea with Iran to the south, Georgia to the north, Armenia to the west and, across the water, Turkmenistan. This place belonged to Asia more than Europe, but UEFA is always keen to broaden its horizons and so the likes of Azerbaijan, and the even more remote Kazakhstan, had been welcomed into the European qualifying groups with open arms. If intelligent life were ever discovered on Mars and they formed a football team, UEFA would be first to stick their flag into the permafrost and claim it as theirs.

The city of Baku was a quaint mixture of Soviet, Asian and Western influences but was spoilt a little by the invasive and pervading stench of petrol which seemed to permeate the entire area. You had to be careful lighting a fag in case the whole place went up in flames. While most of the media party were housed in a modern hotel in the centre of town which had a giant underground nightclub, we broadcasters stayed in the old town right by the Caspian shore. A short walk from our hotel was a tall watchtower which offered great views across the water and from there you could walk up a couple of flights of stone steps into a wonderful medieval looking district full of little coffee shops and restaurants. It was one of those places, rather like Albania and Turkey, where you got the distinct impression that there were stiff custodial sentences in prospect for any man caught in public without a moustache or a cigarette.

We'd been told prior to arrival that, although it was mid-October, the weather would be very pleasant, somewhere around 28 degrees Celsius, and so I travelled fairly light, packing a couple of summer shirts and a thin, cotton jacket for the evenings. The forecast certainly held true throughout our first day there. The sun shone down gloriously, dappling the calm waters of the Caspian Sea as the locals thronged the parks and squares in shirtsleeves. A group of us including Graham Taylor, Terry Butcher, Mike Ingham, Charlotte Nicol and *talkSPORT* reporter Mike Bovill enjoyed a wonderful lunch, dining al fresco in the courtyard of what looked like a 15th century fort.

However, this part of the world, we later discovered, is prone to quite dramatic meteorological extremes. Temperatures as diverse as minus 33 degrees and plus 46 degrees Celsius have been recorded in Azerbaijan which must give the inhabitants some rather complicated wardrobe dilemmas: "Now then, what shall I wear today? Thong and flip-flops or caribou-fur Inuit fisherman's anorak?"

On the day of the game, the prevailing conditions changed dramatically. A bitter wind blew through the city, sheets of frozen rain lashed down from above and the temperature had gone from Iberian to Siberian overnight. Imagine waking up in your holiday apartment in Dubai to be met with the kind of weather that greets away fans to Boundary Park, Oldham in mid December. Even though I put three layers on, none of them were particularly hard-wearing and I might as well have been wrapped in a giant sheet of three-ply Andrex.

As I mentioned before, the Tofig Bakhramov Stadium in Baku is named after the match official who allowed England's third goal to stand in the 1966 World Cup final. Although forever known as 'the Russian linesman', this is a misnomer as Bakhramov was in fact from Azerbaijan. Of course he is also a hero to England supporters, many of whom arrived in Baku wearing the famous red shirt with Bakhramov's name and the number 66 on the back; indeed a statue was unveiled in his honour prior to the game. Given the hugely variable weather conditions in his native country, I'm tempted to suggest that after a lifetime's exposure to a mixture of extreme heat and extreme cold, Mr Bakhramov's shoulder and elbow joints seized up completely just as Geoff Hurst's shot came down off the crossbar and hence the flag stayed down.

Unfortunately the stadium that bears his name offered very little in the way of respite from the icy conditions I was experiencing 38 years later. There were no press facilities at all and we were denied access to the interior of the stadium by the sort of armed guards with whom you do not try to reason. As was my custom I had arrived some three hours before kick-off to ensure that the telecommunications lines we had booked had been installed and that I could set up my equipment with plenty of time to spare. Unfortunately the media tribune consisted of a row of open air seats without an ISDN or telephone line in sight and there was no-one around to help us sort it out. Mike Bovill and I set up a sat-phone the other side of a fence facing away from the pitch but the signal was erratic at best and I felt it safer to file during the match using my mobile phone.

It was impossible to refer to any of my prepared notes as the still torrential rain reduced them to pulp within seconds and when the team sheets finally arrived 15 minutes into the game they dissolved into the mass of wet slush on the table top on front of me. The Azerbaijan players could have been called Sentov, Pissov and Getcharocksov as far as I was concerned.

Happily the mobile signal was strong enough to get the immediate job done and at least I could record the interviews and feed them back from the sat-phone at the hotel later on. When we returned at around 11pm I found a flight of stairs leading from the restaurant to the roof of the hotel and headed up there to send the stuff back. It's not unusual to see radio reporters wandering around rooftops with satellite dishes, since the absence of anything between yourself and the sky generally guarantees an excellent signal without the bothersome trial and error which you often experienced on the ground where large obstacles like Terry Butcher were a constant threat.

Mind you, there was the odd hazard up on the roof too as my IRN colleague Andrew Cheal discovered in Japan during the 2002 World Cup. He'd gained access to the very top of a high rise hotel in Niigata via a ladder and a trap door and had established contact with the forces broadcaster BFBS who were interviewing him live in their sports programme. In mid stream, out of the corner of his eye, he noticed a Japanese security guard appear out of the little door, poke his head around and then disappear back down the staircase. Ever the professional, Chealy completed his interview and then, fearing the worst, checked the door. It was locked tight and he found himself stranded on top of the 23rd floor of a city centre skyscraper with night rapidly falling.

Luckily fellow radio reporter Gary Weaver was waiting for him in the bar, so he decided to call him and get some help to liberate himself from this high altitude prison. As Chealy took out his phone, he noticed with horror and increasing panic that the battery was stone dead. In the end he dialled up the IRN studio on his ISDN unit, spoke to someone there who got hold of Gary's number and phoned him in the hotel bar and he in turn located the security guard so that the door to the roof could be unlocked. The alternative would have been a night spent, literally, on the tiles.

In the far less hospitable weather of Baku, I was keen to get everything filed as quickly as possible and was delighted to hit the satellite first time and as the interviews were being fed I peered enviously through a glass panel into the restaurant below where people were dining and drinking to their hearts' content. I hadn't eaten since breakfast and the thought of food and beer increased my impatience. It was about half an hour later, although it felt more like several weeks, when I finally sent down the last piece of audio.

"Everything okay guys, am I clear?"

"Er, just hang on mate . . . the computer system's just gone down . . . I think we've lost it . . . oh shit, it's gone . . . sorry . . . you'll have to feed the whole lot again."

By the time I'd sent it all down for a second time it was midnight and the pitch black sky was flecked with snowflakes which were being swirled around in the petrol-stinking wind which was blowing in off the Caspian Sea. I had been out in the freezing open air for the best part of seven hours, dressed for a late spring barbecue, my clothes sticking to my skin, chilled to the very bone and as close as I have ever come to experiencing hypothermia. It was a fittingly surreal end to the whole damn journey.

Do you still want to carry my bags?

CHAPTER FOURTEEN

"Scalded Cat"

I left Independent Radio News on October 29th 2004, three days before my 44th birthday, after 17 years working on the sports desk. Given that the future of the organisation seemed to be deliberately and cynically geared towards minimalist mediocrity, I had few regrets as I picked up a redundancy cheque and headed into the unknown waters of freelance broadcasting.

When I first joined IRN in 1987, reporters were ordered to bring their passports with them to work every day in case they were suddenly dispatched to some godforsaken corner of the world to cover a breaking story. By the end of the 1990s, with the honourable exception of the sports desk, they needed little more than a London Transport two zone travel card and by the time I left they weren't even allowed to go to the toilet without a meeting with their line manager and subsequent debrief.

Several others, including my long time sports desk colleague Andrew Cheal, had also decided that ITN's "exciting new direction" represented little more than a bunch of junior accountants running a sweet shop and decided their time was up too. We had a leaving do in a function room at the Cheshire Cheese, fittingly, where many of the faces we'd worked with in the past turned up to make it a brilliant night. By coincidence, at around the same time, Adrian Bevington and Joanne Budd had organised a press reception for the then England manager Sven-Goran Eriksson and I was able to have a drink with many of the people who had helped make my years on the road so memorable and enjoyable.

In truth though, I felt a bit like the only survivor of a treasure laden clipper ship that's capsized and who's forced to negotiate shark infested waters in a leaky, one seater rowing boat. Being a rather lazy and disorganised person by nature, I found the prospect of facing the vagaries of life as a free agent, with all its randomness, insecurity and paranoia, a little bit terrifying. Most freelancers will tell you that they spend much of their professional lives yo-yoing between euphoria and despair. I'm not a natural networker but fortunately I had several personal friends who were generous enough to either give me offers of work or helpful advice on how to get it.

One such was Stephen Booth, a BBC television producer who I'd got to know through a mutual love of music (he's the only other Tanya Donelly fan in British sports broadcasting as far as I know) and with whom I'd sneaked out to see the Pixies in concert at a festival in Lisbon during Euro 2004, after telling my IRN colleague Elliot Cook that, if anyone asks, I was locked in a top level meeting with the FA media department and couldn't be disturbed. Boothy was a great guy to have around on trips such as these and we would spend as much time chatting about our favourite bands as we would discussing the football. It was at that tournament that he, along with his BBC colleague Lance Hardy, hit upon a great idea to spend an evening away from all the football analysis and shop talk.

They organised a group of around a dozen of the most ardent music fans amongst the England media corps at our base at the Marriott Hotel and asked us to compile a list of our Top 50 albums of all time. We would then reconvene a week later over a meal in the hotel restaurant and everyone would go through their selections, with each vote then counted to form a chart rundown of the overall winners. Compilations were banned and so, controversially in my opinion, were live albums. I had planned to include both the Ramones' blistering double set "It's Alive" and "Bob Marley & The Wailers Live At The Lyceum". The only other rule was that, under no circumstances, was football to be mentioned during the dinner.

Despite these bureaucratic setbacks, I must confess that, for those few days in Portugal, I was probably just as concerned with the relative merits of The Queen Is Dead, Ziggy Stardust and Marquee Moon as I was about England's European Championships campaign. And I'm willing to bet that there were a fair few others who felt the same way. As we hung around waiting for the daily media conferences, song selection rather than team selection became the topic of choice and even those outside our little circle of music critics became engrossed in this new obsession. Admittedly, most of them merely dismissed us as a bunch of overgrown schoolboy saddoes trying to recapture the spirit of our youth. Fair point.

Definitely out of the running for a place at the table was the *Daily Mirror*'s Martin Lipton. He had such a feeble grip on contemporary music culture that he once confessed to me that the only CD he'd ever owned was the traditional Greek folk music compilation the rest of us had thrown in the bin after the mad scramble for freebies in Gothenburg in 1995. I once mentioned this to a fellow music loving football journalist and he was aghast:

"He's got no albums at all? That's like having no soul."

"Yeah, and no rock, pop, reggae, funk, punk, post punk, or indie either," I replied, "but, on the plus side, no rap, techno or jazz."

When the Lisbon equivalent of Round Table arrived, I took my seat excitedly clutching a sheet of paper torn from my reporters' pad containing my crucial 50 selections. I won't bore you with the entire line-up, but the Top 10 was as follows:

1. Marquee Moon - Television
2. The Rise and Fall of Ziggy Stardust & the Spiders From Mars - David Bowie
3. Underwater Moonlight - The Soft Boys
4. The Queen Is Dead - The Smiths
5. Even Serpents Shine - The Only Ones
6. The Velvet Underground & Nico - The Velvet Underground
7 Q:Are We Not Men? A:We Are Devo - Devo
8. Unknown Pleasures - Joy Division
9. Talk Talk Talk - The Psychedelic Furs
10. Perverted By Language - The Fall

Also among the panel were such giants of musical critique as Henry Winter (*Daily Telegraph*), Shaun Custis (the *Sun*) and Mike Ingham (*5Live*) as well as myself, Lance and Boothy.

The evening got off to a fairly promising start, in which we nodded our heads in approval of the thoughtful inclusion of quality LPs by the likes of Bob Dylan, The Doors, Led Zeppelin, The Clash, Patti Smith and James Brown. But the spirit of mutual admiration was, to borrow a footballing expression, turned on its head in a disastrous five minute spell during which Messrs Winter and Custis both nominated "A Present For Everyone" by current teenybop favourites Busted, whose fan base included my own two daughters, then aged 7 and 2. This drew howls of derision from the serious musos amongst us who poured scorn and vitriol on the pair.

To be fair, they defended their corner manfully, citing a grasp of the prevailing pop zeitgeist, but all sympathy we might have had for Shaun evaporated completely when he proceeded to name Permission To Land by panto metal has beens The Darkness in his Top 10.

Thankfully he was in the minority and the final overall Top 10 contained some classic albums:

1. Nevermind - Nirvana
2. Never Mind The Bollocks - Sex Pistols
3. The Queen Is Dead - The Smiths
4. The Smiths - The Smiths
5. Sgt.Pepper's Lonely Hearts Club Band - The Beatles
6. Ziggy Stardust - David Bowie
7. Definitely Maybe - Oasis
8. Dark Side Of The Moon - Pink Floyd
9. Hunky Dory - David Bowie
10. Unknown Pleasures - Joy Division

I've often wondered what our fellow diners at the restaurant made of it all, as their enjoyment of the foie gras and pan fried sea bass was interrupted by such nuggets of wisdom as "Generation Terrorists? Surely The Holy Bible was their masterpiece", "you see I consider the mid 70s to be Dylan's golden age" and "ELO? You're having a laugh."

The evening had been a wonderful diversion from the business of covering Euro 2004 and was so thoroughly enjoyed by the participants, that a second instalment was quickly arranged, in which we would have to name our Top 50 singles of all time. Again, I offer you my Top 10:

1. This Charming Man - The Smiths
2. Roadrunner - Jonathan Richman & the Modern Lovers
3. Another Girl, Another Planet - The Only Ones
4. God Save The Queen - The Sex Pistols
5. Marquee Moon -Television
6. Atmosphere - Joy Division
7. Pretty In Pink - The Psychedelic Furs
8. Holiday In Cambodia - Dead Kennedys
9. Complete Control - The Clash
10. Kicker Conspiracy - The Fall

In comparing this with my albums list, I notice that six of the artists are replicated, which suggests that my tastes aren't as eclectic as I thought.

Episode two of the Marriott Music Club dinner had to be expanded due to the increased number of people who wanted to take part and included a few who didn't seem to be genuine music fans which, for snobs like me, rather diluted the quality of the selections. Some appeared to have got the wrong end of the stick completely. One of the girls who worked for the travel company which organised the trip for the England media arrived, dressed to impress, in her finest frock and heavy make-up.

"Hello everyone, I'm here for the singles night."

Among the other highlights were Mike Ingham, *5Live*'s laid back and sagely chief football correspondent, kicking off the evening by announcing that his number 50 was Enter Sandman by Metallica, and someone (though not Henry or Shaun this time) picking Love Me For A Reason by The Osmonds. Disappointingly, I was the only person to nominate The Trumpton Riots by Half Man Half Biscuit.

Despite my misgivings about some of the participants, the final result is, again, a pretty decent selection:

1. Teenage Kicks - The Undertones
2. Tainted Love - Soft Cell
3. God Only Knows - The Beach Boys
4. Waterloo Sunset - The Kinks
5. Life On Mars? - David Bowie
6. Love Will Tear Us Apart - Joy Division
7. This Charming Man - The Smiths
8. The Story Of The Blues - Wah!
9. Don't Fear The Reaper - Blue Oyster Cult
10. Like A Rolling Stone - Bob Dylan

Quite apart from their skills at organising music themed dinner parties, Boothy and Lance were both key production staff at the BBC's *Final Score* programme and, within days of me leaving IRN, invited me to join their reporting team, although I had to start at the bottom in terms of the matches I was covering. I quickly added Swansea, Peterborough and Scunthorpe to my list of football grounds visited but, while very grateful for being given the chance to broadcast on national television, I still harboured a desire to get back to covering games at the top level.

The chance came when my phone rang while I was out food shopping and John Lyles, the then producer on *Sky Sports' Football First* show, offered me a crack at commentating on a Premier League fixture. I had taken the advice of my old mate Bill Leslie, who'd left *Capital Gold* and got some freelance work at Sky, and sent them a demo CD of some radio commentary clips and, amazingly, it was deemed sufficiently promising for them to offer me the chance to work on the programme. So, a few weeks after leaving IRN, I was in the TV gantry at Goodison Park for a Premier League game between Everton and Fulham. After 20 years of having a great face for radio, I now had a great voice for television.

I don't mind admitting that I was beset by the kind of nerves that I hadn't experienced since waiting for the gun to go off before the 1988 Olympic 100 metres final. As a radio commentator I was very much of the gobshite variety, decorating a blank canvas in an aural tribute to Jackson Pollock as I spat out machine gun bursts of staccato narrative. Television, with its added dimension of pictures, required a far more measured approach, in which the overriding rule of thumb seemed to be "less is more". Bill had told me that I would probably reach a point during the game when I felt I wasn't saying enough and that would be the point where I'd probably got it just about right. Furthermore, you had to keep an eye on your TV monitor as well as the action on the pitch itself to make sure your commentary matched the pictures being seen at home. It was no good crapping on about Fulham's poor away record, if the director has selected a close-up shot of David Moyes scowling in the dug-out.

It was also less advisable to leap to opinions, since close-ups and replays could often prove you completely wrong. For example, a player could go down injured after an aerial challenge and you might be tempted to suggest that he made rather a meal of it.

"He's gone down clutching his face as if he's been hit by a truck, but I don't think there was any contact and it all looks very theatrical."

At which point the director will cut to a close-up and the player will roll towards the camera revealing a three inch gash above his eye with his face barely visible through a waterfall of blood.

One of the great things about working for TV rather than radio is the level of backup you get in terms of directorial and production staff. On a typical IRN outside broadcast I would turn up, plug in and spout off; here there was a phalanx of trucks and a crew of around 70 on hand to make things click. It was daunting to think that I could ruin the whole thing by failing to produce a decent commentary. Fortunately John had put me in very good hands for my first Sky OB. I had Grant Best directing the pictures from the truck and offering his advice, experience and guidance, while floor manager Brett Smart organised everything on the ground and made sure I had all the technical and logistical backup to see me through.

Alongside me in the gantry to add expert analysis in the "co-comm" chair was former England striker Garry Birtles, who was a key part of Brian Clough's legendary Nottingham Forest side of the late 70s and early 80s. He was one of those players who'd come late into the game via non-league football, having already taken up a trade on leaving school. He described himself as "the only carpet fitter to have won two European Cups", surely a distinction which will never be matched, unless Lionel Messi packs it all in for a stint at the Buenos Aires branch of Carpetright.

In the end I was lucky that the game was a fairly uneventful and straightforward affair won by a towering header from the unmistakeable figure of Duncan Ferguson, who met a corner from Kevin Kilbane. I thought I'd done okay and, at the end, Garry shook my hand and said "you almost sounded like a professional" while John Lyles later observed that he'd "heard an awful lot worse". *Sky Sports* is the sort of company which, quite rightly, sets high standards and expects them to be met, so this was high praise indeed.

I became good mates with Garry who, like Terry Butcher, was a big AC/DC fan and was thrilled the time my wife was able to score him a couple of tickets for a show by Angus and the boys at the 02. Because of his background following his dad into the carpet trade, Garry had seen a less glamorous side of life and had a totally different set of work and personal ethics from many footballers, especially the modern day ones. He was always immaculately dressed and never wore tracksuits or trainers on the grounds that he'd spent most of his playing life wearing them and was fed up with it. He was also very particular about table etiquette, being very much of the school that believes manners maketh man and that cleanliness is next to godliness. Unfortunately in my case, cleanliness was next to impossible; I couldn't walk past a bowl of soup without half of it ending up down my shirt.

Almost every time we covered a match together, Garry would sit there with a pained expression on his face, tut-tutting his way through the pre-match media room meal as I slurped and slobbered away, occasionally launching bits of lasagne and chilli in his direction. The nadir came before a game at Reading when I managed to decorate my tie with a one inch wide stripe of chasseur sauce from top to bottom. Garry was appalled.

"Look at him, look at him! He's a disgrace," he shouted to our fellow diners.

It became a standing joke. Whenever a group of commentators would gather in the Sky staff canteen, I would walk in to be greeted by cries of:

"Oh God, here he comes, quick take cover."

Whereupon they would all cower under the tables holding up imaginary perspex shields.

In addition to the *Sky Sports* work, I would also cover matches "off tube" for a variety of broadcast outlets who would syndicate English language commentaries to foreign broadcasters and websites. This involved commentating from pictures beamed in on a TV monitor rather than being at the game itself. Although you would be describing the action from Montevideo, Asuncion or Podgorica the whole broadcast would be generated from a small cubicle in a far less exotic location such as Feltham, Wimbledon or Shepherd's Bush. In effect you are seeing exactly the same feed of pictures as any viewer in their living room.

This is an awful lot harder than it sounds, given that you are often at the mercy of a foreign match director and the images that they choose to present you with on screen don't always conform to your expectations. It's generally acknowledged that *Sky Sports* leads the world in its technical coverage of football matches, so I was very lucky to be working for the best in the business, but many outside organisations fell far short of these standards. For example you could be hailing a goal for Peru in Lima and showing off the impressive knowledge you've gained from two days of statistical preparation.

"Jefferson Farfan gets on the end of Solano's pinpoint cross…..Peru lead with only 13 minutes played….it's the PSV Eindhoven striker's 10th international goal….and the crowd at the Estadio Nacional goes wild."

But as you're uttering the words and nodding smugly to yourself at how well that seemed to have encapsulated the situation, the director might cut to a crowd shot of the Peruvian fans celebrating wildly and then an image of the two dug-outs before the pictures finally show an assistant referee with his flag raised for offside. This would force a hasty reappraisal.

"But he'll to wait a little longer to reach double figures…the goal's been disallowed by the Colombian referee…and the crowd is silenced. "

In another instance you might have no idea who got the final touch when a goal is scrambled in after a melee in the six yard box and your confusion is compounded by the director who, instead of tracking the goal scorer, unhelpfully chooses to go straight to a close-up of the frustrated goalkeeper or jubilant coach. By the time they've cut back to the celebration, whoever scored is underneath a huge pile of ecstatic team-mates and you have to wait for each and every one of them to get up until, after what seems like an hour has elapsed, the identity of the scorer is finally revealed.

Another pitfall of trying to commentate accurately from a distance of several thousand miles is the wholly inadequate shirt numbering employed by certain sides; such disparate entities as the Peruvian national team and Doncaster Rovers spring quickly to mind. In both instances the dark numbers are virtually indistinguishable from the stripes or hoops on the playing strip, especially when viewing wide-shots on a fuzzy monitor in a darkened west London studio.

When faced with off-tube commentaries I usually spend the first ten minutes of the game delivering a geography and history lesson while trying desperately to work out the identities of players, many of whom you've never seen before. The viewer will be treated to a fascinating succession of details about the stadium, the town itself, the history of the fixture and the significance of the occasion, whereas what you're actually concentrating on is whether the long haired midfielder is actually number 15 or number 18 and why there seems to be a number 22 on the field when he doesn't appear on the team sheet, which you sometimes receive only minutes before kick-off. The default setting is to concentrate on the players that you do know. I guarantee the next time you watch a South American qualifier between Ecuador and Uruguay, Antonio Valencia and Diego Forlan will see plenty of the ball early on.

One of my most panicky moments came during an Asian Champions League game between two teams from the United Arab Emirates and Qatar which I was covering for various betting websites and other internet clients. Normally when you're actually at the ground, a team sheet will arrive around 45 minutes before kick-off with the two teams listed on it, but if you're commentating off tube these are somewhat harder to get hold of. In some cases your producer will have a contact at the stadium who will either fax or email the details through, although they often arrive dangerously close to kick-off time and you have little time to digest the two sets of numbers. Typically, this was the case here and a sheet of paper landed on my desk less than five minutes before the game started. In such circumstances, the last thing you want is an early goal but of course, sod's law, one of the teams scored inside the opening minute.

Fortunately it was quite clearly the number 19 who had put the ball into the net, so all I had to do was glance down at my team sheet to identify the player. However I noticed, with some alarm, that there was no number 19 listed, and a further check revealed there wasn't even a number 19 in the squad. Given that most of the audience wouldn't be too familiar with the players involved I simply mumbled a vague approximation of the right sort of name very quickly to cover my tracks:

"Al-Ahli take the lead......(enormous pause while I refer to notes).....just 58 seconds played....(ensuing panic at non-existence of goal scorer).........an extraordinary opening to this game.....(realisation that I would have to say something).........and el Huhbudubollah has got the goal."

It turned out to be a misprint on the team sheet and I eventually worked out, by a process of elimination, that the player had been accidentally listed on the sheet of paper in front of me as number 9 instead of 19 and el Huhbudubollah was never heard of again.

Being someone who had thoroughly enjoyed travelling to some interesting and unusual locations to cover events, I must admit it was a little frustrating to be trapped in a booth in London watching pictures of stadiums perched high up in the Andes, located in bustling city streets or surrounded by sun parched deserts. On the plus side though, it was a lot easier to get home. However I was grateful to be in a warm studio when I provided the commentary for a Euro 2012 qualifier between the Faroe Islands and Slovenia. It was early June and most of Europe was sweltering in a heatwave, but the weather was rather different in the Faroese fishing village of Toftir (pop: 823) where the match took place.

The Faroes, a dependency of Denmark, is a tiny cluster of 18 islands located in the north Atlantic, roughly halfway between Norway and Iceland and not a place to which visitors normally arrive armed with an inflatable lilo and a bucket and spade. The average summer temperature is no more than 13 degrees Celsius and I can only assume the wealthiest man on the islands is the bloke who runs the kagoule shop. He had certainly sold out on the day of the game as several hundred spectators huddled in the tiny unroofed stadium, which was being battered by gales and torrential rain. The pitch was more ploughed field than manicured lawn and frankly, water polo would have been a more suitable sport to stage on it.

The main problem I had as a commentator was the fact that large droplets of rain kept falling onto the cameras thus obscuring my view of the match. It was like trying to describe the game through the porthole of a Trident submarine. At one point in the second half, I was anticipating a Slovenian attack when all the viewers and I saw was a hand clutching a cloth stretching across and wiping the lens vigorously. The cameraman presumably thought the director had cut to one of his colleagues and took the opportunity to clean his lens, oblivious to the fact that his pictures were still in shot. Credit to the visiting team, they managed to win the game 2-0 and I can only imagine how good the hot showers must have felt afterwards.

These hazards are of the occupational variety for commentators and you eventually learn to deal with them. There are, however, some people who expect, indeed demand, that we perform with an android-like consistency under any circumstance, and consider even the slightest error, stumble or hesitation to be a total abdication of responsibility worthy of excommunication from the ranks of their profession.

This I know because of a shameful lapse into personal vanity which persuaded me one day to type "John Anderson" + "football commentator" into the Google search engine. I realise that most people have, at some stage, googled their own names but I should have realised that this was asking for trouble, after suffering a bizarre experience during one of my first ever encounters with the internet. My wife, who is a good deal more technologically gifted that I am, got us connected for the first time in 1997 and I was intrigued by the possibilities of this new innovation which, as I loudly told anyone who'd listen, would surely go the same way as Betamax video, Sinclair C5s and Terence Trent D'Arby.

I decided to start with the basics and did a search on the single word "Anderson". Within seconds I was transported to a website devoted to the pneumatic charms of Baywatch actress Pamela Anderson. A single click later and I was watching a video of her then husband, Motley Crue drummer Tommy Lee, steering a speedboat with a part of his anatomy which is not generally employed to perform such a task. Almost reassuringly, I was then able to witness Pamela enjoying the aforementioned organ in its more customary function with commendable gusto. Coincidentally my aunt, who sadly died that same year, was also called Pamela Anderson. She was a dinner lady in Bournemouth.

My subsequent commentary-related vanity search produced results which, in some ways, were even more shocking and unexpected. In the great Pandora's Box which is the internet, it is hardly surprising, with human nature being what it is, that a casual trawl through cyberspace should unearth an endless myriad of pornography.

However, unbeknown to me, there were other "specialist" sites which catered for a sub-species of unfortunate individuals who were afflicted with a (thankfully rare) disorder which renders them completely obsessed with football commentators. From what I could gather, many of these diehard perfectionists appeared to spend most of their leisure time hunched on a sofa with a TV remote control in one hand and a mouse in the other, making largely derogatory comments on chat forums about those whose job it is to describe football matches via the medium of television. Such nuggets of wisdom would include comments like:

"Shocking call on the third goal from Anfield."

"Anderson is simply awful, he sounded like a scalded cat when the equaliser went in."

"How on earth did that local radio screamer ever end up commentating on national television."

"The player identification in the APOEL Nicosia v Sturm Graz game was simply unacceptable."

Their vitriol seemed perversely rather touching. It was as if they genuinely believed we were deliberately setting out to ruin their lives by producing substandard commentaries. They always referred to us by our surnames in the style of that opinionated character from the Harry Enfield sketch who has nothing but contempt for people in the public eye.

"Oi, Tyldesley...no."

The only pleasure they appeared to draw from our efforts was a Fantasy Football style weekly competition in which they tried to predict which pairings of commentators Sky would use at the forthcoming weekend Premier League matches. They would go apoplectic with excitement if it transpired that they had correctly guessed that Rob Palmer and Warren Barton would be at Bolton v West Ham. A league table would then be published and the winner, presumably, was crowned Anorak of the Week.

To be fair they did have their favourites; Mowbray, Mann and Champion seemed to go down well but most of us were considered either too excitable or too dull. I was very much cast in the former category and almost universally held in contempt. There was also an end of season awards thread in which I was invariably nominated in the "Worst Commentator" category.

I found myself becoming increasingly fascinated by this esoteric and clandestine brotherhood (unsurprisingly very few women were attracted) in which a microscopic section of the cyber community devoted so much time and energy to something which most people would scarcely display any more than a passing interest in. I once even entered the discussion myself and volunteered to appear at their annual dinner if I ever scooped the much coveted "Worst Commentator" gong. This gala evening, I envisaged, would be held at a bus shelter in west London, attended by 14 overweight men in Star Trek T-shirts, dribbling into their kebabs before planning a full blown assault on the 24-hour Shell garage's top shelf magazine section en route home to their bedsits.

My interest ended abruptly though, when Jacqui Oatley's appearance as the first ever female commentator on *Match Of The Day* was greeted with the kind of misogynistic bile you would only otherwise expect to hear from the militant wing of the Bernard Manning fan club. On the day the pioneering Jacqui made the headlines (a Fulham v Blackburn game at Craven Cottage in April 2007), I was at the other end of the gantry providing the Sky commentary. Bizarrely this had become front page news and the whole thing had turned into a bit of a circus. A posse of photographers followed us around the pitch as we walked from the tunnel towards our commentary position and, at one point, one of the snappers asked me rather abruptly to get out of the way so that he could get a better shot of our heroine who, to her eternal credit, seemed to be as embarrassed as anyone about all the fuss.

I was tempted to tell him where to stick his telephoto lens but thought better of it and moved across a fraction, secretly hoping all his shots would include my left arm.

I thought back to my first TV commentary at Everton and how nervous I had been and couldn't imagine how Jacqui must have been feeling, given that she had the added pressure of being the subject of every phone-in show and pub conversation that week. After the game I congratulated her and said words to the effect that, whatever the reaction was, she had achieved something that no-one else had done before and nothing could take that away.

Others weren't quite so magnanimous. So hideously unfair and unpleasant was some of the downright sexist criticism directed at her by the self-appointed online commentating "cognoscenti" that I logged off for the last time and vowed never to return. Sadly, I did reappear once to shamelessly plug this book when it was first published in 2009 in the rather cynical hope that these obsessives would buy a copy. They may not enjoy reading this updated version quite as much.

CHAPTER FIFTEEN

"Pimp My Book"

However, it was indirectly through the publication of this book that my career took an unexpected turn and led me towards the 2010 World Cup. I was quite enjoying my new role as a television commentator and internet hate figure, and the fact that I spent much of my time working from home preparing stat sheets and intros offered me the chance to regain some of the valuable family time I had missed during my regular excursions abroad in my previous incarnation. When I came home from the World Cup in France in 1998 my elder daughter Becky was nearly two years old and I calculated that I had been absent for 25 percent of her life. It was great to be able to devote so much of my energy towards her, my other daughter Katie and my wonderful, heroic and long-suffering wife Carolyn.

The realisation dawned on me that I might finally be settling into a less hectic and more measured way of life on the night before a Sky commentary in Middlesbrough in the midst of a big freeze in January 2009. Sometimes I would travel up to a venue the day before a match because of the distances involved, especially in the middle of winter when the threat of poor weather made a journey on the morning of the match too great a risk time-wise. The good thing about TV outside broadcasts is there is always a crew of production staff around and so you are never short of someone to have a few beers and a meal with. On this particular night I was especially keen to watch Watford who were playing in the Friday night live Sky game at Reading, so I dragged a group of slightly less enthusiastic souls out to a local pub and grabbed a table equidistant between the telly and a window overlooking the town's rather insalubrious main drag.

Midway through the second half, with Watford trailing by three goals to nil, I rather lost interest in the game and was drawn towards the procession of pubbers and clubbers who were parading up and down in sub zero temperatures at the start of the weekend break. Every now and again a taxi would pull up and disgorge a bevy of teenage girls who, despite the kind of prevailing conditions that would have sparked a near riot at the Faroese kagoule shop, were dressed as if headed for a cocktail party on a particularly balmy night at Waikiki Beach; with their high heels and gownless evening straps. As the latest group of scantily clad revellers emerged into the winter freeze, I experienced the kind of involuntary reaction which gave lie to a deep seated, yet hitherto undiscovered, sense of my own increasing age and imminent demise.

Instead of making a boorish gesture with my forearm and beerily shouting:
"Cor blimey look at that; I wouldn't mind giving her one!"
My gut instinct was to sympathetically venture:
"Blimey, they must be bloody freezing dressed like that in this weather."
All at once, the reality that I was, by now, a father of two in his late forties who had been married for more than 15 years, overrode the fading belief that I remained a gung ho journalistic opportunist who had cut a swathe through the sporting world for two decades.

Perhaps it was time to contend myself with a career as a below average TV commentator who could earn reasonable money without hitting the heights, in a working environment free of the kind of depressing management bullshit which had so blighted my final years as a staff radio reporter.

And yet, as I watched successive England qualification campaigns unfold, I would feel the odd pang of near pathological jealousy at the missed opportunity of frequenting smoky bars in Al-Amaty, subterranean nightclubs in Zagreb or quaffing lager from a plastic pint glass with Butch on Heavy Metal night at the Minsk equivalent of the Hammersmith Palais. This was made worse by the fact that I would bump into some of the guys who'd been at those games and they would take great pleasure in regaling me with tales of drunken nights in unusual locations.

I did have a role in the 2006 World Cup when I was hired by UKTV as a commentator on their "alternative" coverage of the event, which came live from a small cupboard-like room in an old BBC production complex just off the A40 near Park Royal. The idea was to frame the commentaries within a more relaxed, informal and comedic programme format as an alternative to the official coverage on BBC and ITV. It was never going to be a hit but, to be fair, the production company treated us very well and we were working alongside co-comms of the quality of Ron Atkinson, Craig Brown and Tony Gale. Okay, it wasn't Baden-Baden and there wasn't a wag in sight, but at least I was being paid for seeing games that I would have been watching at home anyway.

One of the matches I covered for them was the final Group E clash between Ghana and USA which would see the Africans, in their first ever World Cup, qualify for the knockout stages with a win. The Ghanaians were a talented but ill disciplined bunch who came into the match with two of their key players, Sulley Muntari and Asamoah Gyan, suspended after both had picked up yellow cards in each of the opening two games. Four more of their players, including star man Michael Essien, would miss any potential round of 16 encounter if they received another booking. I was alongside Galey for the match and, within five minutes, we were wincing in horror as Essien lunged into an awful late challenge and was yellow carded thus invoking a suspension. I ventured the opinion that newcomers Ghana were a little naive in their approach to World Cup matches, given that referees had been specifically told to clamp down on challenges that were over the top or from behind. It was a view that Galey endorsed and we criticised Essien for his rash behaviour.

A week later the *Daily Telegraph*'s Giles Smith, a writer I much admired and whose book *Lost In Music* (a kind of *Fever Pitch* but about rock'n'roll rather than football) eerily mirrored my own teenage years, wrote a feature piece about UKTV's coverage of the World Cup. In it he had a right go at Galey and me, suggesting that the word "naive" to describe Ghana's robust tactics could have been substituted by the word "black". The clear inference was that we were being racist and I was furious. I penned an outraged reply in our defence, pointing out that we were merely referring to a style of football and that our criticisms were borne out by the facts of the match, but the paper chose not to publish it. Some of the "quality" newspapers and their smug columnists seem to take great pleasure in slagging off TV commentators and presenters; but while they were prolific in the dishing it out department, taking it was something they were clearly far less keen on. There is no doubt in my mind that any football commentator would be far better at writing a witty newspaper column, than their printed page counterpart would be at describing a live football match.

Under the inexpert guidance of the "wally with the brolly" Steve McClaren, England had spectacularly failed to qualify for the next big footballing carnival at Euro 2008 in Austria and Switzerland, which left me with a blank summer in which I was really struggling to find any kind of meaningful work. I used the spare time to pen my recollections of 20 years on the road and those musings and memories eventually became this book which first came out the following year.

The small company which originally published the book had a virtually non-existent promotional budget and so I embarked upon a campaign of self promotion. I used all my media contacts in a bid to get airtime and column inches devoted to this new literary masterpiece and codenamed this strategy "Operation Pimp My Book".

With help from many local radio stations, both BBC and independent, as well as high profile newspaper writers like Henry Winter, Charlie Sale and Rob Draper, I managed to drum up some momentum, but what I lacked was national radio exposure. BBC *Radio 5Live* and *talkSPORT* were the obvious targets given the nature of the book and so I set to work.

Attempting to convince *5Live* that a humorous book about sport, travel, and journalism written by a broadcaster would fit neatly into their editorial and listenership demographic should, at first glance, have been a relatively straightforward task. However the sheer weight of the corporation's bureaucracy ensured that it was akin to persuading a churchwomen's guild to publish an article promoting child pornography, satanism and mass murder in its parish magazine.

I'm convinced the BBC has an entire department in which people are paid to prevaricate indecisively about anything and everything. Each time I contacted a programme producer to discuss the idea, I would invariably be transferred to someone else who would then refer me to a third party who, in turn, suggested I spoke to his boss and on and on it went for days until I finally ended up back with the person who I'd originally called. Either that or someone would enthusiastically request a review copy, which I would duly send out, only to never hear from them again despite endless call and emails. There are probably more copies of the book circulating in the corridors of the BBC than were actually sold in Waterstone's or WH Smith. The honourable exception to all of this was the *Danny Baker Show* whose independent production company at least had the good grace to explain that it didn't really fit in with the style of their programme.

By contrast, it took just one short phone call to book a slot on *talkSPORT*'s highly entertaining *Hawksbee and Jacobs* programme; I spent a hugely enjoyable and relaxed half hour in their company and, immediately, the rating for *A Great Face For Radio* shot up on its Amazon homepage. At one stage it broke the Top Ten in football books, outselling tomes by Sir Alex Ferguson, Steven Gerrard, Arsene Wenger and, most pleasingly of all, John Motson. This unfortunately gave rise to another unhealthy obsession, namely checking the numerical placing of the book on a daily basis just like a rock band who've just released their first single. My mood would often depend on whether I'd cracked the Top 5,000 in all books on Amazon or was languishing outside the Top 100,000. As far as I know

JK Rowling and Stephen King didn't suffer too many sleepless nights during my honeymoon period as a published author.

But my visit to talkSPORT Towers in Waterloo on that early November day in 2009 was to yield far more than just an increase in book sales. I was lucky enough to make the acquaintance of producers Matt Smith and Steve Morgan who were planning ahead for the station's coverage of the following summer's World Cup for which England had just comfortably qualified under new coach Fabio Capello.

In the finest journalistic tradition we repaired to the local *talkSPORT* boozer which turned out to be the King's Arms in the middle of Roupell Street, a wonderful little thoroughfare which so closely resembles a Victorian cobbled lane that it was sometimes used as a film set for television costume dramas. It was a pub I'd frequented many times before, since it was a convenient place to meet up with my old mates from Guildford and Woking given its close proximity to Waterloo Station. As well as having enjoyed some epic piss-ups there in the past, it was also in the King's Arms three years earlier that a *Sky Sports* producer had called to invite me to commentate on their Copa America coverage and so I had nothing but fond memories of the place.

At once I got on famously with my two new drinking partners. Matt, *talkSPORT*'s head of outside broadcasts, was an amiable Brummie and Aston Villa fanatic who enjoyed a pint or two of Guinness, which was just as well since he never seemed to be too far away from the next programming crisis. Steve was yet another person with whom I instantly established a rapport based around a mutual love of bands like The Smiths, Joy Division and The Fall. As it turned out we had unwittingly been at the same half dozen or so London gigs over the past year.

During the course of the conversation they explained that they were looking for an experienced and versatile on-site reporter who could handle the day to day coverage of news from the England camp and conduct post-match interviews on match days. I made an eloquent speech outlining my suitability for the job, pointed them in the direction of *A Great Face For Radio* as a kind of CV, recharged their glasses and promised Steve I'd burn him copies of a couple of rare Smiths bootlegs. All of which seemed to have the desired effect, as Matt called me within days with the news that *talkSPORT* supremo Moz Dee had agreed to sign me up as part of the station's team for South Africa.

Two decades after making my debut at Italia 90 and 12 years after attending my last World Cup in France, I would be back on the England bandwagon; much older yet not much wiser but still fired with the boyish enthusiasm which had persuaded me to get involved in this ridiculous business in the first place. I was so chuffed I even forgave myself for humming Toto's appalling 1982 hit "Africa" for the remainder of the day.

My first game as the newly ordained *talkSPORT* England correspondent was a March friendly against Egypt which would also provide my broadcasting debut at the new Wembley. Generally there are two media days in the run up to the match in which the manager, captain and selected players are available for interviews with newspapers, TV and radio. Not much had changed, and our radio conference remained a nicely relaxed set-up with myself and *5Live*'s Mike Ingham granted around ten minutes between us with each interviewee. The BBC were the radio commentary rights holders, so protocol dictated that they would open with their questions and I would follow, although I was at liberty to use sound bites generated by them and vice versa. It was a wholly amicable state of affairs especially since Mike and I knew and trusted each other well.

The only difficulty in getting the second bite at the cherry was trying to make your interview sound fresh and topical without irritating the player by simply repeating all the same questions. Mike's meticulous approach to interviewing meant he often had all the bases covered and at times I was secretly thinking "cheers mate, all I've got left to ask him is his favourite colour and what he had for breakfast."

It was my first exposure to Capello who seemed a polite and affable man but was to prove a very difficult interviewee. His grasp of English was tenuous at times and on occasions he would fail to understand the questions, often referring to his ever present interpreter. This had the effect of disjointing the flow to such a degree that the original point would occasionally be lost and it was hard to pin him down on any given topic. I had a suspicion that he deliberately used the interpreter as a defence mechanism to buy himself thinking time when faced with an awkward enquiry. With all the stops, starts and stumbles and his heavy accent, these interviews rarely came across very well on radio.

I arrived at Wembley on the night of the match to be greeted in the media suite by Stan Collymore, *talkSPORT*'s chief pundit, who usually got the team line-ups confirmed before anyone else which helped enormously. The whole set-up was a lot more grandiose than the cramped press facilities at the old stadium where you'd jostle your way through the narrow confines of the press room to a trestle table and collect a paper bag containing a sandwich, drink and apple like a five-year-old on their first day at school. Here, we enjoyed an excellent hot meal in a spacious room overlooking the pitch. Unfortunately our broadcast point was located in the TV gantry on the opposite side of the stadium. Stan provided much of the pre-match analysis and colour and had to go on air about an hour before I did, so he left with producer Matt Smith to get set up and I remained behind scribbling my intro.

"Are you sure you'll be ok finding the gantry?" Matt called out to me as he left.

"Oh yeah, no problem, I'll be fine," I replied confidently.

In all my years of finding my way around the bowels of football stadiums around the world, nothing had prepared me for the initiative test I was about to face here. This was a Spinal Tap gig at Hampton Court maze. I had to get a lift down a floor and walk around half the perimeter of the ground at pitch level and then take another lift up to the gantry area, which seemed simple enough. Unfortunately the lift numbering system was less than helpful, featuring floors B2, B1, M, 1 and 2. Having eventually established that B1 stood for Basement Level 1, I stumbled out into a scene that was part underground car park, part building site. Everywhere I looked there were fork-lift trucks, stacked wooden pallets, cones, fleets of top of the range Mercedes cars, all manner of motorised grounds keeping equipment and a phalanx of monosyllabic, shrugging men with hi-vis vests and earpieces whose sole function appeared to be grunting haughtily at anyone who dared to ask for directions.

There appeared to be a lift every 25 yards, all of which, rather than containing useful pointers such as "TV gantry", "corporate boxes" or "loading bay", were categorised numerically without a clue as to what that number meant. It was as if the backers of this project, which finally opened four years late and £300 million over budget, had decided that the provision of direction signs was simply one expense too many. After completing more laps of the stadium than the average 10,000 metres runner, I finally managed to ascertain that I needed Lift 14 to Floor 4 and eventually joined Stan and Matt on the gantry.

As ever in World Cup year, the hype surrounding England's chances had gone far beyond what could be reasonably described as logical. Sections of the media appeared to actually believe that Fabio's men would be swept to the final on a tidal wave of ill conceived and unsustainable optimism and then hammer Brazil 8-0 without breaking sweat. Quite why a nation whose footballers have repeatedly failed to replicate our only ever World Cup success, suddenly becomes so absurdly convinced of our global infallibility at the dawn of every successive major tournament is one of the great mysteries of world sport. If they handed out silverware for misplaced arrogance, the Wembley trophy cabinet would have long been reduced to sawdust.

As we all know, since Bobby Moore lifted the Jules Rimet Trophy at Wembley in 1966, England have reached the semi-finals of a World Cup just once. What people forget is the fact that, prior to the 2010 tournament, this feat had been matched by Uruguay, Poland, Belgium, Sweden, Bulgaria, Croatia, Turkey, South Korea and Portugal. I doubt very much that newspapers in Seoul or Montevideo were quite as triumphalist about their team's chances in South Africa as some of ours were.

As one of the more experienced and sagely members of the England press corps put it:

"We always go into these tournaments believing we'll win it and we always fuck up."

Sure enough, England were absolutely hopeless in the first half against Egypt and trailed to Mohamed Zidan's goal at the interval. To be fair to Capello, he made changes at half-time and substitutes Peter Crouch and Shaun Wright-Phillips both scored in a 3-1 win. Subsequent friendly victories over Mexico and Japan, the latter thanks to two own goals, did little to justify the tribal tub thumping.

In between those two matches Capello took his provisional World Cup squad of 30 players to an altitude training camp in the Austrian Alps. This was intended as preparation for England's opening group game against the USA which would take place nearly 4,000 feet up in the South African high veldt at Rustenburg, close to where the England base camp was situated.

The trip included a media day in which the press could attend training and interview several players, so *talkSPORT* sent me off to Graz, which was the nearest reasonably sized town to the training venue at Irdning. The area is located at 2,200 feet above sea level and is a major winter sports centre, but its state of the art training facility, adjacent to the luxury Schloss-Pichlarn Hotel, made it a popular location for many top football clubs as a summer base. Real Madrid, VfB Stuttgart and AS Roma had all trained there, as well as Premier League clubs Fulham and Stoke City. In the rarefied atmosphere and thinner air, it was easy to imagine a Rory Delap long throw flying over one of the surrounding peaks and landing somewhere near the German border.

Irdning is a two and a half hour drive from Graz so we had to board a coach at the crack of dawn to take us through the gorgeous scenery en route to the media conference. You could see why football clubs were so keen to come here, as the training complex was in an absolutely stunning setting. The area is dominated by the Grimming Massif, a huge mountain which towers imperiously over the small town, its pine fringed slopes overlooking a deep valley, dotted with lakes and tiny villages. The air, though not noticeably thinner, was crisp and fresh.

Just prior to the trip, *talkSPORT* had run a competition offering a listener the chance to watch England train in Austria and I was asked to interview the lucky winner, who was a Newcastle fan called Sean. I spotted a gaggle of England fans close to the edge of the main training pitch and our man was among them. He was a hugely affable fellow and completely relaxed in front of a microphone, which isn't always the case when carrying out the dreaded vox pops which are every radio reporter's least favourite job.

I switched on my new state of the art digital recorder and started by describing the magnificent natural scene which surrounded us and concluded the opening question by observing, with one of those irritating smug chuckles:

"I bet this is a little different to back home eh, Sean?"

His response took me back to the stupid question I'd asked Tracey Neville at the Commonwealth Games in Kuala Lumpur in 1998.

"Not really, I live in the Lake District."

Generally, watching England train yields few clues as to what tactics or formation the team will employ. The 15 minutes access granted to the press is primarily for the benefit of the camera crews and photographers and consists of little other than a bit of light jogging and a few stretches; we don't really get to see much of the actual work on the shape of the team. In Austria, given that we'd come such a long way, the FA were more generous with their time and we were granted a longer opportunity to study the session, hoping to gain some vital insight into which of the borderline players would be selected in the final World Cup 23.

The general consensus was that midfielders Adam Johnson and Scott Parker looked sharpest, Tom Huddlestone also appeared to be in good form and Wayne Rooney was busting the net with everything that came his way. On the minus side veteran defender Jamie Carragher seemed chronically short of pace, with wide men Theo Walcott and Aaron Lennon unable to create consistently from the flanks, unlike Johnson whose delivery was superb. Ledley King was accompanied on the trip by a personal trainer and appeared to be a dead cert to miss out due to his lack of fitness. In the end, of course, Capello confounded us all. Carragher, King and Lennon were all included in the World Cup party but Parker, Johnson and Huddlestone were among the unlucky seven who failed to make the cut. It wasn't to be the last time that Capello would baffle the media in the weeks to come.

After the session we were shepherded into a little bar and restaurant in an annexe of the hotel which resembled one of those stereotypical Alpine cottages in which Hansel, Gretel and Heidi had grown up. The only things missing were Belle and Sebastian and the lilting voice of Julie Andrews drifting through the open lattice windows.

One of the players who was put up for interview was Carragher, who had been persuaded by Capello and his assistant Franco Baldini to come out of international retirement at the age of 32. When it was reported that the Liverpool stalwart was considering quitting the national team in 2007, he was accused of being a bottler by *talkSPORT*'s confrontational *Drive Time* host Adrian Durham. Incensed, the Liverpool player called the station to confront Durham on air. The presenter played down his initial comments and the pair established a rapport. Sensing the opportunity to get a high profile name on board for their World Cup coverage, *talkSPORT* signed up Carragher as a pundit. He and Durham would present a daily show from Liverpool drawing on Carragher's status as an England insider.

Of course those plans had to be shelved when the player agreed to Capello's request and was subsequently selected in the provisional World Cup squad. When he came in to the Hansel and Gretel cottage to be interviewed, I decided to have a wry dig at him, knowing that he was the type who would take it in his stride and join in the leg pulling.

"Jamie, can I just start by asking you what on earth you were thinking of by agreeing to represent England instead of doing your *talkSPORT* show with Adrian Durham. It's an absolute disgrace and you've let your country down."

He broke into a broad grin and countered brilliantly:

"I know, I feel gutted about it. It was a big decision whether to have the chance to go to the World Cup in South Africa with England or spend four weeks in a cramped radio studio with Adrian Durham. In the end I went for the World Cup because I'd have probably ended up hitting him."

It was great stuff and I felt very pleased with myself as I set up my sat-phone on a stone wall overlooking the first tee of the hotel's golf course to file back the interviews and some voice pieces. Rather less pleased was a golfer who had just begun his swing at the moment I boomed out the opening line of my report. In his surprise, he shanked the ball hideously into a clump of trees and then stomped off furiously, no doubt contemplating a quadruple bogey on the opening hole.

The Carragher interview went down a storm and was replayed, to much delight, by successive presenters, not least Adrian himself. It felt great, on a personal note, to be working for a station where you were actively encouraged to take chances and have a bit of fun instead of simply asking the routine questions about fitness and preparation. I generally liked to try and get a laugh out of managers and players whenever possible, as it adds a little human dimension to things. You obviously had to be careful about who you were talking to and in what circumstances; it's no good trying to crack jokes when a player's just suffered a heavy defeat. On the right day, you could usually elicit a chuckle from the likes of Harry Redknapp, Ian Holloway and Steve Bruce, but it was definitely not a good idea to try and form a comedy double act with Roy Keane, David Moyes or Mark Hughes.

Once during a post-match *Sky Sports* interview I did with Redknapp at Portsmouth, the whole thing descended into farce when his mobile phone kept going off in mid sentence. He'd be halfway through answering a question when you'd hear a horrible tinny ringtone followed by:

"Sorry....'ang on a mo....awrighht Jamie.... listen I'm on Sky, son.....I'll call you back."

Two minutes later the same thing happened.

"Hi Sandra..yeah fine....can't really talk now....see you later. Sorry John, that was the wife....wondering where I am....I said 'turn on the telly'."

I was absolutely delighted when the clip made the top ten in one of those end of the year blooper programmes.

The Austria trip was a whirlwind affair but, in the space of 48 hours, I'd managed to make acquaintances old and new, gather loads of very useful pre World Cup audio and enjoy some absolutely beautiful scenery. As I boarded the plane at Graz for the journey home, I was flushed with the thought that the next time I climbed a set of airline steps it would be for the rather longer journey to the 2010 World Cup.

CHAPTER SIXTEEN

"They Treat Us Like Refugees"

The travel arrangements for the England media party following the national team in South Africa had been organised by a company called BAC Sport, with whom I had journeyed to many places and received much help over the years from the likes of David Pearson, Brian Scott and John and Keith Warren whose thankless task it was to try to organise a group of around 100 media representatives, all with different deadlines and agendas.

They had booked accommodation for us at the Sun City resort which was about 40 minutes' drive from England's base at the Royal Bafokeng Sports Campus. We were billeted in spacious apartments which two people would share, with the en suite bedrooms separated by a communal living room and kitchen area. Generally, people from the same organisations had already paired up as flat mates, presumably on the basis of who would be least likely to end up killing each other during a possible six-week stay.

As I was the only representative from *talkSPORT* who was based with England, I had no obvious partner and so, by a process of elimination, was paired with another solo traveller. I learnt that he was a Eurosport website reporter I had never met called Tony Mabert, who wasn't due to join the party until a week after we arrived.

I shared a taxi to Heathrow with the *Daily Mirror*'s John Cross who lives close to me in north London and who had been a good mate on numerous football and athletics trips going back ten years. During the journey he looked up from his texting and asked me who I was sharing with.

"Some bloke from Eurosport called Tony Mabert," I replied.

Crossy let out an astonished shriek and turned towards me, his face contorted in horror:

"Oh my God," he spluttered "not Terrible Tony."

After which he broke out into a cackle of fiendish laughter:

"Bloody hell Ando, he's an absolute maniac."

He explained that he'd come across Tony during Euro 2008 and regaled me with lurid tales of how his unpredictable behaviour, violent mood swings and drunken antics had shocked even the most seasoned campaigners within the England press corps. As I listened, I grew increasingly alarmed at the prospect of sharing an apartment with a man who appeared to possess all the social niceties of a 1970s vintage Oliver Reed crossed with Jack Nicholson in *The Shining*.

Crossy continued tapping away on his Blackberry throughout the conversation and, within minutes, I received a text message from *5Live* Football Correspondent Ian Dennis:

"I hear you're sharing with TT, good luck."

As word got around, I was accosted at the check-in by other travelling companions who were keen to inform me of the impending oblivion into which I would shortly be enveloped. Even the *Independent On Sunday*'s Steve Tongue, a former colleague at IRN and one of the gentlest souls on the trip, sidled up to offer his condolences.

"Surely this bloke can't be that bad," I kept insisting.

"Honestly mate, he's a complete nutter," came the unanimous response.

I digested this news on a slightly nervous journey to Johannesburg as I pondered what on earth I was in for during the following weeks. It appeared that Tony's idea of a good night out consisted of necking 17 pints of strong lager, having a fight with a nightclub bouncer, ripping the door off his hotel room and dancing insanely to techno music until dawn.

Given my own past history, I'm certainly not one to suffer bouts of righteous indignation when it comes to other people's social habits, but the idea of having to wake at 7am to do a live chat with the *Alan Brazil Sports Breakfast* to a backdrop of bacchanalian mayhem was a little disconcerting. Having said that, Alan himself would no doubt have heartily approved. At least I had a week to prepare myself.

We landed in Johannesburg very early in the morning, and the two and a half hour coach journey north to Sun City took us through the largely featureless terrain of the high veldt, which was dotted with depressingly primitive squatter camp settlements in which people lived in corrugated iron shacks with tyres or rocks holding down the flimsy roofs. Little breeze-block buildings served as shops and were spray painted with slogans such as "Wendy's Hair Salon" or "Sammy's Bottle Shop" and barefoot kids would run around in the dust as their parents sold fruit from baskets by the side of the road.

One such camp was located, rather incongruously, just a few hundred yards from the gates to the England team HQ. The base which the FA had chosen to house the national team for a sojourn which, we hoped, would last through all the way through until July 12th, couldn't have been more luxurious, with its gym, spa and sauna, pool and designer restaurants. But, for all its undoubted opulence, the whole complex seemed depressingly isolated from the outside world. It was located just off the only major road for miles around and accessed via a long winding, dusty drive. Armed guards stood outside the gatehouse at the entrance and all vehicles were subject to rigorous security checks before being allowed to head up towards the training complex or hotel. All our baggage had to carry official security tags and was searched every morning before travelling to the training sessions.

The city of Rustenburg, a largely blue collar platinum mining centre, was located a few miles to the south and offered little in the way of culture or entertainment. My lifelong friend Phil Edwards, who had been there a couple of times as the rugby correspondent at *Sky Sports News*, described it as a one horse town which the horse had quickly got bored with and galloped off somewhere more interesting. We were told it was not a particularly safe environment, especially late at night and, since taxi firms were charging extortionate fares for a return journey into town, it didn't seem to be worth investigating. Even if they had been allowed to, it was hard to imagine England's millionaire footballers being tempted out for the evening.

Our base at Sun City was further north and represented a slightly less opulent but nonetheless very comfortable environment; although there was a similar feeling that this was somewhat removed from reality, and there was nowhere you could escape to and get a genuine feel of what the South African World Cup was really all about. This vast entertainment complex had been founded by entrepreneur Sol Kerzner in 1979 in Bophuthatswana, an area which was governed by black South Africans much to the dislike of the apartheid government who declared it an independent state. This non-federal status meant that the region wasn't subject to the same laws as the rest of the country and so Kerzner could offer visitors "delights" such as gambling and topless revue shows which were illegal elsewhere in South Africa at the time.

While it quickly proved to be a mecca for wealthy white South Africans who could enjoy the freedoms it offered, Sun City also became a primary focus for the anti-apartheid movement in the rest of the world, who saw it as a symbol of the nation's inequality and prejudice. Many world famous acts such as Frank Sinatra, Queen and Elton John had played lucrative concerts there and been subject to strong criticism for taking the shilling from an inhumane regime. In 1985 a group of rock stars including Bob Dylan, Bruce Springsteen, Lou Reed and, rather inevitably, Bono, released the protest single Sun City under the collective title of Artists United Against Apartheid. The accompanying video intercut scenes of spinning roulette wheels and bikini clad girls relaxing at palm fringed swimming pools with newsreel footage of police oppression and anti-apartheid riots. One of the images which best summed up the anger and injustice so many people felt was a still shot of a poster with the slogan "Sun City – The Fantasy Island In The Midst Of Hell."

The complex had continued to flourish and expand in the post-apartheid era but for people like me, who had bought the Sun City single and supported its manifesto, the bitter associations were hard to shake off. When I told people I was going to be based at Sun City, the reaction was often along the lines of:

"Ooooh, it's just like a mini Las Vegas."

Which I took as a warning rather than an endorsement.

Due to some sort of internal booking mix up, we didn't actually get into our accommodation at the Apartment Village until the second day, and had to spend the opening night at the Cabanas Hotel which was in a different part of the resort by a huge artificial lake.

Despite it being midwinter in South Africa, the days were warm and sunny, and our hosts laid on a welcome reception and buffet in an outdoor eating area surrounded by colourful plant life and hungry baboons, who would leap onto the tables and try to grab bits of food the moment your back was turned. The terrace was patrolled by a group of less than intimidating uniformed guards whose job it was to discourage these uninvited guests. We dubbed them the Baboon Squad and they carried little water pistols in holsters which they would fire at the interlopers while, at the same time, trying to avoiding spraying the diners.

"Freeze punk, or I'll lightly squirt you."

This provided an entertaining backdrop to a thoroughly pleasant first day, and it was great to be able to wind down after a largely sleepless 13-hour flight and long coach journey. But not everyone was entirely satisfied with the arrangements.

One of the most legendary and colourful characters on all the trips I had been on with England is Giancarlo Galavotti of the Italian paper *Gazzetto dello Sport*, who had spent many years based in London reporting on the English game. Although I am sure he thoroughly enjoyed living and working in this country, he never gave that impression. Giancarlo's outward appearance was always that of a disapproving first time visitor who regarded the locals as something of a cultureless sub-species. This he did with such a reservoir of dry humour and hilarious non sequiturs that, despite the grumpy exterior, he was a much cherished travelling companion. His physical resemblance to Benito Mussolini merely added to the effect.

During Euro 2000, on a coach trip back from Eindhoven to our Belgian base after Kevin Keegan's England had squandered a 2-0 lead against Portugal and lost their opening match 3-2, someone asked Giancarlo what he had made of the game. In his heavy, aristocratic sounding Italian accent he delivered a concise and brilliant summation in a single sentence, which none of the other assembled writers and reporters could possibly have bettered:

"It was like a pantomime horse," he solemnly opined, "but with only the front legs."

While he was a popular figure with his fellow journos, Giancarlo was certainly not the darling of the BAC Sport travel staff who suffered long at his hands. Lacking the natural English reserve that most of us possessed innately, he was often a vocal critic of the organisation and arrangements of these trips and would make endless complaints about flight times, hotels, food, transport and such like. On our first day in South Africa he was very unhappy at the inconvenience of having to spend one night at the Cabanas and then being forced to uproot early in the morning.

As the rest of us tucked heartily into our lunch on the sun dappled terrace, Giancarlo seemed less than impressed. He was at an immaculately laid table with a vase of freshly cut flowers at its centre, looking every inch the colonial gentleman in his cream suit, sunglasses and straw hat. A napkin protruded from the neck of his shirt as he contemplated the large glass of red wine and delicious looking plate of seafood in front of him. But before he started eating he turned towards us tutting loudly.

"They treat us like refugees."

On the second night I found myself sitting next to Giancarlo at dinner and he was very helpful in offering what insight he could into his compatriot Fabio

Capello; although the general thrust of it was that this was not a man any of us would ever get to know well. The England coach did things very much his own way and, while outwardly polite and attentive, had little time for the opinions of those outside his inner sanctum of friends and advisors. Even Giancarlo, who had far more reason than the rest of us to be well in with the England coach, admitted that he found Capello something of a mystery.

The first official media conference with the England team was held the day after we arrived and offered us our first glimpse into the gilded prison which would be the players' home for the next few weeks. As ever, the FA's media operations manager Joanne Budd had organised an impressive media centre with separate rooms for newspapers, television and radio. It was a ten minute walk from the training pitch via a somewhat convoluted route which ensured we were kept well away from the hotel, gym and physio rooms.

In addition to the head of team security Ray Whitworth, who was well known to us all, the FA had brought in a perma-tanned American ex-marine with a crew cut and shades who would bark ominously at anyone who deviated even slightly from the designated path, like Sergeant Bilko growling at Private Doberman. It all seemed a little bit paranoid and heavy handed and the feeling of "us and them" was compounded a few days later when Capello himself launched an angry tirade at a group of photographers who he deemed to have strayed a little too close to the window of the treatment room. In fact, they were simply trying to get pictures of the players as they emerged from the main building and any shot aimed at the window would doubtless have resulted in a reflection of themselves. Since *talkSPORT* had a big advertising deal running with *The Times*, I got Brownie points (if you'll excuse the pun) by interviewing their chief sports photographer Marc Aspland, a co-socialiser of long standing, who gave a fascinating snapper's perspective into the England boss, concluding that this was the out of character behaviour of a man who already felt under pressure. Marc said he particularly enjoyed photographing Capello in the dug-out, as his animated, hand waving demeanour produced far better pictures than the dour personas of Steve McLaren and Sven-Goran Eriksson ever did.

There were always plenty of lenses trained on David Beckham whose World Cup playing prospects had been ended by an Achilles injury but had been drafted into the England backroom staff. It was a bit strange seeing him kitted out as coach rather than in a playing strip, and his role certainly seemed to be more ambassadorial than anything else.

The main story as we arrived on that first day of training concerned the fitness or otherwise of midfielder Gareth Barry who had picked up an ankle injury in the run up to the tournament and was doubtful for the first group game against the USA. The Manchester City player sat out the opening session and I was in the middle of updating the situation in a live link with *talkSPORT*'s Mike Parry from the side of the training ground when Ray Whitworth signalled that our allotted 15 minutes had elapsed and we were told to quickly move along. I continued talking as I made my way back towards the media centre, becoming increasingly breathless in the thin air. I apologised for my less than clear enunciation but pointed out that this was an apt illustration of how altitude can affect the human body. I was having trouble getting my words out while walking at a brisk pace for a few hundred yards, but the players would have to perform flat out for 90 minutes under similar conditions. Admittedly, I conceded, they were a little bit fitter than I was.

It had been decided by the FA media department that Capello would do radio interviews before moving on to TV and the papers and so he appeared, polite as ever and shaking our hands, for his first public utterances since the squad's arrival in South Africa. In the midst of a fairly non-committal answer about Barry's chances of being fit for the opening game, he casually dropped the bombshell that skipper Rio Ferdinand had suffered a serious knee injury after an accidental clash with Emile Heskey and had been taken to hospital with his World Cup over before it had even begun.

As soon as the England boss rose from his chair to move on to the next part of the press conference I was on the line to *talkSPORT* breaking this dramatic piece of news to a disbelieving audience. As first mornings go it was quite a start and the story would go on to dominate the news agenda for the next few days.

The problem of course was that, as "our man in the England camp" I became very in demand with programme producers, and a typical day might start with a breakfast show appearance at 7am and end with a late night chat some 16 hours later. It was certainly one of the driest trips I had ever done, as there was just about time to nip down to the nearby 4th Street Cafe after the last report of the day and sink a quick pint or two before collapsing into bed ahead of the next one. It was all a far cry from the heady days of the early 1990s when any amount of sleep that could be stolen between the nightclub closing and the press conference starting was considered a bonus. The legendary Tony Lockwood once decided it was time to grab a quick kip after a big night out in Rotterdam and marched up to the hotel receptionist:

"Hello, I'm Mr Lockwood, room 154. Could I have an alarm call for 7.15am please?"

" It's 7.30 now, sir."

I didn't mind a bit of self-sacrifice though, as it was a joy and privilege to be part of a great team covering the world's biggest team event on national radio.

The ever helpful *talkSPORT* producers would brief me as to the general line of questioning so that I knew which areas to concentrate on, but it still took a little while to adapt to the idiosyncratic styles of the presenters. Breakfast stalwart Alan Brazil was great fun to work with but would occasionally catch me hopelessly off guard with a question that came completely out of left field. On one occasion we were chatting amiably about the latest England news when suddenly he changed tack:

"Tell me John, what do you make of the news that television viewers in North Korea may not be able to watch their team playing in their first World Cup since 1966?"

The honest answer would have been:

"I haven't got a clue, what are you asking me for? I'm in Sun City not Pyongyang."

Fortunately I remembered a Sunday newspaper report I'd read prior to departure and was able to sound vaguely informed as I explained that the country had no live TV rights and would only show heavily edited highlights some 12 hours after the matches had finished. The military dictatorship headed by Kim-il Jong were fearful that anti-North Korean banners or slogans at the grounds might end up being beamed into the nation's living rooms. Another time I was unexpectedly asked to shed some light on a crowd security problem ahead of a match in Pretoria of which I had little or no knowledge. It was all rather unnerving at times, especially for someone like me who takes about two hours and three cups of tea to properly wake up each morning.

I also enjoyed doing the *Hawksbee and Jacobs Show* as they were both very sharp and amusing and we'd sometimes go way off topic in the course of our conversations. Once they were talking about what the players were doing to kill the boredom during the long hours between training sessions and the subject of ipads came up.

"I bet Nobby Stiles never had an ipad," one of them joked.

"Nobby didn't even have shin pads, never mind an ipad," I replied.

Whenever I appeared they would introduce me with a deliberate over emphasis on the second word of my billing as "England camp reporter", as if I were mincing around the team HQ like Julian Clary. Danny Kelly would always refer to me as "our man embedded in the England camp" as if I'd been catapulted Tom and Jerry like into the very brickwork of the team hotel.

You always knew you were in for a challenge when talking to Adrian Durham who had set himself up as England's number one cheerleader. He would proudly tell the nation that Fabio's men were definitely going to win the World Cup and took great pleasure in haranguing me for my more sceptical view of the team's prospects.

It had taken me a little while to get my broadcast gear up and running in Sun City since our high tech apartments had digital telephone technology and it was impossible to install an ISDN line, which relied on physical cabling. Happily the resort manager agreed to let me use one of the older apartments on the other side of the village as a studio. Since Terrible Tony had yet to rear his ugly head, I ended up with five bedrooms, three bathrooms and two kitchens all to myself but, unfortunately, my two separate pieds a terre were a good ten minutes' walk apart. It didn't seem like much but, given that I would be commuting between them at least up to half a dozen times a day, it was an annoying inconvenience, especially first thing in the morning when it was still very cold indeed.

So, as an additional kindness, he also provided me, free of charge, with my own personal golf buggy to make the trips back and forth. Although it looked a little like the Boulder Mobile those two hairy cavemen used to drive on *Wacky Races* and the maximum speed was only 15 mph, this quickly became a status symbol. I took great pleasure in looking down my nose at my pedestrian peers as I drove past, waving regally like the Queen in her State Landau. I came to quite enjoy my early morning drives through the darkness of the Apartment Village; the chilly winter stillness punctuated only by the occasional squawking of the hadadas which were large, purple-grey, long beaked birds whose name was onomatopoeic, mimicking their noisy, distinctive call. The only hazard on the empty roads was avoiding the ubiquitous baboons who would career suddenly out of trees in your direction in the misguided hope that you were a low velocity grocery van.

Sometimes *talkSPORT* would ask me to bring in a guest from one of the newspapers to appear on their shows and I would act as a taxi service to whisk them away to the makeshift studio. I would pull up outside their apartments and knock loudly on the door shouting "Andocabs" but stopped short of actually charging fares.

After Rio Ferdinand's departure, Steven Gerrard was promoted to the England captaincy and was put up for the media in a conference which would generate huge interest especially given what had happened to Rio and the fact that John Terry, who had lost the armband following the scandal involving his alleged relationship with Wayne Bridge's ex-girlfriend, continued to be overlooked. Usually on a big day like this I would wake up full of enthusiasm, my head buzzing with the questions I might pose to the new skipper. However, on this occasion I awoke to a terrible feeling of inner physical turmoil and, before I could even look at the clock, I was in the bog, head down doing a passable impression of a firefighter's hose. Worse was to come, as the other end quickly followed suit, a pattern which was to continue non-stop for the next half an hour. Feeling only marginally better, I finally managed to drag myself onto the coach for an uncomfortable journey to the Royal Bafokeng and ran straight to the toilets the moment we reached the media centre.

I got through the interview just about, although there were times when I honestly felt I was about to throw up, or worse, in front of the new captain of England. The thought also struck me that if I had picked up a contagious virus, I was in danger of passing it on to Gerrard just days before the start of the World Cup. Certainly, if he felt like I did, he'd have been doubtful for breakfast never mind the USA game. Minutes after I'd finished the interview, I was back in the khazi perfecting my Fireman Sam impression. In the end it was diagnosed as an airborne non-transferable virus and happily Stevie G avoided catching it, although we did hear that a couple of players had been struck by a similar dose of the trots and missed training as a result.

All of which had rather taken my mind off the issue of Terrible Tony and, although from time to time people would sidle up and ask mischievously if he had arrived yet, I was pretty well convinced by now that this was an elaborate wind-up. Doubts resurfaced though when Rob Beasley, my old mate from the *Signal Radio* days, and his room-mate, *Sun* photographer Dickie Pelham, put on an incredible display of horrified indignation during one coach journey to training.

"The problem is," Rob explained, "that's he's so unpredictable, especially when he's had a drink. On the face of it, he's quite a nice guy but he just has this knack of winding people up. I've nearly hit him a couple of times."

Dickie maintained a look of stupefied outrage throughout, and they were so convincing that I approached BAC Sport's Brian Scott to voice my concerns at the prospects of my work patterns being shattered upon Tony's arrival. He explained that there was little that could be done unless an actual incident took place.

As you have probably guessed, I had been totally taken in for the second time and Tony Mabert turned out to be a hugely likeable fellow in his late twenties, who was on his first major trip with England. We got on like a house on fire from the word go and he found the whole Terrible Tony thing hilarious. The name stuck and he gained instant credibility among our companions in the village since the wind-up had caused such amusement. I had to take my hat off to Crossy who admitted he'd thought up the whole thing on the spur of the moment during the taxi ride; it had been a brilliantly executed set-up and I actually felt privileged to have been the hapless victim.

In the ten days between England arriving in South Africa and their opening match, we interviewed a good number of the players in the course of our daily visits to the media centre. With a couple of notable exceptions, the pattern which emerged during these interrogations was that of a squad which appeared to be suffering rather than embracing the whole World Cup experience. It was obvious to us very early on that they felt isolated, trapped and just plain bored as they whiled away the hours between training sessions. They were polite and obliging and dealt diplomatically with all manner of questions, but there was none of the France 1998 bonhomie which saw players cheekily inserting song titles into their answers. If there had been, I'm sure "Heaven Knows I'm Miserable Now" would have featured strongly. Or, in the case of those struck down by the vomiting bug, "Crepitating Bowel Erosion" by Carcass.

The FA had provided all manner of amusements within the team hotel, such as table tennis, computer games, DVDs and even a room full of books which, I wasn't surprised to be told, went largely unread.

"Hi JT, I'm torn between Kafka and Proust tonight, what do you reckon?"

"No contest Wazza, try 'A La Recherche Du Temps Perdu'. The structural, thematic and stylistic scope is simply awe inspiring."

But despite the tempting literary diversions, there seemed to be a real lack of spark in the players' eyes. Everything appeared to be depressingly routine and perfunctory, as if the whole thing were a chore rather than a pleasure. The word I used most often to answer those inevitable "what's the mood in the camp like" questions during my many reports from the England HQ was "joyless". There simply didn't seem to be any sense of freedom about the place. The Dutch players, for example, were based at the Sandton Hilton right in the middle of Johannesburg's most fashionable district.

They were free to visit its shopping centres, cinemas and restaurants, mixing with fans and locals without any ill effect. And, of course, Holland went all the way to the final.

By contrast England's choice of base camp seemed unnecessarily withdrawn and secretive; indicative, I felt, of aloofness and arrogance rather than warmth and embrace. It's an irritating national trait which doesn't just apply to football and the sooner we lose this "sceptred isle" mentality the better as far as I'm concerned. The two most honourable exceptions to the procession of tracksuited zombies that passed before us were David James and Joe Cole who both seemed genuinely pleased and excited to be part of the show. The veteran goalkeeper was very honest and open about the frustrations he felt at the lack of variety in daily life at Rustenburg. He likened it to the Bill Murray film *Groundhog Day*, in which a weatherman relives the same 24 hours over and over again; James even joked that he expected to wake up every morning to the sound of "I Got You Babe" by Sonny and Cher.

Cole also brought a humour and vitality to proceedings, even though he was clearly not a Capello favourite. Technically the midfielder was unattached to a club, having been released by Chelsea and yet to join Liverpool, but the feeling among fans and the media was that he represented that spark of creative unpredictability which could light up the England midfield. It was an opinion sadly not shared by the England coach, a man who doesn't so much throw caution to the wind as nail it to the mast.

One of the rare diversions for the players came in the shape of a safari trip to the nearby Pilanesburg reserve. Even this was marred by a rather silly dispute in which the FA accused camera crews and photographers of being overly intrusive in following the squad around. No doubt they were horrified at the prospect of headlines such as "England Squad Mildly Amused By Antics Of African Wildlife", or "World Cup Stars Observe Rhino At Close Quarters". Cole seemed less worried about the presence of the media than he was about a perceived lack of predatory action from the local mammals.

"It was a bit disappointing," he told us. "I was hoping to see a real tear-up."

I was unable to go on the trip but was told that the following media party enjoyed a rather more lively encounter with a rogue elephant who lurched a little too close to their Land Rover for comfort, forcing the driver to beat a hasty retreat.

"We got charged by a bull elephant," the *Telegraph*'s Henry Winter explained later, "but it's ok, we got a receipt."

Before I left for South Africa my younger daughter Katie had begged me to get some autographs for her and I asked each player we interviewed to sign the photo on his profile page in the team handbook, which they duly did. It was perhaps telling though, that James and Cole were the only two who asked what her name was, so that they could write a personal dedication.

A little light was shed amid the gloom when defenders Matthew Upson and Tottenham's Michael Dawson, the latter having flown in to replace the injured Ferdinand, visited an orphanage at a local township to meet the kids, have a kick around and hand out some goodies. The FA and several English clubs, including Spurs, had put up money generated by players' fines to fund the building of proper homes and the provision of foster parents for kids who has lost their mums and dads to AIDS and HIV.

Dawson was personally involved in the scheme and had been corresponding with a boy called Aubrey who he was very excited about meeting for the first time. As the England player waited inside the Tottenham house on the estate the little lad, who'd been off playing football up the road, eventually ran in wearing a bright red Manchester United top with Wayne Rooney's name emblazoned across the back. Dawson joked that he wished it had been his name and after much hurried searching, a Spurs shirt was finally located for the photographs. But, to his great credit, Aubrey insisted that he was a United fan and refused to put it on. He did, however, treasure the signed England shirt which Dawson subsequently handed him.

We got great interviews with both players who were genuinely touched by what they had witnessed and posed for countless photos with the children. Many of the media party also joined in an impromptu football match and were gob-smacked by the skill and enthusiasm the kids showed. I still haven't fully got over the fact that I was comprehensively nutmegged by a six-year-old.

All of which begs the question, why oh why did this sort of initiative not become a more regular feature? The players and media mingled with a shared sense of humbled and awestruck admiration at the positive attitude of people whose lives were a billion times less privileged than our own. The business of preparing for football matches was put squarely into perspective and the kids enjoyed a day they'll never forget. Unfortunately this was to be the only such excursion undertaken by the England players in South Africa and a year later Jamie Carragher quite rightly bemoaned the lack of opportunities the players ever get to experience a real taste of life in whatever country they're visiting. Travel broadens the mind, it seems, unless you are an England footballer.

CHAPTER SEVENTEEN

"Thirty Five Days Without Chips"

The first real indication of whether England were in any shape to justify the ill informed and jingoistic hype which some were peddling on a daily basis back home would come in a warm-up game against the Platinum Stars, the local South African League side. The game took place at one of the most incongruous locations in world football. The Moruleng Stadium, which had only been opened eight months earlier, sits some 30 miles away from Rustenburg in what can only be described as the middle of nowhere. We turned off the main road expecting to see the ground immediately, only to plough on along dusty tracks dotted with the odd baobab tree for what seemed like an eternity, before finally turning a corner to be greeted by a shiny new flat pack arena in the midst of the parched nothingness. Imagine crawling for miles through the Sahara desert in search of an oasis and stumbling upon a mirage in the shape of Northampton Town's Sixfields Stadium.

Thousands of locals were thronging around the ground when we arrived (God only knows how they got there) and surrounded the bemused looking England players as they got off the coach. As the game got underway we got our first chance to experience the sound of the vuvuzelas (or Uwe Seelers as we quickly nicknamed them after England's 1970 World Cup nemesis). These brightly coloured plastic tubular horns emitted a dreadful, cacophonous and relentless drone which almost completely drowned out the natural sound of the crowd and had moved some observers to insist that they should be banned for World Cup venues. While I agree that these instruments of torture created an ambience akin to that of a crowded bus boarded by a three-year-old clutching a Fisher-Price saxophone, I also had to concede that this appeared to be part of the football-going experience in South Africa and, as such, should be accepted, however grudgingly.

Amid a backdrop of deafening vuvuzelas and the sun setting gloriously behind the distant mountains to create an otherwordly, pinky-blue haze, England's performance was decidedly lacking in any vibrancy, tempo or colour and they were flattered by a 3-0 win in which the home side missed an early penalty. Given the remote location, I had to provide updates from the match live into the *Hawksbee and Jacobs* programme on my mobile phone, a task rendered near impossible by the incessant noise within the stadium. Barely able to hear a thing, I had to simply guess not only at what they were asking me, but when to take my cue:

"*talkSPORT*'s England correspondent John Anderson is at the Moruleng Stadium, where I gather there's heavy security after the stampede which caused injuries to fans at a Nigeria friendly yesterday."

(Five second pause)

"That's right fellas, England leading 1-0, Jermain Defoe scoring after only three minutes......"

In the end, the heavy security was not needed as a hugely good-natured crowd enjoyed a glimpse of players they would only ever see otherwise on TV and many of the supporters lined the route from the dressing room to the waiting coach to get treasured autographs and photos. More proof, if it were needed, that getting England players directly involved with locals is unlikely to result in an outbreak of the plague.

Among the throng at the Moruleng Stadium that afternoon was American 400m hurdles legend Ed Moses who was in attendance as the public face of a local charity initiative. My years covering track and field had begun just as Moses' decade long domination of his event was drawing to a close and the only time I saw him compete was at the Seoul Olympics when, as a 33-year-old, he finished third. So it was a real pleasure to have the chance to interview one of the sport's all time greats and he was absolutely charming. Like many of his compatriots he was clearly not a follower of soccer, but I felt I had to ask for his thoughts on the forthcoming match between England and his native USA. In that brilliantly diplomatic, yet non-commital style which so many American sports people have utterly mastered, he opined that he hoped it would be a good match and may the best team win. In the end of course, neither of those aspirations were to be fulfilled.

England had qualified for the tournament fairly comfortably from a group which featured Ukraine, Croatia, Belarus, Kazakhstan and Andorra, all of whom had only become UEFA members within the preceding 15 years. The qualification draw had been made in the interregnum between Steve McClaren's departure and Fabio Capello's appointment, so the Italian had inherited a very favourable list of opponents. In this sense at least, Capello was to prove to be a very successful manager, since he always seemed to emerge from these lucky dip scenarios like a man who'd tripped over into a steep ravine and uncovered a diamond mine at the bottom. Stick him in a room full of FIFA dignitaries, local Europop divas and indigenous dance troupes and he was guaranteed to come up trumps.

The draw for World Cup 2010 was no exception, as out of the hat came USA, Algeria and Slovenia. It was an outcome which could scarcely have been more benign if the panel of sporting stars, which included David Beckham, had held up pieces of paper bearing the names of St Kitts and Nevis, East Stirlingshire and Firs Farm Primary Under 9s. England would surely top the group and stay in Rustenburg for a winnable round of 16 tie against the likes of Ghana, Serbia or Australia.

I had already had a good look round the venue for England's opening game, Rustenburg's Royal Bafokeng Stadium, as we had gone there on our first day in South Africa to collect our accreditation passes from the media centre which was located within the arena compound. This relatively routine exercise was rendered rather farcical by some chaotic local disorganisation, which saw the entire written press corps initially unable to have their credentials processed due to a computer glitch. We radio reporters were in and out in ten minutes while our newspaper cohorts had to sit around grumbling for what seemed like hours, which amused me no end as it was normally the other way round. Unfortunately for Capello and the players, the problem was finally resolved and Fleet Street's finest eventually got their laminates.

To relieve the boredom of the wait, Henry Winter and I decided to try and have a look around the stadium itself, fully expecting to be turned away at the gate by security staff. But, rather like the experience in Atlanta in 1996, we walked unchallenged straight into the stadium, down the tunnel and onto the pitch. On our way back we popped into the dressing room that England would occupy, which was small, very spartan and only seemed to be half built. Men with wheelbarrows were scuttling back and forth down the breeze blocked corridors to the accompaniment of churning cement mixers and the whole place smelt of wet paint. We sniggered at the thought of how this might go down with our squad of pampered millionaires but, to be fair to the workmen, they had managed to transform the place by the time the match arrived and there were no complaints, as far as I know, from the players.

There was plenty to complain about during the match itself though, as Steven Gerrard's early opener was cancelled out by a goalkeeping howler of epic proportions from Rob Green who somehow allowed Clint Dempsey's tame shot to squirm through his hands and over the line. England lacked the necessary know how or invention to recover from this blow and had to settle for a 1-1 draw in their opening match.

With commentary provided by the excellent Jim Proudfoot, my role for *talkSPORT* on match days was to conduct interviews after the game in the Mixed Zones which, by and large in South Africa, were spacious and well organised. Obviously everyone wanted to get some reaction from the hapless Green, although we were fearful that he might try and avoid the waiting throng after his blunder had cost England victory. But, like Gareth Southgate and David Batty in previous tournaments, he showed himself to be a brave and honest man as he stood tall and faced the media in the midst of his darkest hour as a player. Not only did he answer our questions, but he did so brilliantly. He was totally honest about his culpability and expressed his deep regret at causing the disappointment that everyone felt so deeply. He also offered a fascinating insight into the psyche of those who have to stand at one end of the field with a number 1 (or in Green's case 12) on their backs.

Goalkeepers, he explained, actually prepare for failure. Their mistakes are usually so much more calamitous than those of any other player, that they have to develop a mindset which enables them to instantly forget the error and concentrate on not making another. In order to achieve that they must go into every game with an acute understanding of the worst case scenario, a burden which must take great mental fortitude to bear. Strikers can miss half a dozen chances in a match but still emerge as the hero with a last minute winner; goalkeepers do not have that luxury.

Green's laudable amenability and frankness came as a stark contrast to the likes of Ashley Cole and Glen Johnson who skulked through the Mixed Zone without even acknowledging the interview requests never mind acceding to them. Unforgivably, this was to be their default attitude for the remainder of the tournament. Cole has always been generally unhappy at the level of attention his private life has attracted in the media over the years, even though much of it had been prompted by his own stupidity and indiscretion. As a result he exercised a self-imposed omerta which extended to anyone with a notepad or microphone. I wondered what he honestly felt he had to fear from the gathering at the Royal Bafokeng Mixed Zone in the opening game of a World Cup:

"Ashley, a disappointing result for England but, more importantly, what the hell's going on with you and Cheryl?"

One major advantage of working in the Mixed Zone with a talkSPORT cube around your microphone was the fact that many of the players and their friends and family were regular listeners to the station and so they were more willing to stop for a chat. The profile of IRN had been such that it might as well have stood for Indonesian Rural Network.

It was a poor start to the campaign but, with Algeria and Slovenia to come, the general belief was that England would still emerge with seven points from the group and, in all probability, avoid the prospect of a last 16 showdown with likely Group D winners Germany, who duly thrashed Australia 4-0 in their opening game the next day.

Happily the Algeria match was in Cape Town which offered us a few days away from the depressing confines of Sun City and a real taste of the World Cup atmosphere. We flew south early on the day before the game with a local airline called Kulula whose stewardesses had a wonderful line in Groucho Marx-esque humour that had us roaring in the aisles with their in-flight announcements:

"In the event of a sudden loss of cabin pressure, masks will descend from the ceiling. Stop screaming then pull the mask over your face. If you have a small child travelling with you, secure your mask before assisting with theirs. If you are travelling with more than one child, pick your favourite."

"Ladies and gentlemen, we've reached cruising altitude and will be turning down the cabin lights. This is for your own comfort and also to enhance the appearance of your flight attendants."

"Please note this is a strictly non smoking flight. Anyone caught smoking during the flight will be asked to leave the aircraft."

"Ladies and gentlemen, we have landed in Cape Town. Please take all your possessions with you, as anything left behind will be shared equally between the crew."

It was wonderful to arrive in one of the world's greatest cities where, at last, we could feel the pulse of a vibrant location alive with World Cup joie de vivre. The only media activity on the eve of match days is the obligatory FIFA press conference at the stadium in which the manager and captain of each team sit at a top table and answer questions from the floor. There are no one-to-one TV or radio interviews and the whole affair is beamed live worldwide, so there's no pressure on me to deliver much and the fact that Mark Saggers and co were already in Cape Town presenting *talkSPORT* programmes from their hotel offered me a rare night out.

The ensuing years since my last on site World Cup assignment had mellowed myself and many of my travelling companions. No longer would the success of a night out be measured in how much you could drink, how late you got back and whether you could pick a fight with a 6' 8" Ukrainian nightclub bouncer. The last of these had actually happened to me during the Sydney Olympics in 2000 when I was trying to get into the Judgement Bar, a conveniently placed all night watering hole in the city's lively Paddington district. My passage was barred one night by a lantern jawed, trench-coated monolith who mistook my hyperactive demeanour in the queue for drunkenness and suggested in no uncertain terms that I was unwelcome. Unwilling to accept this latest indignity from a breed of men I have seldom had anything but utter contempt for, I argued loudly, but ultimately in vain, that he should be welcoming foreign guests into the bar rather than casting them aside.

Finally, when I realised no amount of logic or rationale would permeate his igneous exterior, I reverted to the good old fashioned Tony Lockwood-esque scream of frustrated abuse:

"You and your type are a disgrace to Sydney, Australia and the entire Olympic experience."

A couple of nights later I was greeted by an even longer queue outside the Judgement and at the head of it stood our friend arms crossed, his expression no more compromising than last time. This called for a change of tactic as I shuffled my way to the front.

"Excuse me sir, you may remember me from the other night. I would just like to apologise unreservedly for my behaviour. You are clearly not a disgrace to the Olympics, simply someone who is exercising their instructed duties in a fair and honest manner under difficult circumstances. I would be terribly grateful if you could see your way clear to letting me through and accept my solemn undertaking that I will act with the utmost responsibility once on the premises."

"No worries mate, in you go."

The atmosphere was a good deal less confrontational as a group of us enjoyed a pleasant pub crawl up and down Cape Town's Long Street on the eve of the Algeria game. This strip of bars, restaurants and clubs was thronged with fans from many different nations, including the heartwarming sight of England sup-porters behaving impeccably and respectfully amid the hubbub. At one point a large white van which must have contained around 20 flag-waving Algerians, either inside the vehicle or on its roof, parked outside a bar full of England fans and exchanged songs and banter for a full 20 minutes without a hint of malice. It was also great to have a few beers with some American supporters whose knowledge and passion for the game gave lie to the fact that the USA is a completely soccer free zone. They loved English football and enthused about it in that wonderful way of theirs:

"You know Robbie Savage at Derby? I kinda like that guy" or "I bet St James' Park is a real cool place."

Although it was wonderful to spend one night as part of the whole scene, it merely highlighted the sense of isolation we and the team were experiencing at our high veldt outposts near Rustenburg. It really felt as if we were the World Cup wallflowers, peering longingly into someone else's celebration but unable to join in. Unfortunately, the next day's match at the gleaming white bowl of the Green Point Stadium did little to suggest that the overall mood was about to be lifted.

In nearly 25 years watching England, I can't recall a more thoroughly inept, clueless and uninspired performance than the goalless draw against a side who started the tournament as 350-1 outsiders. Algeria, in only their third World Cup, were a hard working but decidedly average team whose two main stars had just been relegated from the Premier League with Portsmouth. Yet after 90 minutes of largely futile toiling, Capello's England had bestowed on them the mantle of impenetrable obduracy so admired by his fellow Italians.

As if the game itself wasn't bad enough, at the final whistle Wayne Rooney foolishly reacted to the understandable boos from the crowd by directing sarcastic remarks into a television camera. Later one of those disgruntled fans, a mortgage broker from south London called Pavlos Joseph, actually broke through a security cordon, entered the England dressing room and reportedly called the players a disgrace to their faces. Capello must have been tempted to play him up front for the next game against Slovenia, since he was the only Englishman that day who managed to breach a stubborn rearguard and find the target.

Again, a sizeable proportion of the team passed up the opportunity to talk to the media after the game although those that did offer their thoughts (Carragher, Lampard and Gerrard if I remember correctly) were honest in their appraisal of a horrendous night which had left England with two points from two games and in danger of failing to negotiate a World Cup group for the first time since 1958.

Almost as bad was the prospect of leaving Cape Town's very genuine splendour and returning to the mind-numbing fake opulence of Sun City, which really did seem to be the place to go if you wanted to completely avoid the World Cup and spend a few weeks in a culture vacuum. I'd already had a metaphorical belly full of golfing Afrikaaners and inveterate gamblers and, quite literally a belly full of everything on the 4th Street Cafe's pleasant but limited menu by the time we returned. Needless to say my subsequent broadcasts sounded more like autopsies than eulogies as we picked through the bones of a performance whose only redeeming feature seemed to be that at least nothing could possibly get worse.

It was amid this background of national self-loathing that we reached, perhaps, the defining point of this increasingly unhappy campaign, at the first proper media conference since the Algeria debacle. I am led to believe that the method of selecting players to attend these gatherings is a little akin to the centre circle huddle which forms just prior to a penalty shootout. Those brave or foolish enough to take a kick step forward, while the rest skulk around at the margins hoping not to make eye contact. After the nightmare in Cape Town it was plainly obvious that any volunteer would be thrust directly into the firing line of an understandably aggressive volley of questioning. The England media department must have felt a little like Peter Cook's brilliant *Beyond The Fringe* portrayal of a squadron leader sending a junior airman into a kamikaze mission:

"I want you to lay down your life, Perkins. We need a futile gesture at this stage. It will raise the whole tone of the war."

With the 22 others doubtless staring fixedly at the ground, Perkins turned out to be John Terry, who of course had been stripped of the captaincy and yet seemed to remain the de facto leader of the squad. Whether he actually volunteered or was pressed into attending remains a moot point but, as had now become the practice, his first port of call was the radio room. Rather than wearing the expression of a condemned man, he strode in, sat down and for the next ten minutes or so, proceeded to leave Mike Ingham and I completely enrapt at the brilliant warts 'n' all assessment he gave us of the match itself and the mood of the England camp in general.

In a wide-ranging and very honest appraisal, he admitted the performance had been an embarrassment and, in answer to a leading question, suggested that the team would need to express their feelings strongly to Capello during the team meeting later that evening, regardless of whether it might anger or upset the manager. He also felt, as most fans and journalists did, that Joe Cole warranted a bigger role in a squad which seemed to be lacking his talent and creativity. When the interview concluded Mike and I, who are not in the habit of executing airborne high fives and shouting "ker-ching", simply exchanged a knowing glance which acknowledged that this particular piece of audio would have the nation hanging on its every word. It brought back memories of the feelings we had when

Kevin Keegan explained his reasons for quitting the England job in a stairwell at the old Wembley after defeat by Germany in 2000.

Sure enough, within seconds of the interview going to air, *talkSPORT* and *5Live* listeners were soon avidly entering the debate. Most of them, as I understood it, seemed to be very supportive of the former captain, expressing that it was about time someone from within the camp had the strength to articulate their true feelings about the situation. I certainly shared that belief and so, interestingly, did virtually everyone at the England media centre that day. As we waited on the bus to return home we almost unanimously agreed that this had been one of the most interesting and forthright interviews ever given by an England player. No one, at any stage, suggested this was insurrectionist bolshy talk from a traitorous outsider.

However, during the course of that evening, some of the senior football writers (known as the "number ones") got wind of a feeling within the England management team that Terry had overstepped the mark and was speaking out of turn. As a result, the papers ran stories claiming he was deliberately undermining the manager as a reaction to being stripped of the captaincy. One tabloid (you can probably guess which one) even described him as a mutineer. To be fair to the writers, Capello's opinion on the matter was made clear in a later interview with ITV's Gabriel Clarke in which he said the Chelsea defender had made "a big mistake".

Even so, I felt Terry should still be praised for making a stand rather than be cast in the role of a national traitor. As acts of treason go, suggesting Joe Cole would be of benefit to the team was hardly the Gunpowder Plot and it wasn't as if Capello was a popular manager leading a squad of World Cup winners in waiting. I voiced these opinions on *talkSPORT* the next morning, adding that you could almost forgive footballers for churning out bland statements in interviews if, as soon as they produce something more insightful, they are likened to Philby, Burgess and McLean. Surely we should be encouraging senior players to give us forthright views rather than criticising them.

As you can imagine, this was not a terribly popular view among the English media inmates of Sun City, although some of my newspaper colleagues did confide to me that they held similar views. The *Mirror's* John Cross (one of the "number twos") wasn't among them though, and appeared on the same breakfast show to take me to task for what he saw as naive and misguided comments. I have absolutely no qualms about Crossy doing so, as it was his honest opinion and opened an interesting side debate about the different ways that the media approach stories. But when I put up a post on Facebook along similar lines, one particularly charmless individual shouted across the breakfast hall that I was a Johnny Come Lately who didn't have a clue about modern day journalism.

Those sort of comments are water off a duck's back frankly, but I was more than a little upset as some people who I had known and respected for a long time then used Facebook to decry me as a "typical broadcaster, who stands on the margins slagging off the papers." Even *Daily Mail* columnist Charlie Sale, the patron saint of Fleet Street agents provocateur, came up to me and said "I hear you've been upsetting people."

And so the next leg of the journey was a rather unhappy one as I travelled to Port Elizabeth for the make or break meeting with Slovenia, feeling a little ostracised by some of my fellow travellers. After a couple of hours of moping I cleared my head with a very pleasant stroll along the seafront of this quiet and charming city, positioned where the Indian and Atlantic Oceans converge. When I returned was invited along by a group of newspaper guys to dinner in the hotel which, to the joy of all of us, was hosting a curry night and this was followed by a drink with my *talkSPORT* colleagues Matt Smith and Mark Saggers. By the time I got to bed, I felt as if my spell in the leper colony was over. It is one of the great inevitabilities of these trips that people will, from time to time, fall out but it is equally true that these outbreaks of animosity rarely last very long. Indeed, I have found that there are few things in this life that can't be put right with a few beers and a curry.

A first half goal by Jermain Defoe secured a 1-0 win over the Slovenians at the Nelson Mandela Bay Stadium and ensured that England completed their long walk to the knock out stages. The euphoria was tempered slightly by news of a very late winner by David Beckham's LA Galaxy team-mate Landon Donovan for the USA against Algeria, which meant that qualification would be via second place and so, rather than Ghana in Rustenburg, our round of 16 opponents would be Germany in Bloemfontein.

The situation had many of us drawing parallels with Italia 90 when England scraped through the group stage with little honour but eventually came within a couple of spot kicks of the final. The reality was though, that a largely unconvincing single goal win over a nation with the smallest population in the whole tournament was hardly a crushing endorsement of Capello and his team, nor a result likely to have the average German fan weeping into his stein of Krombacher.

But at least we were through, and there were happy scenes in the 4th Street Cafe the following night when we regulars ("evening Ando, pint of the usual in your monogrammed pewter mug?") were joined by Adrian Bevington, Joanne Budd and Mark Whittle from the FA media department who had managed to escape the shackles of Royal Bafokeng for the evening. The three of them were sitting at a table, each tucking into a pint of lager and a huge plate of chips.

When I asked why they had opted for this less than healthy meal option when there was far more tasty and nutritional fare available on the menu, Jo neatly encapsulated the entire Capello regime in a single sentence:

"We've gone thirty five days without chips."

Of all the people cursing England's failure to win the group, the BAC travel staff had as much reason to complain as anyone. Their hopes of a cosy tie in nearby Rustenburg had been completely scuppered in the blink of an eye by Donovan's late goal in Pretoria, and they now had to implement Plan B which involved transporting us via a seven-hour bus trip to the very unlovely city of Bloemfontein which was nearly 400 miles to the south.

This meant a very early start and it was literally at the crack of dawn when we boarded the coach. *TalkSPORT* of course wanted a piece from me into the breakfast programme but I explained that it would have to be via a mobile phone from the bus as we would be an hour into the journey at the time they wanted me to come on the show. As ever the station's producers decided to milk a little humour from the situation. Danny Kelly was presenting that morning and I was introduced with a piece of music which I was old enough to identify as the theme tune from the 1970s ITV sitcom *On The Buses*. When it faded out and Danny crossed to me I was in hysterics and reacted by adapting the famous catchphrase of the programme's misanthropic Inspector Blake, played by Stephen Lewis:

"I 'ate you, Kelly."

Whoever chose the DVD we were shown to break up the journey had a delicious sense of irony too given the assignment that faced England, as we settled down to watch *Where Eagles Dare*. The 1968 wartime epic features a gallant band of men storming the ramparts of a German fortress and emerging victorious. Sadly Capello's modern day marauders where unable to enlist the services of Clint Eastwood in their bid to achieve a similar outcome.

From what I could glean on our journey through the city, Bloemfontein itself had not travelled a great distance in the post-apartheid era in terms of social regeneration. We traversed a large urban area which appeared to be a black ghetto with its inhabitants living hand to mouth on the streets in the midst of crumbling buildings and crushing poverty, redolent of 1960s East St Louis or Detroit. Our base was an equally anachronistic slice of Afro-Americana on the outskirts of the city called the Windmill Casino and Entertainment Centre. This charmless monstrosity of gambling halls and generic restaurant chains fronted by a gaudy neon approximation of the Moulin Rouge, was billed by one travel guide as "an elegant experience for those who dare to flirt with chance and blow kisses at Lady Luck." For non gamblers like myself who fart at chance and blow raspberries at Lady Luck, this was a wholly dispiriting experience, reminiscent of some hell hole in the American Midwest where Bible Belt out of towners turn up in 4 x 4s and talk loudly about the right to bear arms and the virtues of capital punishment.

On the day we arrived, a section of the car park had been turned into a fashion catwalk and a succession of very bored looking amateur models were showcasing the kind of eye wateringly garish party gowns which Lady Gaga would have dismissed as simply too dressy. It was like being in the direct firing line of a terrifying phalanx of giant decorative toilet roll covers and you needed sunglasses to shield your eyes from the fluorescent outfits as much as the warm sunshine.

Across the way we could see the entrance to the casino itself where, in bold letters above a large slot in the brickwork were the words "Gun Drop Off". This seemed to imply that it would be considered absolutely fine to wander around the complex brandishing a Glock semi-automatic pistol but not to carry it within the inner sanctum of slot machines, card tables and roulette wheels. To add to the peculiarity of the setting, there was a huge red and white big top behind the hotel with a large sign which said "McLaren's Circus", a reminder that at least Capello's circus was in town rather than looking on forlornly at home.

Not that we had time to check out McLaren and his bunch of clowns falling off a tight rope clutching an umbrella. Within an hour or so of arriving we headed off to the Free State Stadium for the pre-match media conferences, which turned out to be a rather embarrassing and petty game of tit for tat, which did little to suggest that Anglo-German football rivalries had cooled ahead of this latest showdown.

As the "home" team according to the draw Germany's press conference came first, but neither coach Joachim Low nor captain Philipp Lahm appeared before the world's media. This was in contravention of FIFA's rules which stipulated that the manager and at least one player must attend the pre-match grilling. Instead the Germans sent out their goalkeeping coach Andreas Kopke, explaining that they had been denied access to the stadium pitch for training and were forced to conduct the session elsewhere and the key figures did not have time to get across the city for the conference. The cynics amongst us drew the more plausible conclusion that this was a ploy to agitate England, given that Kopke was the man whose save from Gareth Southgate's penalty had broken English hearts in the Wembley semi-final at Euro 96.

Although Capello and Gerrard both represented England when their turn came, it was an appearance which consisted of a mere seven minutes of fairly surly and non-committal answers before they departed. This left a packed and baffled room of international reporters feeling rather cheated, given the insipid nature of the responses; as Capello revealed, none too sensationally, that he respected the Germans, they were a very good team and he hoped Wayne Rooney would be a key figure. Inevitably this led to renewed accusations of aloofness and arrogance against England from the foreign press, with which it was hard not to sympathise. The FA denied a snub, claiming they had fulfilled their responsibilities but you couldn't help feeling they had stoked up a war of very few words.

Back at the Windmill I even began to harbour notions of regret that I wasn't in Sun City preparing for a match in nearby Rustenburg but, alas, the Royal Bafokeng would host USA versus Ghana that night. Unfortunately the casino had the only giant screen television on site and so became the default venue for the media pack to assemble and watch the game. After apologising profusely to the doorman for not having a gun to drop off (although of course the irony was lost), I ventured in and sat down with some colleagues to enjoy what turned out to be a compelling affair won by the Ghanaians courtesy of Asamoah Gyan's extra time goal, which guaranteed African involvement in the quarter-finals.

However, just seconds after Hungarian referee Viktor Kassai blew his final whistle, the casino management decided that they had had quite enough of the World Cup and the wall panel on which the flat screen TV was mounted started to move upwards. Behind it stood a row of some eight or nine topless cabaret dancers who began to enact a rather clumsy version of the Can-Can for the benefit of a largely dumbstruck audience. The whole situation led me to imagine a scenario in *Thunderbirds* whereby part of the wall on Tracy Island would slide across to one side, revealing not Thunderbird 1, 2 or 3 but a clandestine bordello in which Virgil and co would get their rocks off after a hard day's rescuing.

I'm not sure what they put in the drinks at the Windmill Casino bar, but I woke up the next morning with a peculiar yet profound sense of inner well being and a calm confidence that England would finally beat Germany in a knockout tie for the first time since 1966. Of course it flew in the face of logic and was totally misplaced as the Germans completely outplayed Capello's bemused and pedestrian team. Even the injustice of Frank Lampard's "goal that never was" did little to dispel the universal notion among the row of English reporters at the half-time urinals (and I'm sure the millions back home) that we were getting a right good kicking from a vastly superior side. Capello's supposed knack for turning things around when struggling at the interval appeared to be restricted to friendly matches, and Thomas Mueller's brace rendered the 4-1 scoreline, if anything, even more emphatic than the mere numerals suggested.

For me, the scene in the Mixed Zone after the match underlined the gulf between the two nations every bit as graphically as the events on the field of play. Successive England players shuffled past the throngs of reporters, their heads bowed, shoulders hunched. Some chose to cower under giant pairs of headphones, others had the laces of their brand new trainers undone and they were all clutching black plastic bags stuffed with their personal belongings. Had they not been instantly recognisable global superstars, you might have mistaken them for a party of thoroughly bored schoolboys trooping back onto the coach after a reluctant visit to the British Museum. Certainly England's World Cup dreams were, yet again, history.

Compare and contrast this with the appearance of the German players, who emerged in brilliant, almost dazzlingly white tracksuits, walking tall, their hair immaculate. They exuded a kind of unvanquishable aura that I don't think I have ever seen in an England side and obligingly conducted interviews in several languages with anyone who cared to ask. Many of these players, such as Mueller, Mesut Oezil, Jerome Boateng and Sami Khedira were comparatively young men and yet in every single respect they totally outshone old stagers like Gerrard, Lampard, Cole and Terry who had, so presumptuously, been labelled England's "golden generation".

Capello's media conference the next day simply underlined the malaise. He suggested the players were tired after a long season and had therefore been unable to give of their best, but stopped short of attaching any personal blame to himself or his preparations for the dismal campaign. Furthermore, he had no plans to quit and, in that respect, was in a position of some strength. Unfortunately prior to the World Cup the powers that be at the FA, in their infinite wisdom, had decided to remove an escape clause in the Italian's contract which meant that they now couldn't afford to sack him even if they wanted to; effectively locking the two parties into a loveless marriage. It was an arrogant and needless piece of business seemingly based on the assumption of World Cup success which opened up the governing body yet again to accusations of setting back the course of the English national team.

I'm really not sure what passes for logic when the FA comes to formulate such decisions and have yet to encounter anyone who does, however I do have a radical plan to ensure the same mistakes are not repeated. Instead of forming committees, think-tanks and Team England leaderships or wasting thousands on consultancy fees the FA should simply do the following.

Walk into any pub, betting shop, secondary school classroom, factory floor, railway station or public park anywhere in the country and refer whatever issue is at hand to whoever happens to be around. I would be absolutely astonished if the response to whether it would be a good idea to remove a sacking clause in Fabio Capello's contract prior to the World Cup had not been a resounding: "Would it, bollocks."

There you go, FA mandarins; a cheap, quick, democratic, unanimous and utterly sagacious solution to all your current and future problems.

My final broadcast from Sun City expressed the opinion that England should now tear up the team sheet, impose international retirement on the remnants of the golden generation and concentrate fully on the new breed of young players coming through. If this meant missing out on one or even two major tournament qualifications then so be it; the nation needed long term rather than short term solutions. They didn't of course and as if to illustrate the point France, who had had an even worse World Cup than England, came to Wembley in the autumn that followed with a new look side and played us off the park.

Although my role as England correspondent had come to a premature and disappointing end, I still had two weeks to kill in South Africa since my wife and two daughters had arranged to come over for a holiday starting the day after the final. So I decamped to the *talkSPORT* lodge in the northern suburbs of Johannesburg enjoying a leisurely time with its motley crew of inhabitants, namely Matt Smith, Jim Proudfoot, Ian Danter, Ray Parlour, Mark Saggers, Adrian Durham, Ian "Moose" Abrahams, Stan Collymore, Liam Fisher, Jonny Norman and Ant D'Angelo.

I felt quite guilty as there was precious little for me to do while the others were working around the clock to produce commentaries and programmes on the remainder of the tournament. Fortunately my old friend David O'Sullivan from local station 702 was on hand to ensure that my evenings were well spent in a variety of local hostelries, most notably the Radium Beer Hall in Orange Grove, one of the city's oldest pubs which had been a home to radicals and free thinkers during the early apartheid era (secretly serving beer to blacks in a room at the back), and rocketed into my list of the Top 20 pubs in the world.

The days were less exciting with the others away covering games or presenting programmes for long periods although Ray Parlour paid me the greatest footballing compliment I've ever received as we kicked a ball around on the lodge's sloping lawn, asserting that I had "a nice touch". The other main diversion consisted of watching *Sky News'* coverage of the manhunt back home involving gunman Raoul Moat, who was hiding out in a forest near the north east town of Rothbury.

I felt a little sorry for the local residents who had to contend not only with a dangerous killer on the loose, but also the fact that their entire town had been turned into a giant outdoor television studio by the likes of Sky, the BBC and ITV. Reporters descended on the area in droves to stand in fields and by roadsides to explain to us 24/7 that a large swathe of greenery continued to conceal the fugitive from view and that nothing much was actually happening.

Terrified townsfolk would cower in their homes harbouring the twin fears that either Moat or Kay Burley would suddenly appear at the doorstep and shatter their daily lives. Arguably even less gripping than the coverage of the siege was the World Cup final itself which saw Holland exchange total football for total mayhem in their attempts to kick Spain off the field at Soccer City. The indefatigable Matt Smith had managed to secure me an observer seat for the game and I was delighted when Andres Iniesta's extra time goal won it for the Spaniards. My journey through the packed media tribune to grab a beer in the press lounge after the presentation took me via a section of Spanish reporters who were hugging each other, scarcely able to hold back the tears at their soccer mad nation's finest hour. I genuinely felt a surge of warmth towards them, as I had for the French when they beat Brazil in the 1998 final. But of course it was tempered with the depressingly recurring realisation that I would almost certainly never experience such a feeling towards my own team in my lifetime.

Covering England does your head in at times. World Cup 2010 had been an unmitigated disaster with an unpopular manager leading an unhappy and unmotivated squad through four matches in which they had underperformed every time. And yet such is the draw of the game that we'll be back, probably with similar unrealistic notions of glory, time after time and hoping against hope that one day we will share the joy felt by those Spaniards who were in Johannesburg on July 11th 2010.

I have often tried to explain this strange magnetism to friends and relations for whom football is not a beautiful game, but a bewildering and pointless exercise in self delusion and torture. Why, they ask, would anyone attach so many hopes and dreams to the process of propelling a piece of leather up and down a rectangular patch of grass?

My best stab at summing up what it means to millions of ordinary people is to relate the story of a fairly routine trip to Elland Road to cover Leeds in a League game twenty or so years ago (I can't even recall the opponents). After the match I took a bus from outside the ground to the station and, on alighting, was accosted by two girls in their early twenties who were obviously dressed up for a night out.

"Do you know how Leeds got on today?" one of them asked.

"They won 3-1," I replied.

"Brilliant, we'll get a shag tonight then."

CHAPTER EIGHTEEN

"Back In A Coffin"

Even if Fabio Capello had become an ice cream salesman rather than a hugely successful footballer and manager, I am sure he would still have ended up a very wealthy man. The proprietor of "Gelati Catenaccio" would simply have strolled across the street to the local tabacchi and purchased a lottery ticket with the correct Euromillions numbers and lived happily ever after.

This King Midas of managers had again plucked a favourable hand from the draw for Euro 2012 qualification, emerging with less than testing fixtures against Switzerland, Bulgaria, Wales and Montenegro. Although the last named were certainly the most formidable of the so-called minnows, the path to Poland and Ukraine looked a smooth one and comfortable early wins against the Bulgarians at home and the Swiss in Basel suggested as much. Even a tame goalless draw with the impressive Montenegrins at Wembley felt like little more than a blip.

The Wales games were billed as derbies but, in reality, were mere formalities especially given that their star man Gareth Bale missed the game in Cardiff, which England won 2-0. Even after a hiccup at home to Switzerland which saw the visitors go two goals up before Capello's men scrambled a draw, England entered the final group game against Montenegro in Podgorica needing a point to qualify.

In a 12,000 capacity stadium in Europe's newest democracy, England produced the kind of display which suggested that Baldrick rather than Baldini had a hand in the cunning plan, such was the combination of stupidity, slapstick and farce which followed. Comfortably 2-0 up with seconds to go to half-time, England conceded a sloppy goal and then, with 15 minutes left, Wayne Rooney committed the kind of act which even his not yet two year old son Kai would have considered a bit on the petulant and rash side.

Rather than remaining calm and riding out the last quarter of an hour of a largely successful mission, Rooney launched a quite inexplicable and ludicrous assault on defender Miodrag Dzudovic who, incidentally, was an employee of the splendidly named Spartak Nalchik. This, in case you are wondering, is a Russian football club and not a trendy milk bar from *A Clockwork Orange*. This agricultural scythe through the back of the hapless Montenegrin's legs rendered referee Wolfgang Stark's breakfast decision of whether to have cereal or toast an infinitely harder one than which card to brandish into Rooney's gnarled features.

A late Montenegro equaliser meant the ten remaining Englishmen were hanging on at the end and, although the point needed to qualify was duly secured, the sense of celebration was tempered by the fact that the Manchester United striker would incur a three match ban, thus ruling him out of the entire group stage at the Euros.

Happily the 32-year-old Dzudovic, unlike his assailant, proved himself to be a man of honour and integrity as he added his testimony to the FA's plea to have the ban reduced and UEFA duly cut the suspension to two games after a contrite personal appearance by Rooney himself. It meant he would miss the opening group games against France and Sweden but be eligible for the final match against co-hosts Ukraine. Capello, who also attended the hearing in Switzerland, had incidentally won another lottery rollover by avoiding the two really tough groups in the finals.

It was to be one of his last acts as national team coach. In December 2011 the England captain John Terry was charged with a racially aggravated public order offence after allegedly verbally abusing Anton Ferdinand during a QPR v Chelsea game in October. The subsequent decision by the courts not to hear the case until after Euro 2012 left the FA with a moral quandary; should they ban Terry from playing for England or strip him of the captaincy which might be seen as prejudging the trial, or allow him to continue which could be construed as a potential embarrassment should he later be found guilty, especially if England were to win the tournament?

In the midst of all this, another courtroom drama was about to unfold. Harry Redknapp, who many considered the ideal replacement for Capello when the Italian's England contract expired after the Euros, and who had powerful supporters both within the game and the media, was due before Southwark Crown Court on tax evasion charges stemming from his time as manager at Portsmouth. His co-defendant was the former Pompey chairman Milan Mandaric.

The trial began in late January and I was assigned to report on proceedings for *talkSPORT*. I arrived on the first day to queue for a pass for the press seats in the small courtroom and collected a little yellow ticket bearing the number 12 which was one of only 26 which were issued to the media. I am told these collectors' items now fetch a decent price on ebay.

Alongside me in the media gallery were not court or crime reporters but sports journalists such as myself; I bumped into my old mate Rob Beasley, now working for the *Sun*, and assumed he was there to cover the case. But it turned out that he was the star witness for the prosecution, having conducted taped interviews with Redknapp and Mandaric while he was on the *News Of The World* which the Crown alleged were incriminating against the pair.

Before the defendants had even taken the stand there was drama in the court, as a *Guardian* reporter was taken to task for tweeting the name of a juror. This led to the judge, who was clearly less than impressed at having to peer out at a row of football hacks, banning any interaction on social media from within his courtroom. I had already told *talkSPORT* that I was extremely uncomfortable with tweeting the proceedings since it meant you weren't concentrating fully on the complicated evidence and, furthermore, one error or typo could land you in serious trouble. It was, given the events at the end of the trial, to prove a wise decision and I'm pleased to say the station fully backed my stance.

The highlights of the trial came when Redknapp gave evidence in person in his own engaging, amusing and scatterbrained manner. There was laughter in court as he described how he had named a Monaco bank account "Rosie 47" after his late, lamented dog and the year of his birth, and then went on to suggest that anyone would be lucky to have a wife as loving and loyal as the hound in question who he described as "more than just a dog". The Tottenham boss also inadvertently announced to the court that his banking security password was his mother's maiden name, forcing his accountant to make a hasty call urging him to change it pronto. There was also a bizarre moment when, in mid interrogation, Redknapp turned on one of the police officers who was seated nearby and claimed he was trying to play mind games by constantly staring in his direction.

From the witness stand, Redknapp portrayed himself as a man incapable of understanding the ways of high finance, claiming he had never read a contract in his life and was blissfully unaware of the clauses within them, even to the point where he had been surprised when they triggered huge bonus payments in his favour.

I had been reporting these exchanges on *talkSPORT* during the breaks in proceedings from the pavement outside the court and, despite the freezing temperatures and snow flurries, was thoroughly enjoying my stint as a court reporter. After a two-week trial Redknapp and Mandaric were both cleared on two charges each of tax evasion and within minutes of the not guilty verdicts being returned I rushed down to announce live on the Richard Keys and Andy Gray show that the pair would walk from the court as free men and that Redknapp's path to becoming the next England manager was now clear.

However if you had been tuned into *BBC News 24* you would have heard a rather different version of events. In this age of texting and tweeting there has developed a ridiculous and unhealthy obsession amongst broadcasters to try and be first with any breaking news. As a result, on the final day of the trial, the BBC positioned its main reporter in front of a camera outside the courtroom and dispatched a junior member of the production staff inside to text the decisions of the jury to him so that they would win the race with ITV and Sky to deliver the verdicts.

When the jury foreman answered the first charge against Redknapp, she did so in such a quiet voice that we in the press seats flashed anxious, confused glances at each other, genuinely unclear as to whether she had actually said "guilty" or "not guilty". The three other verdicts which were delivered far more clearly confirmed the pair had been cleared on all counts and they hugged each other in the dock.

However the BBC representative inside the court had heard "guilty" for the first charge against Redknapp and texted accordingly. Downstairs the reporter announced the wrong outcome live on air, accompanied by a graphic at the bottom of the screen which read "Harry Redknapp found guilty of tax evasion", before eventually correcting himself and claiming there had been "confusion" surrounding the verdict. The only actual confusion was in the mind of the BBC producer who had sanctioned such a muddle-headed decision in the first place. Maybe they should come up with a new slogan "BBC News 24: First, Fastest and False".

When Redknapp emerged onto the steps of the courthouse to give his reaction, I managed to position myself in such a manner that all the TV pictures prominently featured my *talkSPORT* microphone cube, and many of the newspapers the next morning displayed my ugly mug to Harry's left. It reminded me a little of the Bobby Robson back pages I had muscled into before Italia 90 and I thought about framing the two images side by side, with the words "John Anderson: Annoying Football Managers Since 1989".

Five days before Redknapp's acquittal the FA had dreamt up a less than satisfactory compromise to the John Terry dilemma by deciding that he would lose the captain's armband (for a second time) but continue to be available for team selection, effectively handing the decision over his international future to the manager.

On the final day of the trial at Southwark, as we were queuing to enter the courtroom, I was chatting with some fellow reporters about how we imagined Capello would react to this situation. I suggested that it was possible he might resign on a point of principle and this was greeted by howls of laughter and derision from the group, which included an award winning sports news reporter from a broadsheet newspaper. Within 12 hours Capello had quit. Terry, he maintained, should be treated as innocent until proven guilty and the FA's decision rendered his position as national team manager untenable. As it turned out, Terry's subsequent acquittal at Westminster Magistrates' Court in July seemed to vindicate his stance, although the FA later banned the Chelsea captain for four matches after finding him guilty of using abusive or insulting words.

I was back on *talkSPORT* that evening reacting to Capello's departure and describing February 8th 2012 as one of the most extraordinary days I have ever experienced in more than a quarter of a century as a sports reporter. What now seemed inevitable was that, on the very day he was cleared of tax evasion, Harry Redknapp was now officially the rightful heir to the England job and would lead the nation into battle at Euro 2012. Cry God for Harry, England and St George.

In the meantime Stuart Pearce was appointed interim boss for the friendly against Holland on February 29th which had been rescheduled after its postponement following the riots in London the previous summer. I had never really warmed to Pearce as a player, given his general reluctance to talk to the media, and was far from impressed with his performance at the press conference which followed his temporary appointment.

His assertion that he would love to lead England in the Euros but didn't feel sufficiently qualified to take the job long term seemed disingenuous, and his appointment of Scott Parker as captain, with no disrespect to the Spurs midfielder, came across as a needless and rather petty snub towards the more experienced Steven Gerrard. Pearce was hugely popular with the fans for the passion he showed as a player, but in his grey managerial suit he struck me as someone desperately trying, but miserably failing, to appear urbane and innovative. The fact that he constantly referred to the FA as "the federation", as if it were something out of *Star Wars*, merely compounded this impression. The only saving grace was that, after four years of Capello, at least we had an England manager who didn't need an interpreter sitting alongside him during interviews.

England were outclassed by the Dutch at Wembley with Arjen Robben running riot and the 3-2 scoreline was hugely flattering to the home side. A late comeback failed to paper over the cracks and it was clear to all and sundry that Pearce was not, even in the short term, the right man for the job.

Redknapp meanwhile was taking the concept of "England manager as impossible job" to extraordinary lengths. It seemed you didn't even need to hold the position to be blighted by its curse and even being mentioned in the same breath would bring on a titanic dose of the collywobbles. After an impressive 5-0 win over Newcastle the weekend after his trial, the Spurs boss contrived to win only one of the following nine Premier League games and suffered a calamitous FA Cup semi-final defeat at the hands of Chelsea. They did eventually finish in fourth place, but missed out on Champions League qualification as their London rivals beat Bayern Munich in the final.

Even those who had championed Redknapp as the obvious choice now began to have doubts and on May 1st the FA announced that Roy Hodgson would be the new England manager, a decision which, amazingly, had been reached without anyone in the media getting any wind of it. There were a few raised eyebrows, but a glance at the West Brom manager's CV suggested he was far better qualified to lead the national team than his more flamboyant counterpart. He had managed 16 teams in eight countries, including at international level with Finland, the United Arab Emirates and Switzerland, leading the latter at the 1994 World Cup.

Hodgson impressed greatly at his official unveiling as he handled all manner of questions with honesty, grace and wisdom, even when quizzed about his spell as a young player and coach in the apartheid-era South Africa. I often try to end my radio interviews with a light hearted question and enquired whether, since it was Mayday, he felt he had come to England's rescue. His reply gave the piece a lovely finishing flourish:

"That's a remarkable question, but I'm not sure England need rescuing. I just hope that I can recapture the spirit of 1966 rather than 1066."

Unfortunately this articulate and engaging figure was to learn very quickly about the perils of taking on a job which makes the Prime Minister look like a Lollipop Man. The *Sun*, in its never ending campaign to belittle and trivialise just about anything, chose to concentrate on Hodgson's speech impediment and published a front page headline of staggering disrespect and insensitivity.

"Bwing On The Euwos: We'll See You In Ukwaine Against Fwance."

This displayed all the sophistication and subtlety of *The Simpsons'* school bully Nelson Muntz ("you can't pronounce your R's..ha, ha") and was met with anger and revulsion by anyone with an IQ above 7. The FA publicly castigated the paper but even that failed to prick the conscience of the *Sun's* editorial team who went on to run a front page lead in which the puerile, overpaid, tennis fan Jonathan Ross (or "Wossy" as he's hilariously dubbed) dismissed it as a bit of a laugh. I'm quite sure he did find the whole thing hysterical, given that his television show consists entirely of him dribbling saliva over celebrities with films to promote and delivering excruciating, scripted double entendres about his gay backing band "they love reading the papers, you'll often find them getting stuck into a Mail on Sunday" (ooh, my sides).

Just 15 days after taking the job, Hodgson was back in the Wembley media centre to reveal the 23 players he had selected for Poland and Ukraine. Much of the focus centred on whether he would pick John Terry, Rio Ferdinand, both or neither, given the accusations that the Chelsea skipper had racially abused the Manchester United defender's brother and fears that selecting them both might engender a potential split in the squad. The evening before the announcement journalists got wind that it was Ferdinand who would be sacrificed and that Manchester City's in-form full-back Micah Richards wouldn't figure either .

Before I set off to Wembley for the conference I tweeted the following:

Given what we know, could this be the 23: JH JR RG; GJ PJ JT GC JL AC LB; TW AOC FL SG GB SP JM AY SD; WR DW AC JD.

When the squad was confirmed via the FA's website, I was astonished to learn that I had got the names 100% right and, as far as I know, was the only person among the collected scribes and reporters to have done so.

Hodgson explained that Ferdinand had been omitted for "football reasons" and became a little perturbed when the line of questioning focused almost entirely on his exclusion. The player had hardly figured during the qualification campaign, he reasoned, and he was keen to defer loyalty onto those who had helped England reach the finals.

As well as vilification at the hands of the tabloids, Hodgson quickly learnt another harsh lesson about life as England manager, namely the injury curse which always seems to strike on the eve of a major tournament. Even before naming the squad he had been robbed of the services of Jack Wilshere, Kyle Walker, Chris Smalling and Darren Bent but it didn't end there. Third choice goalkeeper John Ruddy was the first to fall after breaking a finger in training (ironically his wedding finger, since he had been given leave to get married the following weekend) and he was followed by Frank Lampard who broke down with a thigh injury. Hodgson could have been mistaken for thinking he had walked into an episode of *Casualty* rather than the England job, and even worse was to follow.

Gareth Barry limped out of the 1-0 friendly win against Norway in Oslo with a stomach strain which didn't heal in time to make the plane and in the following warm-up game, another single goal victory at home to Belgium, Gary Cahill broke his jaw after a collision with team-mate Joe Hart, following a cynical push by visiting midfielder Dries Mertens. The fact that the Chelsea defender was replaced in the squad by the inexperienced Liverpool full-back Martin Kelly rather than Ferdinand, a veteran of 81 caps and three World Cup campaigns, led to serious questions about Hodgson's judgement as manager.

What could not be queried was the fact that the new boss produced hard working, well drilled teams which, although unlikely to rival the 1970 Brazilians in the glamour stakes, were certainly hard to beat. Two wins and two clean sheets against decent opposition in the warm up matches suggested that, at the very least, England would be no pushovers in the weeks to come. The games also illustrated the good form of Ashley Young and Joleon Lescott and the promise of young players like Danny Welbeck and Alex Oxlade-Chamberlain.

Other positive factors emerged in the days leading up to the squad's departure for their base in Poland. The FA, conscious of the negative perceptions surrounding the squad in South Africa, had chosen a location right in the very heart of the beautiful and historic city of Krakow as their home from home. This would offer the players a wonderful backdrop and a degree of freedom to get out and about during the tournament. In keeping with this new spirit of glasnost, a week before flying out, they hosted a pre-tournament golf day and barbecue for the players and media at their English base at The Grove, just north of Watford. Given that I am to golf what Tiger Woods is to marriage counselling, I respectfully declined the invitation to embarrass myself on the manicured greens of Hertfordshire, but gratefully accepted the chance to enjoy some free food and drink in the evening.

It is fair to say that spending a few hours in the company of 40 or 50 assorted scribblers, snappers and TV and radio "talent" wouldn't figure highly in many footballers' lists of "50 Things To Do Before I Die" but, although most of the squad stayed within their own groups, they were very courteous and well mannered throughout. What was plainly obvious from this gathering was that Steven Gerrard and John Terry were the Alpha males, mixing with charming ease amongst our group and chatting amiably with everyone who approached them. It was Gerrard's 32nd birthday and he joked that he would be really pissed off if anyone produced a cake or sang "Happy Birthday" since he was beginning to feel his age, especially in the company of youngsters like Oxlade-Chamberlain and Welbeck.

Terry, whose private demeanour appeared to be completely at odds with his turbulent and controversial public image, told us he was gutted for his Chelsea team-mate Lampard who'd suffered his injury that day, but was looking forward to seeing him fit again on the club's pre-season tour of the United States. He said the players particularly enjoyed trips to America since the vast majority of locals didn't have a clue who they were and so they could stroll around freely like normal tourists, which was next to impossible anywhere else in the world.

In as much as I could tell from the evening, it seemed that Phil Jagielka, Gary Cahill, Joe Hart, Theo Walcott and Wayne Rooney were the more outgoing ones with Leighton Baines, Scott Parker, Glen Johnson and Joleon Lescott of the quieter variety. Not one of the players touched a drop of alcohol all night but Gary Neville was relieved to be told by a member of the FA media department that the rule did not extend to the coaching staff. He had been part of the triumphant golf quartet which also included the less probable figure of *Daily Mirror* football correspondent Martin Lipton who was barely as tall as his putter. Neville's appointment by Hodgson appeared to be a masterstroke in that he was a hugely respected figure both as a former player and *Sky Sports* pundit who was able to bridge the generation gap between the sexagenarian manager and his squad. Having said that, when Neville made his England debut in 1995, Oxlade-Chamberlain was not yet two years old.

Things had got so bad on the injury front that the former Manchester United star had actually been called upon to play at centre-half in a training match. When we asked him how he had fared the answer was disarmingly honest.

"It was embarrassing," he said, "an absolute shambles."

Since May 25th when Ruddy had pulled out, the withdrawals had come at a rate of exactly one every three days. Cahill's absence was confirmed 72 hours before the squad's departure for Poland and I had fears that the traditional photo shoot on the steps of the aeroplane would result in the players collapsing domino-like down onto the tarmac with only third choice goalkeeper Jack Butland emerging unscathed to make the trip.

Happily everyone boarded the plane safely and I was already in Krakow by the time the squad arrived, having been awoken by the alarm clock at 02:30 that morning for a ridiculously early departure from Stansted. Unfortunately we had been booked on Ryanair who did their best to scupper my travel plans with their absurd baggage policy. I was carrying all my radio equipment plus enough clothes to last a four-week trip which would include at least four different cities, six different hotels and a minimum of eight internal flights, but was permitted only one case in the hold and one item of hand luggage. Fortunately BAC, who had organised the trip, agreed to pay the extra amount required to ensure that I was able to travel to the Euros with more than just a toothbrush, a pair of underpants and my broadcasting equipment.

If Ryanair could charge its passengers a tenner for each gulp of air inhaled and each millilitre of urine expelled during the flight they doubtless would, so next time you're planning a short hop to the continent and actually want to take a change of clothes, it would probably be more convenient to go business class via Singapore.

The motto of Ryanair: The Cheap Fares Airline is a little misleading given that it doesn't mention the plethora of "optional extras" it charges on top of the fare itself, and I would suggest that their next campaign carries the banner headline Ryanair: Making Air Travel A Thoroughly Unpleasant Experience Since 1985.

And they weren't the only sinister forces at work to try and ruin our preparations for the tournament. Prior to our departure, the BBC's *Panorama* programme had helpfully broadcast a documentary entitled "Euro 2012: Stadiums Of Hate", which purported to highlight frightening levels of racism and anti-Semitism among football supporters in the host countries, Poland and Ukraine. There was footage of seemingly racially aggravated violence during a league match at one of the Euro 2012 venues in Kharkiv and the former England defender Sol Campbell, never the most adroit in front of a microphone, warned fans that if they travelled to the tournament they might end up "coming back in a coffin". You got the impression that you would be savagely attacked by Molotov cocktail-wielding neo-Nazi thugs within seconds of setting foot in Warsaw or Kiev airport.

I have travelled extensively covering football in Eastern Europe and would not dispute that there are problems with a minority of extreme right-wing supporters in certain countries, although it is generally restricted to the rivalries among domestic clubs. It is certainly no worse than anything I have experienced among English fans and I personally have hardly ever witnessed any racist incidents on foreign soil beyond the confines of stadiums on match days. Even at a first glance the *Panorama* programme seemed to be scaremongering on a grand scale; a kind of *Daily Mail* on television approach from programme makers who had a pre-planned agenda and had conveniently forgotten that it wasn't so long ago that travelling English fans were guilty of exactly the same kind of behaviour.

Imagine the fuss in this country if Ukrainian or Polish TV had made a similar film telling their citizens it was not safe to visit the London Olympics, illustrated by footage of violence from the riots which blighted our capital in 2011. In the end of course, nobody came home from Euro 2012 in a box and, aside from an altercation between Polish and Russian fans early in the tournament, there were no serious incidents to cast a shadow over what was a very enjoyable trip for anyone who undertook it. All the supporters I spoke to had only positive things to say about their stay, and the Fan Zones at each tournament venue were beautifully organised, safe and enjoyable places to share the communal joy of watching football. My *talkSPORT* colleague Stan Collymore, who is of mixed race and an outspoken opponent of all forms of intolerance, told me he never encountered the slightest hint of malice or aggression from anyone during his four weeks in Ukraine.

Throughout my own journey the only manifestations of this supposed culture of hate were a couple of swastikas daubed on a wall in Poland, hardly the sort of thing which would have you cowering in a corner of your hotel bedroom for fear of venturing into the streets outside. The best bit of graffiti I spotted was a wonderfully crafted and ornate piece of lettering in a myriad of colours which spelt out the message "Fuck UEFA".

Upon our arrival in Krakow a group of us strolled into the city's magnificent main square which is dominated by the 14th century St Mary's basilica which looks down upon a bustling medieval piazza surrounded by a myriad of bars and restaurants, many of which were located in atmospheric subterranean locations. It didn't take long to reach the opinion that, if you were to pick a spot in Europe in which to be based for the next few weeks, you could do an awful lot worse.

After a splendid al fresco lunch, we went to check out the England team HQ at the Stary Hotel, a luxurious six-storey, 53-room building which had been converted from a 15th century merchant's house and was located a stone's throw from the thriving hub of this fantastic city. It was a world away from the secluded base the FA had chosen in South Africa two years ago, although there were fears that the players might be disturbed by the hubbub which engulfed the square at night when stag and hen parties would convene to sample the delights of the bars and clubs. The other potential threat to their beauty sleep was posed by a bugler who would climb one of the twin towers of the basilica and sound a blast from his golden trumpet on the hour every hour, 24 hours a day. This tradition dated back to the Middle Ages when his shrill blast would alert Krakowians to the threat of fire or invading Mongol hordes.

Most of the players came from big cities like London, Manchester, Birmingham and Liverpool and none of the ones we interviewed lost a wink due to either high altitude trumpeters or invading posses of drunken teenagers. What they did tell us was how much they enjoyed the city centre location and how relaxed they felt at their home from home. The sense of calm was also due to the almost complete lack of expectation from fans or the media going into the tournament.

If one good thing came out of that World Cup humiliation at the hands of the Germans in Bloemfontein, it was that never again would we enter any tournament with the kind of blinkered jingoism which had been such a ludicrous precursor to so many past campaigns. This group of players shouldered the lowest hopes of any England team since Test matches against the West Indies in the 1970s, and the general belief among supporters was that we would do well to qualify from the group and anything else was a bonus. My own rather gloomy prognosis was that England would lose to France and then draw with both Sweden and Ukraine, forcing an early trip home. My fears were compounded by the fact that the team hotel was next door to a shop called "Soap Bubble World", suggesting England's might well burst prematurely.

There was a large crowd outside the Stary to greet the England team bus as it arrived from the airport, including a noisy, green-shirted Irish contingent who attempted to wind up their English counterparts by chanting:

"One Maradona, there's only one Maradona."

Now whatever you think about England fans, there is no denying their wonderful ability to trump most rivals when it comes to verbal jousting via witty chants and songs. Within seconds came the riposte:

"Down with the Euro, you're going down with the Euro."

They did later get a dose of their own medicine at the Fan Zone in Kiev before the match against Sweden though, when despite being totally outnumbered by yellow-shirted Scandinavians, they began to sing, to the tune of "Go West":

"You're shit, but your birds are fit."

To which several thousand Swedes instantly retorted in perfect English:

"Go home, to your ugly wives."

The bus driver's initial attempt to negotiate his vehicle around the very tight final bend into the street outside the hotel was hopelessly misjudged, forcing him to reverse back down the narrow cobbled thoroughfare and try again. His second attempt was a success but as one wag in the crowd observed:

"I hope England take corners better than that against France."

The bus itself was liveried with the England crest and the slogan: One Prize, Two Countries, Three Lions. You could have gone on: Four Players Out Injured, Five Penalty Shootout Exits, etc.

Further proof that I was going to enjoy my stay in Krakow came when I was invited out on that first night to a traditional Polish restaurant by my old mate Olly Foster and some of his BBC TV colleagues. Appetites were clearly large in this part of the world since the main course consisted of mounds and mounds of pork knuckle, sausages, black pudding, ribs, fried potatoes, picked vegetables and onions served up in what appeared to be a wooden canoe. All of this was washed down with pints of the frothy local beer Zywiec which, in keeping with this most phonetically baffling of languages, is pronounced jeev-yetz. Not surprising really in a country where the town of Lodz is pronounced Woodge.

On their second day in Krakow the England squad attended a formal welcome reception from the city's mayor at the magnificent Gallery Of 19th Century Polish Art located in the old cloth hall at the very centre of the main square.

Immaculate in their dark, tailored suits, the squad made the short walk across the square through a crowd of excited locals and lined up rather awkwardly beneath the huge canvasses depicting agricultural landscapes and epic scenes of religious and military iconography. At one point I thought I heard Andy Carroll lean over to Jordan Henderson and whisper:

"Unless I'm very much mistaken Jordan, that portrait bears the trademark brushwork of Poland's foremost romantic painter Piotr Michalowski."

Of course I could have misheard.

The squad stood patiently as the speeches were translated back and forth between Polish and English, applauding respectfully at the right moments and then mingling politely with some of the invited guests who were absolutely delighted to be rubbing shoulders with these foreign superstars. It was a small but significant gesture which helped give the squad a sense of their surroundings and ensured that, if Poland went out of Euro 2012, the whole of Krakow would be rooting for England. It is perhaps an unfortunate by-product of such sporting pre-eminence that the players' diets are so closely monitored these days that none of them were at liberty to take advantage of a quite magnificent spread of food which adorned a huge table at the centre of the room. Never fear though, the English media party were on hand to ensure that this splendid feast didn't go to waste. I had only been in Krakow for 48 hours but was already in danger of coming home looking like Luciano Pavarotti. Incidentally, Joanne Budd later informed me that chips were back on the menu in the team hotel.

Prior to the reception, we had attended our first media conference since the team arrived, with Joe Hart and Stewart Downing put up for us to speak to. Joanne's latest media centre marvel had the added advantage of being housed in the hotel we were staying at, and the radio room interviews were conducted in what was actually a normal room in which the bed had been replaced by a large table at its centre which virtually filled the space leaving us rather squashed in at one end. When the 6'5" Hart sat down, his knees were virtually pushing into my chest and we managed to heave the table back a few feet so that we could both enjoy a greater level of comfort.

The England number one is a hugely likeable figure who exudes quite astonishing levels of pragmatism, taking absolutely everything in his stride. His motto seems to be "so be it" and he must be a dream to manage, given that nothing at all seemed to faze him. You got the impression that if you positioned a rocket launcher on the penalty spot, tossed him a pair of gloves and asked him to intercept the flying missiles, he would simply say "no problem, let's get on with it." Downing, a more introspective character, revealed that the issue of Rio Ferdinand's non selection had not been discussed, with Roy Hodgson simply telling the squad to concentrate on training, the games ahead and the players that were there.

More local integration followed when the squad were put through their paces in front of a crowd of 3,000 locals at their Hutnik training ground on the outskirts of the city and then invited a host of local schoolchildren onto the pitch for a photo and autograph session. There were reports that the Dutch team had suffered racial taunts at the same venue the previous day but England were greeted with nothing but warmth and appreciation.

What the training revealed to us as journalists was that, while Danny Welbeck and Wayne Rooney looked deadly in the shooting practice, Carroll would have had trouble locating the rear end of a bovine mammal with a four stringed instrument. Twice he miskicked completely from low crosses into the box and then hit a shot so high that it evaded not only the crossbar, but also the 30 foot high green netting behind the goal and almost hit the roof of the parked team bus.

Within three days of arriving England had gained ten times more positive PR than they had during the whole of the World Cup and that was further boosted by a solemn duty which every visitor to this part of the world should try and undertake. In addition to the myriad attractions at its centre, Krakow is the nearest major city to the Auschwitz-Birkenau concentration camp and the players were offered the opportunity to make the trip along with a small media group who would share the pictures, quotes and soundbites among everyone to avoid the whole thing becoming an unnecessary circus. I was quite pleased not to be among them, as the emotions I took from my visit nearly 20 years previously remain etched so indelibly into my psyche that a return trip would almost seem mawkish. That view seemed to be shared by skipper Steven Gerrard and a couple of other senior players who elected not to lead the England party to Auschwitz because they too had already experienced the horrors of it.

Instead it was Wayne Rooney who led the players' contingent which also included Joe Hart, Phil Jagielka, Leighton Baines, Theo Walcott, Jack Butland and Andy Carroll. I am told it was Rooney's idea that the players should wear dark clothing as a mark of respect, which suggested that he himself was displaying a growing sense of maturity and responsibility. Visibly shaken by the experience, he told the press corps:

"It's hard to understand, so tough. When you see the amount of children's clothes and shoes, it's such a sad experience. You have to see it first-hand to understand, and of course it puts football into perspective. It will never be forgotten. We know that kids nowadays are interested in footballers, and if a few more people understand what happened because we came here today then that has to be good."

The party also included Roy Hodgson, FA chairman David Bernstein and, most poignantly of all, the Israeli former Chelsea manager Avram Grant whose own family lost 15 members among the 1.3 million innocent people who were murdered in this grotesque death factory. Grant spoke individually to each of the players and then addressed the group outside the ovens which were used to burn the corpses.

"It's very important you are here," he told them. "People will see you have come here, and then others will follow. It's important to talk about this and spread the message of what happened here."

At Birkenau, Hodgson and Bernstein donned skull caps and placed lit candles on the railway tracks which, for so many poor souls, represented the final stop on their journey through life.

The remainder of the squad, led by Gerrard, visited Schindler's Factory where the German businessman Oskar Schindler saved over a thousand Jews from certain death during the Holocaust. Having witnessed first hand the inhumane treatment of Jews in the infamous Krakow Ghetto, he managed to liberate many of them by employing them as labourers at the enamelware and ammunitions works he had founded in the city. Here they were treated with the dignity and respect which had been so cruelly denied their compatriots and were spared shipment to the concentration camps. Again, the players involved in the visit acted with great respect and humility. Joleon Lescott, who cut an impressive figure in every respect during the tournament, came away from the visit with an entirely different concept of the word "ghetto" from the one he had previously only heard via the lyrics of his favourite rap artists:

"Most youngsters today have a glorified image of a ghetto but the ghettos we have learned about today are not like that. I did not have a full understanding of what the word means. For a lot of people today it has been lost in translation. You see it in films and learn about it in music but to learn the origins of the word ghetto opens your eyes. People were chosen to go to Auschwitz. This is my first experience of something like this."

As professional sportsmen, footballers inhabit a world in which statistics can tell a thousand stories. Here is one brutal fact which perhaps best illustrates the sickening events which enveloped Krakow just three generations ago. Prior to the outbreak of war in 1939 there were more than 60,000 Jews living in the city, representing a quarter of its population. Today the Jewish community numbers around 200.

CHAPTER NINETEEN

"Hopefully He'll Hear Us Up There"

Within four days of arriving in Krakow we undertook the first of several commutes between Poland and Ukraine, rising early to fly the 820 miles to Donetsk for England's opening group game against France. Our arrival at Sergey Prokoviev International Airport, named after the famous composer who was born in the region, marked a new milestone in my own personal travel odyssey; Ukraine was the 50th country I had visited.

The city of Donetsk is a rather nondescript place in the south east of the country whose economy is reliant on heavy industries such as coal mining, and the proliferation of pitheads dotted around the place reminded me a little of mid 1980s Stoke-On-Trent. In fact it had been founded by a 19th century Welsh engineer called John Hughes who arrived in the area in 1869 with a group of 100 or so miners and ironworkers and began its industrialisation. For a while the town he founded was known as Yuzovka which is a Russian approximation of Hughesovka.

There didn't appear to be an awful lot going on in Donetsk, where the main attraction seemed to be the magnificent Donbass Arena itself and the stadium certainly was a sight to behold.

The home of 2009 UEFA Cup winners Shakhtar was built by the club's oligarch owner Rinat Akhmetov to the tune of nearly $400 million. By day it gives the appearance of a flying saucer that has landed in a well manicured garden of flower beds and fountains and by night, when the exterior is lit up, it resembles a giant diamond and sapphire engagement ring.

The paucity of entertainment on offer in Donetsk was borne out by a conversation I overheard between a guest and the receptionist at our Ramada Hotel which stood on a fairly nondescript street close to the Kalmius River.

"Excuse me, could you direct me to the city centre, please."

"This is the city centre, sir."

Next to the hotel was a towering billboard which featured a bevy of attractive women dressed in sporting apparel extolling the virtues of some kit manufacturer or other in a bid to equate their gear with all things cool and chic. My eye, however, was not drawn toward the pouting models in their lycra shorts, but to a large slogan above their heads which read "Perfection Has No Limit." Now forgive me for being pedantic here but surely perfection is a finite concept which, by its very definition, denotes something of a completely flawless nature which, ergo, cannot attain any higher status. I was tempted to write to the company's PR department to point this out and helpfully suggest that a more literal example of something which genuinely does have no limit is the glib, crass and remorseless destruction of the English language by advertising agency "creatives".

The Ramada had a large, ornately decorated bar on the ground floor which, given the lack of entertainment in Donetsk, quickly filled with thirsty hacks gathering around the TV sets to watch Spain draw with Italy and the Republic of Ireland's opening defeat against Croatia. Sitting behind us with a group of French journalists was former Arsenal star Robert Pires, whose presence the next day in his country's Media XI contributed hugely to a 6-0 defeat handed out to their English counterparts.

Among the local treats served up in the bar were varenyky; ravioli shaped dumplings filled with meat, vegetables or potatoes, which were delicious. I did stop short though of ordering one of the other items on the menu, listed simply as Ukrainian lard. Unfortunately the Ramada was one of those places where, if you wanted to order lunch it was best to do so at breakfast. On the day of the game, *talkSPORT*'s programme director Moz Dee arrived at the hotel for lunch with a group of the station's sponsors. I was invited to join them but explained that the service was rather slow and I would prefer to grab something at the stadium rather than run the risk of waiting around for the food and arriving late. It was a good move since I later learned that the whole party had had to abandon their table when the starters still hadn't been served an hour and a half after they sat down.

What Donetsk may have lacked in vibrancy it certainly made up for with heat and humidity, and it was hard work helping to lug the broadcast equipment from the bus drop-off to the stadium in temperatures of around 35°C. Being British, I engaged a young waitress at the inevitable McDonald's franchise inside the media centre in a conversation about the weather. I enquired whether this was a normal summer temperature for the region and, after she confirmed that it was, I continued my meteorological interrogation:

"I bet you have really cold winters though."

"Not so cold," she replied, "usually minus 20."

She looked rather puzzled when I explained that if such temperatures were to hit London, the entire city would lapse into cryogenic paralysis, forcing all ten million inhabitants to undergo an involuntary three-month hibernation during which not a single bus, train, car or plane would move an inch.

"Do you want ice in your Coke?" she shrugged without a hint of irony.

England performed ably against the French in a match which many, myself included, expected them to lose. Roy Hodgson pulled a surprise by starting with the 18-year-old Alex Oxlade-Chamberlain ahead of his Arsenal team-mate Theo Walcott and, although Joleon Lescott's header was matched by a Samir Nasri goal, you suspected the England boss was delighted with a point against his toughest group rivals in a "mustn't lose" rather than "must win" game. The FA media department played a blinder in the Mixed Zone afterwards, seeking me out for one-to-one interviews with Lescott, Scott Parker and Oxlade-Chamberlain who, for a teenager, spoke very maturely about his and the team's performance. As a reporter it is almost as satisfying when a youngster talks a good game as when he plays one, and the son of ex-England international Mark Chamberlain was following in the assured footsteps of a young Michael Owen or Philip Neville.

We returned to Krakow the same night and the buses which transported us to and from the venues and airports had been very thoughtfully stocked with fridges full of beer, although they did initially lack the complimentary presence of a bottle opener. Luckily Gerry, one of our minders from the South Africa trip two years before, was back on board and possessed the enviable gift of being able to open beer bottles with his pen. Although this caused the tops to fly around the crowded seats like shrapnel, such was the need for refreshment that it was well worth risking the loss of an eye for.

More evidence of the relaxed nature of this England camp surfaced the next day when the FA released videos of the players winding down in the hotel, including footage of Joe Hart and Alex Oxlade-Chamberlain flashing their six packs during a game of head tennis in the pool. Outside, the locals engaged in a new pursuit which involved seeing how many England players could be spotted wandering around in the main square. You could almost imagine Sir David Attenborough crouching behind a statue with a pair of binoculars offering commentary in those wonderful hushed tones of his:

"If we wait very quietly we may be lucky enough to spot one of these elusive creatures. And there, in the distance, beside the Hard Rock Cafe we see a male of the species displaying that familiar white plumage. Unless I'm mistaken it's a Phil Jagielka (*Defendorus Evertonis*) emerging from the nest into the late afternoon sun in search of cappuccino. What a magnificent sight he is."

The next item of prey on the menu of the England players were Sweden who had lost their opening game 2-1 to hosts Ukraine courtesy of two goals from the evergreen Andriy Shevchenko. The Scandinavians had something of a hex over the English, having never lost a competitive game between the two nations but if that run could be ended, Hodgson's men would be a big step closer to the quarter finals.

Among the media group which follows England on a regular basis is Peter Wenmann, the London-based football correspondent for the Swedish daily *Aftonbladet,* who reports back to a nation which has long been obsessed with the English game. I first got to know him during Euro 2004 and he was a regular at the 4th Street Cafe during the World Cup in 2010. No matter how late I would emerge from my final *talkSPORT* appearance I was almost certain to find Peter and his partner in crime Steven Howard of the *Sun* sitting at the bar indulging in copious amounts of alcohol and some wonderfully irreverent chat. So fond was our Swedish friend of a night on the beers that Henry Winter, a brilliant wordsmith on and off the printed page, suggested that the paper Peter worked for should be changed from *Aftonbladet* to *Oftenbladdered.* In fact the word literally means "the evening sheet" but Peter would proudly inform us that in Russian it translates as evening prostitute.

One night in the run-up to the Sweden game, I found Peter in the outside seating area of our base at the Andels hotel in Krakow, which overlooks a square by the main railway station and was always a bustle of activity. He was trying to ascertain whether there were any Swedish cultural or historical figures for whom the English had a hatred, for a preview article he was writing. Nobody, it seemed, had a bad word to say about any of his fellow countrymen and he wondered if I could think of any annoying Swedes. After some deliberation, I finally did come up with one suggestion:

"What about that awful pop duo Roxette who did 'The Look'? They had a blonde singer and a spiky haired guitarist and were absolute shit."

While Peter declared himself to be rather crestfallen that I had such a negative opinion of one his nation's most successful musical exports, he did at least have something to focus his article on and, after ordering another bottle of red wine, ran off to file.

The next day he showed me his column in the paper which declared me to be the only Englishman in Krakow who could summon up any animosity towards his country.

To illustrate this, the piece carried a large photo of Roxette, underneath which was the caption "Not For Mr Anderson." I joked that I might start getting hate mail from outraged Swedes, and in fact I probably would have done if I had admitted to Peter that I can't stand Abba either.

The Sweden game was at the Olympic Stadium in the Ukrainian capital Kiev which, although the city has never hosted an Olympics, did stage football matches during the 1980 Games in Moscow hence the rather grandiose name. Though far busier and livelier than Donetsk, Kiev seemed to have modernised architecturally at a much slower rate and many of its huge, monolithic buildings still evoked memories of the Soviet era.

A fine example of such an edifice was the massive slab of concrete and metal known as the Hotel Ukraine which loomed ominously over Independence Square in the heart of the city like a giant tombstone. Less than a decade earlier, the square had been the rallying point for the Orange Revolution in which political protesters had rallied in opposition to electoral and social corruption. Now, it hosted the city's Fan Zone and pulsated in vibrant shades of yellow and blue which were the national colours of both Ukraine itself and Sweden, whose base was in the city. At the heart of this throng stood a towering monument to the traditional protective female spirit Berehynia; imagine a replica of Nelson's column topped by Horatio wearing one of Lady Hamilton's best frocks.

It wasn't just the exterior of the hotel which brought to mind its Stalinist past. Upon arriving at the reception desk I expected to be met by a cheery smile and the usual greeting along the lines of:

"Good afternoon sir, welcome to the Hotel Ukraine."

Instead, a grim descendant of Rosa Klebb thrust out a gnarled hand, palm upwards and barked a single word:

"Passport."

It was like an immediate post-war visit to Checkpoint Charlie and, having handed over said document and paid for my wi-fi connection in cash (nothing could be charged to the room or paid for with a credit card here), I meekly enquired whether I might be able to have my key.

"Key upstairs," she growled with a look which suggested that I had just asked permission to graze a herd of sheep in my room.

Although the reception area itself was relatively modern, once you left its confines you were transported into a world of Cold War minimalism and austerity. Upon exiting at my floor I was greeted by Rosa's scarier older sister who was sat at an empty desk in the middle of the lobby and silently handed over the key. This, in stark contrast to the smart cards generally used to open hotel doors these days, was a huge, clunky monstrosity with an even larger wooden fob which weighed about half a ton. It looked like a prop from a Harry Potter film and I strongly suspected it would have fitted neatly into the keyhole of the boiler room at Hogwarts.

The room itself had clearly not changed since the days when low ranking Politburo accountants would gather at the hotel for their Christmas parties and dance jackboot to jackboot to the lilting strains of Soviet military anthems and then enter the raffle to win a year's supply of tractor oil. All the furnishings were stark, wooden and featureless; the wiring wouldn't have earned a safety certificate in the days of Michael Faraday and the television set looked like the sort at which my parents would gaze longingly in Rediffusion shop windows in the early 1960s. I switched it on to try and catch the Republic of Ireland v Spain game but, although the excitable Ukrainian commentator came through loud and clear, such was the picture quality that it looked as if the match was being played out in a post-apocalyptic blur of nuclear fallout and toxic waste. Shadowy figures running about were barely visible behind a fuzzy, oscillating haze of blue and green sludge. I decided it would be wiser to venture out and find a place where the TV set hadn't been personally built by John Logie Baird.

As I walked to the lift, one of the loudest claps of thunder I have ever heard ripped through the night, heralding a deluge of monsoon proportions which continued for the next half an hour or so. This relentless precipitation confined me to the four walls of the Ukraine and so I followed signs to the bar. These led me not to a comfortable watering hole in which to relax and watch the game, but to a small door outside which stood a little sign which read "Erotik Show". I peered into the room which was empty but had at its centre a small stage with a pole rising upwards from its centre. The flat screen televisions remained resolutely switched off.

Fortunately, tucked away in a corner of the reception area was a tiny counter where you could buy plastic cups of extortionately priced lager with the saving grace that it did have a 21st century TV set where you could watch Ireland getting well and truly thrashed by an ominously impressive Spanish side. Within a few minutes I was approached by a figure closely resembling the Creature From The

Black Lagoon who splashed across the floor leaving pools of liquid behind him and prodded me with a wet finger.

"All right, Ando?"

As I turned I was just about able to discern that this soggy mass of pulp was in fact ITV News reporter Steve Scott whose own attempt to find an alternative venue had not been as well timed as mine. He'd got as far as the other side of the hotel car park when the heavens opened and had sheltered for a few minutes before valiantly dashing back in. Although he'd only been under the open skies for a matter of seconds, he looked as if he'd just completed the Olympic 400m individual medley still wearing his suit. I bought him a beer and he slowly but gradually dried out as we watched Spain complete a 4-0 win.

Later I bumped into a group of colleagues and mentioned the mysterious Erotik Show and they said they had been in to have a look.

"Was it any good?" I asked.

"Nah," they replied. "Wasn't showing the football."

The following day I had to get across town first thing in the morning to appear on *talkSPORT*'s breakfast show which was being broadcast from an apartment very close to the stadium where presenter Mark Saggers and his producer Dennie Morris were staying. This required a ten minute cab ride through empty streets which, even in London, would have cost little more than a few quid. When I was dropped off, the driver asked for 150 of the local currency hryvnia which worked out at a rather steep £12. Haggling was useless since he had all the charm of a loveless sergeant major and, when I waved a 200 hyrvnia note in front of him, he finally mustered two words in English.

"No change."

I protested in vain and demanded a receipt to which the response was similar.

"No receipt."

"Yeah, no seat belt, no sense of direction and no fucking manners either," I replied as I slammed the door.

This was a country where getting ripped off was a non-negotiable, occupational hazard; confirmation of which came from Saggs and Dennie who had been stuck in Kiev since before the tournament began and were already wearying of the place and its dour, inflexible locals. They did however know lots of good places to eat and all my trips to Kiev were brightened considerably by splendid lunches in their excellent company. I also later discovered the city's underground system which was cheap and efficient once you had worked out the Cyrillic place names, but whose map looked a bit like a child's attempt to draw a swastika in wax crayon.

The match itself joined the great pantheon of topsy-turvey, haphazard England 3-2 results which included the 1970 World Cup quarter-final against Germany, group matches against Portugal and Romania at Euro 2000 and, more recently, the "Wally With The Brolly" Euro 2008 qualifier against Croatia. The difference of course was that this time England won.

Andy Carroll's inclusion from the start paid handsome dividends for Roy Hodgson as he produced a wonderful header from Steven Gerrard's cross and England were in total control at half-time. Then, enter stage left, the unmistakeable shambling reappearance of Giancarlo Galavotti's pantomime horse, as woeful defending allowed Olof Mellberg to strike twice and leave England trailing by the hour mark. Hodgson then threw on substitute Theo Walcott and, in my guise as the *talkSPORT* touchline reporter, I greeted his arrival by saying that it was about time he delivered something akin to the hat-trick he scored as a teenager in Croatia in 2008. He didn't disappoint, first unleashing a spectacular shot to equalise and then producing the cross from which Danny Welbeck cleverly flicked in the late winner.

It was an insane, breathless match which you had to watch through your fingers at times, but the result meant Sweden were out and England needed just a point against hosts Ukraine back in Donetsk to qualify for the last eight. The Mixed Zone was buzzing afterwards and we got some great audio with Walcott, Welbeck and Gerrard who was ushered over to my spot in the throng personally by none other than Club England's Managing Director Adrian Bevington. You could tell the Liverpool midfielder was revelling in the captaincy, a mantle he had worn in such awkward circumstances at the World Cup two years previously. He was smiling, upbeat, honest and talkative this time, and producing performances which not only repaid Hodgson's faith in him, but marked him out as a potential Player of the Tournament contender.

The fact that we spent a second night in Kiev before returning to Krakow brought home the hectic schedule that we as reporters and the players were undertaking. The plane from Kiev landed at lunchtime and we were to spend just two nights in Poland before an early flight back out to Donetsk for the final group game against Ukraine. The big news story in that period of course was that Wayne Rooney, who had thus far been suspended, would be eligible for the match and the FA organised a press conference with the England striker at our hotel.

I received a call from their media department informing me that there would be no separate radio interviews with Rooney. BBC *5Live*, with whom *talkSPORT* had equal rights holder status at Euro 2012, had been afforded the never adequately explained title of "broadcast partners" by the FA and, as such, were granted separate audiences with players which we didn't get. They had already pre-recorded a piece with Rooney which was embargoed until after the conference and therefore non-exclusive, and so another radio appearance was deemed unnecessary by the powers that be. I knew that Rooney was a fan of *talkSPORT* and argued that we should be allowed to do our usual five minutes with him but this was denied us on the grounds that I would then have audio that the BBC didn't have access to.

In the end, the situation actually worked to our advantage because I was advised that I would get a slot at the main televised conference after the likes of Sky's Nick Collins and ITV's Gabriel Clarke had asked their questions. I was able to fire off four consecutive questions at Rooney which yielded three or four minutes of excellent material and, to all intents and purposes represented a "one to one". The only difference was that, instead of the quiet ambience of the radio room, there was the background accompaniment of cameras clicking whenever Rooney produced a puzzled expression or a smile, as the photographers looked for the most emotive or appropriate shot. You will have seen and heard this many times on TV at big media conferences when a sudden movement, a wiped away tear or a big grin elicits a flurry of clicking and flashing from the snappers. They call it the Nikon chorus.

Some broadcasters get in a real flap about background noise during interviews, insisting on complete silence and empty rooms, but I have always felt that a bit of natural sound can actually enhance a piece and takes the listener a little closer to the heart of the event. Obviously you don't want to conduct the interrogation at the side of an airstrip where Harrier Jump Jets are taking off and landing, but the sound of people kicking balls around in the background or a little wind, rain and traffic adds to the aural sculpture in my opinion. When I was in Brazil covering Manchester United's ill fated appearance at the 2000 World Club Championship, I ran an effects mike out onto the balcony so that every piece I filed was accompanied by the sound of the waves lapping onto Copacabana beach. What's the point of being somewhere colourful and exotic like Rio when you sound like you're in the non-fiction section of North Finchley public library?

In addition to my improvised interview the FA, to their enormous credit, agreed to our requests to get Rooney live on the *Alan Brazil Breakfast Show* later in the tournament, which meant that, in the end, *talkSPORT* got more mileage out of England's star striker than *5Live* did. He expressed great regret at the incident against Montenegro which led to his suspension and admitted that he had feared he would miss out on Euro 2012 completely when the initial three match suspension was handed out. As a result he was more determined than ever to help England get the result they needed to reach the quarter-finals.

I cursed my luck as I rose the next day at the crack of dawn for another visit to Donetsk. I was used to long hours since my day would generally start with a spot on the *Breakfast Show* at around 7.30am and would end with some late night malarkey with Andy Goldstein and Bobby Gould on *Sportsbar*, in which the chat often revolved around my own social activities on the trip as much as tournament and team news and were great fun to do. On this morning though it seemed unduly harsh to be setting off again less than 48 hours after arriving back from Kiev and tiredness was beginning to take its toll.

The deja vu of the coach ride, airport check-in and departure lounge coffee bar was beginning to grind others down too and there were a fair few moans and groans about the grinding repetitiveness of it all from a good many of our party as the Groundhog Day scenario took effect.

But then came the awful moment when the whole situation we were in, the whole seemingly urgent pursuit of stories, the whole concept of what we saw as important, irritating or amusing and indeed the whole tournament itself paled into meaningless insignificance. While we had been travelling, working, laughing, drinking and moaning our way through Euro 2012, one of our former travelling companions was reaching the end of a enormously brave and dignified but ultimately losing battle against the odious cancer which had gripped him for the past 18 months.

As we stood around waiting for our flight to Donetsk, word came through that Danny Fullbrook the *Daily Star*'s football correspondent had died in hospital in London at the tragically early age of 40, leaving behind a ten-year-old son.

I must confess that I didn't know Danny anywhere near as well as many who were alongside me that day, but my memories are of a larger than life character with a booming voice who was never shy about offering his opinion but, however much you may have disagreed with it, would never hold a grudge and was always the first to have a laugh about it all over breakfast. The nicknames bestowed upon him amongst our brotherhood spoke for themselves; he was generally referred to as "Fearless" or "Foghorn".

In some ways I was a slightly peripheral figure among the tight knit and increasingly young group of newspaper reporters who would spend hours chewing the fat at endless training grounds and media conferences season after season, but Danny would always made me feel welcome with an invitation to join them for a drink or a meal. He was the sort of person who would take any amount of piss-taking in exactly the right spirit and would dish it back in spades.

I remember a night during the 2010 World Cup when Henry Winter and the *Guardian*'s Kevin McCarra hosted a barbecue at their apartment in Sun City, during which the *Mirror*'s John Cross had somehow managed to end up with a large rip down one leg of his designer jeans. As the beers began to flow, this became longer and longer as people took turns to grab the trailing strip of denim and tug at it until Crossy was left with one half of his trousers looking as if it had been put through a shredder.

"Bloody hell lads," he complained, "they cost me £120."

"Blimey," I retorted, only half joking. "I don't spend that much on clothes in a year."

Danny's voiced then bellowed across the room.

"We can tell, Ando!"

Henry had asked me to provide the music for the evening so I set up my ipod with its speakers and compiled what I thought was a lovingly crafted and eclectic succession of crowd pleasers. Unfortunately not everyone in the room was a fan of the likes of Morrissey, The Cure, Lou Reed and the Manic Street Preachers and there were soon complaints from the younger fraternity that the selection wasn't modern enough. In a bid to appease the mob I put on Sabotage by the Beastie Boys but to no avail. Danny marched across the room towards me.

"That's quite enough of that, Ando," he shouted before firmly hitting the pause button and walking off again to loud applause.

It was almost impossible to imagine that, just two years later, he was no longer with us. A fair few tears were shed on the shuttle bus as it crossed the tarmac and we boarded the plane in near silence.

Once we were in the air one of Danny's closest friends on the trip, Shaun Custis of the *Sun*, broke the hush via the intercom system. Choking back the tears and in a voice cracking with emotion, Shaun delivered a wonderful speech about Danny's qualities as a travelling companion, the fun and laughter he had spread on such trips and how deeply he would be missed. Finally and poignantly he concluded by saying:

"We all know how much Danny liked a lot of noise, so let's all join in a minute's applause and hopefully he'll hear us up there."

In a touch of real class before the pre-match press conference at the Donbass Arena, Roy Hodgson and Steven Gerrard both delivered their unscripted and heartfelt tributes. Danny had been a lifelong and fervent supporter of the England manager's former club Fulham and had once done a newspaper column with the captain. Relationships between football people and the media aren't always a bed of roses but this was proof, if it were needed, that Danny was one of the good guys.

On the day of the funeral around a dozen of the lads on the Euro trip flew back to London to pay their final respects at Mortlake Cemetery where hundreds of people attended including Frank Lampard who had visited Danny several times in hospital. Back in Krakow the rest of us gathered at a restaurant in the Jewish quarter and raised a glass in his memory. The *Daily Mirror*'s Oliver Holt made a short speech and summed it all up when he said:

"This is just the sort of evening Danny would have loved."

He certainly would have done, since it carried on into various local bars where we discovered the attractions of hazelnut vodka and ended at around four in the morning with Henry Winter and Olly Foster recreating the famous *Chariots Of Fire* college run scene around the perimeter of Krakow's main square.

England beat a very poor Ukraine side with Rooney, almost inevitably, getting the winning goal and clinching top spot in the group above France, who were beaten by Sweden, and a last eight clash with Italy in Kiev. With the Ukrainians having joined co-hosts Poland on the Euro scrap heap the Mixed Zone was a good deal more chaotic than in previous matches and we managed to scramble a few words with Rooney and Joleon Lescott who, to his credit, would always stop for a word.

The match ended at around midnight local time and an hour and a half later we were on the coach for the flight back to Krakow which landed at around 0530. This gave me a thoroughly invigorating one and a half hours' sleep before I was up to talk to Alan Brazil and Ronnie Irani. On the coach back to the hotel I had been chatting to Nick Collins about the rigours of having to file first thing in the morning after virtually no sleep but I was the lucky one. All I had to do was set the alarm, jump out of bed and wait for the studio to call the ISDN line which had been installed in my room; once the piece was finished I could roll over and go back to sleep. The demands of television were such that Nick had to put on a suit, comb his hair, and head to the square outside the hotel where he had to try and look fresh-faced and upbeat in the harsh glare of the early morning sun.

There was a five-day gap between the Ukraine match and the quarter-final so, at last, we did have a little time to relax. The media conferences during that period were hugely upbeat affairs with England having exceeded expectations by topping Group D and Joe Hart was again a joy to interview. He revealed that Rooney had insisted on marking his return to the side by choosing the music in the dressing room prior to the Ukraine game:

"Wayne got hold of the ipod and within seconds 22 pairs of headphones went on."

During an interview with Scott Parker, *5Live*'s Ian Dennis asked for his reaction to the news that Harry Redknapp had been sacked as Tottenham boss. The midfielder admitted he was disappointed as Redknapp had brought him to the club and inspired the late development which had helped him revive his England career to the extent that he was a first choice at Euro 2012.

After the interview we were asked by the FA to edit out that section since they were always a little wary of straying into club matters with players who were on international duty. I don't particularly agree with their stance but nonetheless agreed to remove it. Another thing that I had trouble comprehending was an anachronistic system of embargoing certain interviews, which dated back to the pre-internet days when newspapers ruled the roost. Under pressure from senior football writers, the FA would agree to hold quotes back until the following day so that the papers had fresh material.

Nowadays with 24-hour sports channels, countless websites and iphone apps. this seemed a rather archaic process and I have always believed that everything should be available to everyone at the same time. However, the Parker interview had been earmarked as one that we couldn't broadcast immediately and I must confess that I was more preoccupied with filing the piece we had done during the same session with Theo Walcott who was an excellent talker and always very good value for a quote.

Hours later when I got round to sending down the Parker stuff I informed the *talkSPORT* newsdesk about the embargo but completely forgot to ask them to edit out the bit about the situation at Tottenham. The next day I was called by an irate FA Head of Media Relations Mark Whittle who informed me that the station's website was carrying a banner headline declaring "I'm Sad To See Harry Go Says Parker." Apparently the player had seen the story and was upset that we had reneged on an agreement not to use the quotes. All I could do was hold my hands up and admit that it was completely down to human error on my part and that, ignorant of the directive, *talkSPORT* had acted in good faith. I emailed an apology to the FA and Parker which was accepted and we moved on.

The tournament had moved on too with the two favourites in ominous form; Spain reached the semis with a comfortable 2-0 win over France while Germany swept aside Greece in a one sided match which prompted me to use on air the Edmund Blackadder quote:

"The German reputation for brutality is well founded, their operas last several days."

Portugal were also through after beating the Czech Republic, with Cristiano Ronaldo scoring his third goal in two games.

Our flight to Kiev had been delayed due to the fact that the Polish aviation authorities had chosen that day of all days to undertake its annual staff security exercise at Krakow airport, searching every plane with military precision before anyone could get on board. Given the increased traffic in and out of the city during the tournament, it was a bit like organising a sponsored walk in Monte Carlo city centre on Grand Prix day.

This involved us spending a less than agreeable half hour in a stationary and non-air-conditioned shuttle bus. When it finally did get moving the driver inexplicably carried out an emergency stop, as if a party of blind nuns had suddenly wandered across the tarmac, and I was thrown headlong to the ground amid an airborne flurry of glasses, pens, keys and notepads.

The pre-match press conference demonstrated Roy Hodgson's linguistic skills as he fielded as many questions in Italian as English and, from what I could make out from the former, the key words were "partita", "importante" and "Balotelli". Only when a local asked him a question in Ukrainian did we finally discover a language that the England boss couldn't speak.

For our second stop in Kiev we were billeted at the magnificent Fairmont Grand which couldn't have been further removed from the Ukraine Hotel. There were no Rosa Klebbs or Erotik Shows here; this was a luxurious five star pied-a-terre overlooking the Dneiper River, the banks of which had been transformed into a makeshift beach and were teeming with picnicking holidaymakers. During our previous visit to the city, some of the other lads had been lucky enough to find themselves staying at the Fairmont at the same time as the Swedish WAGs who, as you might imagine, scrubbed up pretty well. I'm told that when a group of them ventured off towards the beach, a posse of England fans decided to take a sandwich and make a day of it.

I doubt that any of them attracted the attentions of the leggy Scandinavians but, had they done so, the hotel would have catered for their every need. I hardly ever use minibars in hotel rooms due to the extortionate prices, but generally take a look out of curiosity to see what's on offer. In amongst the mortgage defying selection of spirits, chocolate and peanuts in the little fridge in the Fairmont was a small package which bore the euphemistic label "intimacy kit". I was intrigued but, rather than open it, I googled the name and discovered that it was likely to contain several condoms, a lubricant called Astroglide, some towelettes, massage oils, two packets of Smints and, best of all, an alleged aphrodisiac called Pinnacle Horny Goat Weed. I can just imagine the chat-up line at the beach:

"Hi Ulrika, would you like a Smint? I'm as horny as a goat."

I learned that the more upmarket versions also contain a feather tickler, a "personal massager" and a cream version of Viagra. Apparently these pleasure packs are known in the trade as shag bags.

Even a Fairmont Hotel intimacy kit couldn't have enhanced England's performance against the Italians and they were duly battered 0-0 at the Olympic Stadium with Andrea Pirlo proving to be Andrea Peerless in midfield. For the sixth time in my career I had to endure an England penalty shootout defeat but somehow this one simply didn't hurt anywhere near as much as the previous five. It was plain to everyone that victory for Roy Hodgson's men would have been a travesty and the fans understood that their team had pretty much settled into the logical scheme of things. For many years England have been a quarter-final team at best but finally we had learned to accept it.

The reaction from the manager and his players was commendably grounded in common sense too. Hodgson felt they had not let anyone down and that he had learnt a lot about his players during his short spell in charge. He was realistic enough to admit that England were a long way behind Spain and Germany in terms of quality but could shed little light on the continuing failure from the penalty spot, other than to compare them to the last hole of the Open when, sometimes, players simply can't hold their nerve.

Gerrard said that, while it had been his best tournament individually, that didn't make up for the pain and frustration he was feeling; the players had put in the maximum effort but needed to improve on the ball if they were ever to win a major tournament. Finally and tellingly, he rated the experience as far superior to the last World Cup and said the atmosphere was much better.

For many of us it was the familiar scenario of seeing some of our travelling companions return home as the England roadshow rolled out of town. For me it meant less pressure, fewer early starts and a more relaxed regime. As tradition had come to dictate, Mike Ingham and I used a little of this down time to explore some of Krakow's more obscure record shops.

One of these was called High Fidelity and certainly bore a resemblance to the store in Nick Hornby's novel. It was located in a side street with a tiny sign, as if the owner deliberately didn't want people to find it. When you got inside it resembled someone's front room with stacks of vinyl and CDs in haphazard piles. When Mike started to flick through a rack of LPs the owner, a guy called Piotr whose heyday had obviously been the 1970s judging by his hairstyle, got rather agitated and insisted that non-one except him was allowed to touch the records. Apparently you had to tell him what you were looking for and he would try and find it.

Understandably a little nonplussed by this, Mike came up with the most obscure jazz artist he could think of and this seemed to impress Piotr who then signalled that it was okay to handle his precious albums. It was as if you had to undergo an initiation test before he would take you seriously and it seems we had passed. For the remainder of our visit he was charm personified but you did wonder how on earth he made a living with such an uncompromising sales technique.

The following day we left Krakow for the final time and I would heartily recommend it to anyone who's planning a long weekend away. For once, we were spared the Groundhog Day airport experience and took the three-hour train ride to Warsaw for the semi-final between Germany and Italy. We had been promised a first class compartment but it turned out to resemble the kind of carriage in which Trevor Howard and Celia Johnson began their brief encounter. The landscape wasn't much more inspiring and the game of I-Spy ended prematurely after G for grass, F for field and S for sky, leaving us with two hours and 55 minutes to twiddle our thumbs. This was made more bearable by the discovery that Poland had its own version of Jaffa Cakes, which is probably pronounced Jzchvya Kszcs.

There was nothing boring about the match itself though; it was a wonderful game of football which further underlined England's limitations. Pirlo was again in imperious form but, as he so often does, Mario Balotelli stole the show with two stunning goals which earned the Italians an unexpected place in the final and saw the Germans consigned to a third successive major tournament semi-final exit.

In the Mixed Zone after the match I was determined to try and grab a word with the Manchester City striker and claimed a decent spot alongside a handful of other English hacks. Next to us were a group of Italians one of whom, to my immediate left, began complaining that I wasn't giving him enough room. I explained that he had plenty of space and I wasn't about to move but he droned on and on about it. Eventually he said to me:

"I need more space, because my recorder doesn't work very well and I have to be nearer to the players."

"Well get a new one then," was my less than sympathetic response.

Eventually Balotelli arrived and stopped in front of the Italians. After a couple of minutes the guy I had been arguing with asked him a question and got a very short reply. I deliberately cut across him and jumped in:

"How does it feel to be in the final Mario?"

Amazingly he then moved away from the Italians and towards our group, offering us an uninterrupted interview which was far longer than the one he had granted his by now irate compatriots. He didn't say much of any great consequence but it didn't matter, as *talkSPORT* had an interview with the hero of the hour and I had the personal satisfaction of being at least one Englishman who had got the better of the Italians at Euro 2012.

And so we made our final Poland-Ukraine commute, arriving at Warsaw's Chopin Airport for a third visit to Kiev for the final. It was the second time we had flown from an airport named after a composer and it brought to mind a phone conversation which, I'm told, Ringo Starr had with Paul McCartney a few years ago:

"Hello Paul, it's Ringo."

"Hi Ringo, guess where I am?"

"Dunno."

"John Lennon International Airport."

One wonders whether this form of nomenclature might catch on. Welcome to Burt Bacharach Heliport, Missouri or the Bjorn and Benny Ferry Terminal in Malmo or the Morrissey and Marr Tram Depot, Wythenshawe.

We were on a scheduled flight with the Ukrainian national carrier Aerosvit which, but for one letter, would have had the perfect name. For reasons none of us understood, they orchestrated one of the longest check-in procedures I have ever experienced, as a huge queue of media representatives snaked its way back from the two available desks. Graham Taylor arrived rather late and we invited him to join us for the wait. This enraged a Swedish cameraman who accused the former England manager of not only queue barging but also using his status to do so, which was frankly ridiculous.

"I know who you are," he kept shouting, with increasing anger.

"You don't know anything about me," replied Graham, "so piss off."

I don't think I've seen him react like that since the famous incident with the linesman in Holland which was featured in the famous "Do I Not Like That" documentary.

At least, for our final visit to Kiev, I would be spared the prospect of struggling with uncompromising taxi drivers or indecipherable tube station names. Our hotel, The Rus, may have been another imposing, monolithic slab of Stalinist unsightliness but it had the advantage of being so close to the stadium that some of the rooms on the upper floors had a view of the pitch. Mine, as always seemed to be the case, was the furthest one from the lift and overlooked the car park, but Phil McNulty, chief football writer on the BBC's website, joked that he could have covered the game without leaving his bed.

I have always been pally with those members of the England press corps who share my love of music and Phil was no exception. We would while away coach trips and flights amiably discussing all things from Led Zeppelin to Rage Against The Machine, but there was one topic of conversation which would be guaranteed to rent us asunder. Phil belonged to a strange, but mercifully small, brotherhood of men who I referred to as English football's militant wing of the Bruce Springsteen fan club. By contrast, I had had never understood the attraction of "The Boss" and would extol the virtues of Lou Reed as the true hero of American rock as opposed to Springsteen who, to use Morrissey's line, "says nothing to me about my life".

Unfortunately Phil's hero was in the midst of a huge European tour while we were at Euro 2012 and he and his fellow acolyte John Richardson of the *Sunday Express* would crap on endlessly over breakfast about the previous night's gig in reverential awe. Eventually, battle-scarred by days of hyperbole, I would pre-empt their eulogies by making up my own version of events:

"I'm told that in Barcelona he did a nine hour set, which is his third longest ever, including a 53 minute rendition of Rosalita, and 12 encores featuring a cover version of the whole of side two of Sergeant Pepper. Apparently, by the end of the gig, Springsteen was the only person left in the stadium since everyone else had to get up and go to work the next day. But he still found time to perform a song he'd written especially for the occasion in support of striking postal workers in Bilbao."

I must confess I found it absolutely hilarious when, later in the tour, Westminster council turned off the power during Springsteen's duet at Hyde Park with Paul McCartney. In among all the wailing from Bruce fans on Twitter were a few kindred spirits who saw this as a relief rather than an outrage. The best of them noted:

"At last, the album everyone's been waiting for: Spingsteen and McCartney Unplugged."

The night before the game, all of the *talkSPORT* gang were taken to an out of town restaurant which resembled a collection of 18th century hunters' lodges. Each group of diners had a little refuge to themselves, connected by a cobbled courtyard, the walls adorned with axes, pelts and antlers. It was the type of place you would have seen in the opening shot of a 1970s Hammer horror film, shrouded in mist and dimly lit; the eerie stillness of the cold night broken only by the far off thunder of hooves. As the scene moved inside, you would get a glimpse of Ingrid Pitt or Madeline Smith lying on a bed, falling out of her top with a gaping neck wound.

Unfortunately, the only female company we encountered during our meal resembled Irene Handl and Bella Emberg. They were the lead singers of a five piece folk ensemble wearing traditional Ukrainian dress who invaded our already cramped cabin and belted out indigenous songs with a near psychotic gusto.

Almost as pain inducing was the eye wateringly steep bill which, given that the meal consisted of pickled vegetables, kebabs and cups of what tasted like watered down jam, could have seen at least two noughts knocked off.

We returned to the city centre for a few beers at the Arena complex near our hotel which was a lively collection of bars and clubs but was also a pickpocket's paradise. We later learned that several people returned home minus their mobile phones. On the same night Elton John and Queen had staged a free open air concert in Independence Square and we could hear bits of it as we walked down the street towards our destination. Queen had replaced the irreplaceable Freddie Mercury with somebody called Adam Lambert who, apparently, had been a runner-up on *American Idol* and looked like the bastard son of Elvis Presley and Liza Minelli. We caught his duet with drummer Roger Taylor as they attempted to replicate Freddie and David Bowie on Under Pressure. It was so awful that I was tempted to go back and fetch Irene and Bella who would have made a far better job of it.

I was up early the next day for a stint on the *Breakfast Show* with Saggs, after which he and Dennie took me to a place where rabbit ravioli was on the lunch menu. When in Rome.

Those who actually were in Rome that day saw their team caught like a rabbit in the headlights against a far superior Spanish side who chalked up the biggest ever win in a major tournament final. Their 4-0 victory in a riveting display of supremacy placed them amongst the pantheon of football's greatest ever teams and drew the inevitable, if tedious, comparisons with Brazil's team of 1970. Who was better? Who cares? Marvel at both.

I arrived home with a great sense of satisfaction; it had been a fantastic tournament, England had done as well as could have been expected, Krakow had been a superb base, the trips into Ukraine, though fraught at times, had been fascinating and both the last two games had been a joy to behold. And, amazingly, no-one had come back in a coffin. Next month on *Panorama*: Going To The Shops, Death Stalks The Deli.

As ever, the return to reality was reassuring but brief. Only three weeks to go until the Olympics......